3 3052 09717 1930

Blacktop Cowboys

Blacktop Cowboys

RIDERS ON THE RUN

FOR RODEO GOLD

TY PHILLIPS

THOMAS DUNNE BOOKS/ST. MARTIN'S PRESS

NEW YORK

PUBLIC LIBRARY
FORT COLLINS, COLORADO

THOMAS DUNNE BOOKS.
An imprint of St. Martin's Press.

BLACKTOP COWBOYS. Copyright © 2006 by Ty Phillips. All rights reserved.
Printed in the United States of America. No part of this book may be used or
reproduced in any manner whatsoever without written permission except in
the case of brief quotations embodied in critical articles or reviews. For infor-
mation, address St. Martin's Press, 175 Fifth Avenue, New York, N.Y. 10010.

www.thomasdunnebooks.com

www.stmartins.com

"Turn the Page," written by Bob Seger, copyright © 1973, renewed 2001 by
Gear Publishing Company.

All photography by Bart Ah You

Book design by Gretchen Achilles

ISBN-13: 978-0-312-33036-1
ISBN-10: 0-312-33036-7

First Edition: November 2006

10 9 8 7 6 5 4 3 2 1

TO MY MOTHER,
WHO ALWAYS HAD A THING FOR COWBOYS

CONTENTS

CONTENTS

Introduction

At any given moment, there are thousands of rodeo cowboys traveling throughout North America in elaborate truck and trailer rigs. Each year, many of these cowboys cover more than seventy-five thousand miles on the road and in the air. They are men with colorful names like Speed and Jet, Rowdy and Howdy, Rope and Cash. Now, they all will grin and tell you they do it because they're too lazy to work and too scared to steal, and that rodeoin's somewhere in between. Of course, it goes much deeper than that. Most of them are reliving the young lives of their fathers—yesterday's rodeo stars and today's walking wounded. Truth is, most rodeo cowboys are born, not made. They are branded at birth for life at two speeds: 85 mph or a standstill. And it's a hell of a ride. For any week spent living on the road, a cowboy might buy himself all of one minute's showtime in arenas often scattered across several states. At its essence, the rodeo life is an elaborate game of poker. The gamblers ante up their entry fees, always betting on themselves. The steers are dealt in blind draws. The difference between winning and losing always comes down to tenths of a second. Once the pot is divided and the crowds are gone, the cowboys pack up and drive hundreds of miles through the night to find another arena by sunrise. To play the game again. For those who can afford it, it is the time of their lives. For those who cannot, it is a gritty existence loaded with crushed hope, mounting debt, and the simple worry of how to get to the next rodeo town. Yet, even for the luckless, it is the time of their lives. This is the story of one loose-knit band of cowboys, mostly steer wrestlers, on the road during the 2004 season. It begins one January afternoon in the Southern California rodeo town of Norco. . . .

CHAPTER 1

The Road to Denver

NORCO, CALIFORNIA
SUNDAY, JANUARY 18

Luke Branquinho unzipped his pants and began pissing into a fresh pile of horse manure. A bubbling green liquid oozed atop the parking lot dirt in small streams, a spent mixture of alfalfa hay and countless Coors Lights. The bleary-eyed cowboy stood beside a Ford F350 pickup in a half-hearted bid for privacy. He steadied himself by gripping the truck's bed with his right hand. His left arm hung limp by his side.

A couple hundred yards away, small groups of people made their way from the grandstands at Ingalls Arena. The remnants of the California Circuit Finals rodeo crowd followed a strip of asphalt that snaked its way down a steep hill and led to their cars. Children, many dressed as cowboys and cowgirls, talked to their parents in excited tones about the wondrous things they'd just seen, far too young to have any idea what cowboy life really meant.

As Casey Branquinho sat in the driver's seat of his truck, waiting on his brother, a woman walked over to the rig. Her son, Levi Rosser, had just won the bulldogging event and twenty-six hundred dollars. Still pissing, Luke turned his head toward her and smiled.

3

"Hey," he called out, "tell your son congratulations for finally getting some this weekend."

"He didn't get some this weekend," she said.

"Well, maybe he's a queer."

"He's not a queer," she said. "He's just kind of private."

"Maybe he needs me to come over and counsel him."

"No, Luke, that's really the last thing he needs," she said, touching Casey on the arm before turning to walk away. "Good luck in Denver, guys."

Luke finished his business, wiped his hands on his jeans, and walked to the passenger side. He opened the door and poured himself into the rig. He leaned back into his seat, winced a bit, and began massaging the flesh behind his left shoulder with his right hand. He reached into his coat pocket and pulled out his last silver can of pain relief. He popped it open, took a long drink, and then set the can in a cup holder and resumed the massage.

A few hours earlier, Luke had been in prime position to win several thousand dollars. He had bolted into the arena, slid off his horse, and grabbed his steer's horns. But when he reached out for the animal's nose, he felt his left shoulder give and he let go of the steer. The pin from a surgery years earlier was all that kept the shoulder from coming out completely.

Casey shifted the truck into gear and looked over at his brother.

"How's the shoulder?"

"Sore."

"Yeah," Casey said, nodding as he guided his truck and a forty-foot trailer through the parking lot.

Before long, the dirt and gravel gave way to city streets that emptied into the endless hum of Interstate 15. Outside, the setting sun struggled to push light through the smoggy air that hung above the mountains east of Los Angeles.

ONTARIO. VICTORVILLE. BARSTOW.

The brothers spoke sparingly. Dark circles of exhaustion hung beneath their eyes. The 2003 rodeo season officially ended that January afternoon in Norco. And the off-season lasted all of about two hours: long enough for Luke to get drunk and for Casey to ready his horses for a long drive. The 2004 Wrangler ProRodeo Tour winter opener was set to begin in Denver the following day.

Settling in for the trip, both men reached out for their cell phones. Luke's rang before he could dial a number. He looked down to see who was calling: It was his old buddy and traveling partner, Travis Cadwell.

"Hey Trav. . . . Just out here rodeoin' buddy. How 'bout you? . . . That's good. . . . No, we're just leavin' Norco now. . . . Well, I was fixin' to win the steer wrestling, but my fuckin' shoulder came out. . . . Yes it did. . . . You're a dumb skinny fucker, you know that? . . . Yeah, exactly. Whatever. . . . No, Levi won it. . . . I don't know. . . . When you gonna break out, at San Antonio? . . . Tucson? . . . All right. Hey, I got another call, I'll talk to you later."

Luke pushed the wrong button and lost the call. He gave up, leaned back in the seat, and closed his eyes. Casey turned up the volume on the radio to hear the Carolina Panthers put the finishing touches on their NFC Championship Game upset over the Philadelphia Eagles.

"This is the deepest penetration for the Eagles today," the announcer said.

Luke looked over at Casey with the dumb grin drunk people wear.

"I got some deep penetration last night."

"With who?"

"I can't remember," Luke said. "I think I drank too much."

Luke's phone rang again. Recognizing the number, he quickly took another drink of his beer and put the phone to his ear.

"Hey there. . . . What? . . . Fuck! You're naked? . . . I want to see you naked. . . . Can I see you naked tomorrow night? . . . Well, that sounds good to me, too. . . ."

Suddenly, Luke dropped the phone to his waist and exhaled in frustration.

"These fucking phones!" he screamed.

He looked over at Casey again. "She was, fuck, she was about to talk dirty to me, too."

"Who is that?" Casey said.

"Lindsay," Luke said, dialing her number.

"Lindsay?"

"Arizona."

"Oh, yes," Casey said, smiling and picturing the pretty young brunette woman.

Luke put the phone back to his ear.

"So, I get to see you naked? . . . You'll do a little dance for me? . . . You will? . . . Yeah, we'll dance. Well, you'll dance and I'll watch. . . . Stay naked 'til I get there. . . ."

Casey shook his head and laughed. Then he looked at Luke.

"Her nipples would be hard if she was naked in Denver," Casey said.

Luke looked over at his brother, paused for a moment to imagine the sight, then returned to the phone call.

"Casey says your nipples would be hard if you were naked in Denver. . . . They are? . . . Goddamn it! . . . We're about fifteen hours away. . . . Okay. . . . I'll see you tomorrow night."

MOUNTAIN PASS. LAS VEGAS. CEDAR CITY.

As the cowboys rode north, the temperature moved south. By 2:15 A.M., it had dropped to eighteen degrees. The edges of I-15 disappeared beneath the banks of blackened snow. Roadside sagebrush fluttered in a frozen wind. Skeleton trees, their fallen leaves long covered by snow, glimmered in the dim light of a setting moon.

Casey spotted the neon sign of JR's Truck Stop and pulled off the freeway. After filling his tanks with $150 worth of diesel, he parked in a vacant field, near a parking lot of truckers sleeping in their rigs. Another truckload of cowboys—Brad McGilchrist, Levi Rosser, and Austin Manning—pulled in and parked behind Casey's rig. The men unloaded their horses, covered them in blankets, and led them around in circles to walk off the miles. The early-morning soundtrack alternated between hooves digging into gravel and men spitting Copenhagen juice onto the ground. Every minute or so, the distant headlights of a freeway car threw light on the lonesome silhouette of a cowboy walking his horse at night.

Casey's trailer door swung open and Luke stood in the doorway, scratching his head and rubbing his eyes like a miner emerging from a hole in the ground. He'd managed some sleep in one of the trailer's beds, but every bump in the road had ravaged his sore shoulder and jarred him awake. Sober and somewhat rested, it was his turn to drive. He climbed into the driver's seat and the insulin-dependent diabetic checked his blood sugar numbers. They were fine. So he chewed up a couple of Rolaids tablets to fix a problem created with the previous night's dinner at Chili's. Then he swallowed an aspirin to ease the throbbing in his shoulder. Now he was good to go.

As he drove Casey's rig back to the freeway, Luke reached

into his shirt pocket, pulled out a cell phone, and called Levi, whose rig was nowhere in sight.

"Hey, what the hell are you doing? . . . Well, hurry up. . . . All right, all right. Are you driving? . . . Good, we can roll on. . . . Huh? . . . I don't know, eighty or so. . . . You just keep up."

Luke hung up the phone and flipped it onto the dashboard. He pushed the gas pedal farther down, the landscape blur quickened, and twenty-five thousand pounds of bat out of hell roared up the base of a mountain pass at 85 mph.

BEAVER. COVE FORT. RICHFIELD.

Levi's truck flew up alongside Luke's. Luke looked to his left to see Brad, Levi, and Austin—all young cowboys making their first real run at full-time rodeo life—rocking out to music and fingering holes in their hands to simulate intercourse. Luke nodded back at them, shaking his fist and sticking his tongue in his cheek in a mock blowjob. The windows between them muted the late-night party unfolding inside Levi's truck. Luke shook his head and smiled as Levi surged ahead and rode off in the fast lane.

"I remember when I was out for the first time," Luke said to himself.

Even at twenty-three years old, Luke was no rookie. In 1998, he won the California High School all-around, steer wrestling, and team roping titles. He joined the Professional Rodeo Cowboys Association in 2000 and missed the National Finals Rodeo that year by about six hundred dollars—a tenth of a second at some rodeos—before making rodeo's grand stage each of the next three years. Entering the 2004 season, he'd racked up more than four hundred thousand dollars in four years, an unheard-of amount for a young steer wrestler. Yet his success came as no surprise to those around him.

Long as anyone can remember, any time there was a group

of kids playing together, Luke was the one bossing the others around; even older kids listened to him. As he grew up, he seemed ready for new stages of life before others his age. Before he was in kindergarten, he drove tractors around the family's fourteen-thousand-acre cattle ranch outside Los Alamos, California; his father, John, laughed as heavy equipment appeared to move around without a driver until it hit a large bump and Luke's head popped into view over the dash. Luke was five when he leaned a shotgun over the side of a moving pickup and shot his first wild boar.

All his life, he's won at everything he's set his mind to: Baseball. Blackjack. Bulldogging. The game never mattered, just the winning. While most cowboys ride into an arena hoping for a victory, Luke parades in believing he cannot lose. And it's that cocksure attitude that allows him to concentrate on his life's other true passion: being a smart-ass. His face usually wears a good-natured smile; serious comments rarely leave his lips; anyone hanging around him for the first time quickly could become convinced he views life as one long joke.

His friends started calling him Fatty after seeing the six-foot, 260-pound cowboy without a shirt on. The nickname stuck, and today more rodeo people call him Fatty than Luke. His bulky frame—the result of weight-lifting sessions and bad eating habits—has done little to hamper his sex life. His early years as a professional cowboy established him both as a powerhouse steer wrestler and a prolific playboy. The latter is hardly unusual for cowboys and cowgirls on the PRCA circuit, where sexual scouting reports are a frequent topic of mealtime discussion. Asked how a night with Luke went, one barrel racer bragged to one of Luke's friends that Fatty was a champion outside the arena, too.

Both he and Casey still spend a good deal of time at their parents' cattle ranch, and neither has bothered buying a house because essentially they live on the road. It's an E-ticket lifestyle that offers little in the way of reflection, mostly because there's always someone around. But that changes in the sleepy hours of the dying night. When everyone else in the rig is asleep, and you're sharing the darkened interstate with tired truckers, cowboys, and other restless souls hyped on coffee, energy drinks, and God knows what else.

As the clock neared 4 A.M., Luke flipped through his CDs, looking for something that fit the mood. Moments later, a saxophone wailed through the speakers at the opening of Bob Seger's weary road song, "Turn the Page." Luke leaned back into his seat, stretched his shoulder, and stared into the distance. The odometer rolled, and the pavement kept coming. When the vocals started, he sang along in a scratchy whisper to a tune that seemed to capture the soundtrack of his life:

On a long and lonesome highway east of Omaha,
You can listen to the engine moanin' out as one long song.
You can think about the woman or the girl you knew the night
before,
But your thoughts will soon be wandering the way they always do.
When you're riding sixteen hours and there's nothing much to do,
And you don't feel much like riding, you just wish the trip was
through.

Say here I am, on the road again.
There I am, up on the stage.
Here I go, playing the star again.
There I go, turn the page. . . .

GREEN RIVER. CRESCENT JUNCTION. FRUITA.
Casey lay in a bed and stared at the ceiling, his body shaking with every bump in the road. Alone in the darkened trailer, he'd

spent several hours trying to cast the saddest memory from mind. This wasn't about a woman; not one he knew, anyway. A couple years back there had been love, but there was no one now. A man gets his fingers burned and pulls back from the fire. Hell, even the puppy that was tearing up Casey's bed seemed like a pretty big commitment to him. But this memory had nothing to do with loneliness and broken hearts. This was about that terrible summer night last year in Wyoming. Finally, Casey gave up on sleep, and began working through it again in his mind.

He pictured himself behind the wheel of the rig as it came down from the Black Hills of South Dakota. He and two other cowboys, brothers Tim and Doug Pharr, were on their way from Deadwood to Cheyenne. That put them on Highway 85 at about 10:30 that night, between the tiny eastern Wyoming towns of Lusk and Newcastle where there's nothing but a rise of blacktop stretching across the wide-open prairie.

Once again, in his mind, Casey watched the stocky mule deer as it walked across the road. After it reached the shoulder, it acted like it would keep going. Casey kept the rig at 65 mph as he got closer. Then, at the last moment, the deer turned and wandered back onto the road. Casey never hit the brakes. Upon impact, the deer rolled beneath the truck, lifting the front wheels off the ground. Wrestling the steering, Casey fought to keep the rig on the road, swerving from white line to white line. He felt the trailer go over; it skidded on its side along the pavement in a deafening, spark-throwing roar.

Once the motion stopped, Casey and Doug got out of the truck and ran to the trailer where Tim had been sleeping. They called out to him, pounding the metal with their hands in the otherwise eerie silence of a pitch-black night. They heard nothing. Moments later, Casey heard the cowboy's voice through the metal wall, saying he was okay. Casey walked to the back of the trailer to check on the three horses, knowing they probably were in pretty bad shape. He couldn't open the mangled trailer door. He made his way to the roof, figuring he'd have to cut the horses out. But the roof was gone. And so were the horses.

Tim and Doug set out across the prairie to try to find the animals. Casey stayed with the rig where there was little to do but fear the worst. The bad news started coming an hour later when Tim called Casey on a cell phone from the scene of another crash. Three miles from the rig, Tim had seen headlights pointing off the roadway and thought it was someone who stopped after finding the horses. But as he got closer, the destruction began to take shape. The mangled car. The dead horses. All the blood in the world.

Casey listened to the details, his stomach sinking with the uneasy pain only guilt can bring. Hours passed before a sheriff drove to Casey for an interview. Casey sat in the patrol car's passenger seat and told the man what had happened. Then the sheriff got a phone call. Casey listened to one end of the conversation, piecing things together, knowing the worst news was coming. The sheriff hung up the phone, looked at Casey, and told him the woman who had been driving was dead. Her daughter was critically injured. Casey sat there, shaking and crying, alongside a dark Wyoming highway much like he was doing now in the back of this trailer, lost in the sadness of another lonely old night on the road.

GRAND JUNCTION. GLENWOOD SPRINGS. DENVER.

(Thirty hours later) As dawn broke, Denver wore a fresh coat of snow. A steady wind blew, and dark gray clouds made the sky above the city look like a raging sea. Heavy snow fell throughout the morning, slowing interstate traffic to a crawl. The lone exception was Luke, who was driving Levi's new thirty-thousand-dollar truck, blowing past cars in the icy fast lane of Interstate 70.

The cowboys had found a greasy breakfast and were headed back to the grounds about an hour before the rodeo started. Luke, driving because he knew the city a little better than the others, pulled off the interstate onto a crowded road a couple blocks from the Denver Coliseum.

"So," Austin said from the backseat. "How's Lindsay?"

"Real good," Luke said, smiling at Austin in the rearview mirror.

"Tell me you showered first," Levi said.

"Yes sir, I did," Luke said. "Showered, scrubbed, and I even shaved my balls."

Austin's calm voice interrupted from the backseat: "Red light."

Luke and Levi didn't hear him. Luke kept driving.

"You really shaved your balls?" Levi said.

Luke looked over at him and smiled. His expression said yes.

Now the voice from the backseat had lost its calm. "RED LIGHT!" Austin shouted. "RED LIGHT!"

Luke whipped his head forward to see three lanes of traffic heading his way. He slammed on the brakes and Levi's shiny new truck slid atop the dirty ice into a crowded intersection. Levi winced as the scene before him unfolded in slow motion. Two drivers trying to turn onto I-70 veered to avoid a crash. A trucker, who had seen Luke coming, stopped his rig in time. Luke missed the collision by about five feet. The trucker, now looking down into the cab of Levi's truck, started laughing as other drivers began honking their horns.

The cab grew quiet. Luke calmly reached down and shifted the truck into reverse. He turned his head and put his arm on the seat, and backed the truck out of the intersection. As he did, he looked over at Levi, who had yet to say a word.

"That trucker thought it was funny," Luke said with a shrug.

"Motherfucker," Levi said, shaking his head from side to side.

"These Colorado stoplights are tricky," Luke said. "What were we talking about, anyway? I can't even remember what we were talking about."

"Your balls," Levi said. "We were talking about your shaved balls."

"Oh yeah," Luke said, laughing to himself.

A minute later, Luke pulled into the Coliseum lot and parked. Levi stared straight ahead and stuck out his hand.

"Give me the fucking keys," he said.

Luke handed the keys over without saying a word. Then all three cowboys began laughing hysterically. It was time to rodeo.

A trailer door slammed shut, and tiny piles of snow rained onto the ground. A cowboy buttoned his NFR jacket, grabbed his horse's reins, and began plodding through the Coliseum lot. Step by step, cowboy boots and horseshoes crushed the powder into ice, carving out a new trail. Horse and rider simultaneously exhaled warm breaths that appeared and vanished like ghosts in the frozen air.

The heavy footsteps eased onto a thin path worn to the pavement by hundreds of other cowboys and horses. The path ended at the base of a large wooden door: the back entrance to the Coliseum. A gloved hand reached out for the handle. The door swung open. And the cold white world outside gave way to the warm browns of old wooden stalls and fresh dirt backstage.

The man led his horse through a long corridor, plotting his course to avoid scattered piles of horseshit. The ammonia stench of animal urine overpowered all other smells, watering eyes and noses alike. The man pressed on, passing cowboys and cowgirls gathered in loose groups of three, four, and five. He stopped occasionally to wish friends well, continuing only after leaving the group laughing at some self-deprecating statement. Finally, he reached the warm-up area—a circle of dirt about a hundred feet across and located just outside the arena. He climbed onto his horse and blended into a parade of riders getting their horses ready to run.

He settled in behind Luke and Bryan Fields, two NFR qualifiers from the previous year who were busy laughing at each other's jokes. Casey, a short rope hanging around his neck and a longer one curled around his arm, stood and talked to a man across a fence. McGilchrist sat on a bale of hay, took the hat from his head, and prayed. Levi and Austin warmed their horses, looking around and taking it all in.

Suddenly, the crowd roared as the lights went out inside the Coliseum. Seconds later, the glow of green lasers and fireworks flashes filtered backstage. As rock music blared, the muffled voice of announcer Boyd Polhamus carried into the warm-up area as the 2004 rodeo season got under way.

Denver, like most rodeos, features seven main events. There are four timed competitions—steer wrestling, team roping, calf roping, and barrel racing—and three rough stock events—bareback bronc riding, saddle bronc riding, and bull riding. Most rodeos begin with bareback riding and steer wrestling, then work through the other events until it comes to bull riding, which usually serves as the finale. Though bull riding clearly holds the most crowd appeal and tension—at least partially because it's the only event where the animals actually try to kill the competitors and the prospect of death always looms one bad break away—each event has its core of followers.

Steer wrestling, revered for its combination of speed and strength, was invented about a century ago by a cowboy named

Bill Pickett, who performed the novelty act in a traveling Wild West show. Team roping has built an enormous following as rodeo's only true team event, a sport that originated on ranches where two men were needed to treat or brand large cattle. Saddle bronc riding is the sport's classic competition, having evolved from the task of breaking horses on sprawling cattle ranches of the Old West. Barrel racing has its own set of fans, being the only flat-out race as well as the only event that features female competitors. Bareback riding, possibly the most physically demanding event in rodeo, has been compared to riding a jackhammer with one hand.

After Denver's first round of bareback riders had taken their turns, the main gate at the other end of the arena swung open. A couple dozen steer wrestlers made their way in and walked toward the timed-event chutes.

Levi and Austin were among the first bulldoggers to go, and both threw their steers to the ground in little more than five seconds: good showings, but not fast enough for any money. Their second runs didn't win them anything, either.

Of the three rookies, McGilchrist had the best opener. Two solid runs earned him a spot in the short round, and he rode away from Denver with a check worth more than five thousand dollars and a top five spot in the early season standings. However, he would spend the next few months in a serious drought that would see his name slip a few spots in the standings each week until it left the top fifty altogether.

As Luke rode his horse into the arena before his run, he worked his left shoulder in a slow circular motion, trying to ease the pain. A 600 mg dose of ibuprofen helped that somewhat.

"This cowboy has been to the NFR three times," Polhamus announced to the crowd.

"How many single ladies do we have in the audience? . . . Okay, how many married ladies do we have who like to look?"

The second question drew a rousing response, but Luke seemed not to notice. In fact, at that moment, all signs of the sarcastic playboy disappeared, replaced by the deadeye look of a cowboy locked in concentration. He glanced over the chute to check on his hazer, a man whose job is to ride along the other side of the steer and herd it toward the bulldogger. Looking back at the steer, Luke took a few deliberate breaths and nodded to the gateman. The steer broke from the chute with Luke on its tail. He leaned far right in the saddle as he reached out and touched the steer's back. He slid his hand up the steer's back and locked his right arm around one horn, grabbing the other horn with his left. He kicked free of the stirrups and planted his feet on the ground. He skidded to a stop, wrenched the steer's neck, and the animal flopped onto its side. He looked up to see his time on the scoreboard: 4.5 seconds. A nice beginning.

Casey sat on a fence and awaited his turn to rope a calf. The steer wrestlers had finished, but Casey had to wait until rodeo's true fan favorites—the mutton busters—had their time in the spotlight.

Here's the thing: For cowboys, rodeo is a competition, a battle against beast and time where the easy money always seems within reach but rarely is. For some rodeo fans, watching that competition unfold is mildly interesting at best. In terms of generating crowd attention, it takes a backseat to, say, a bronc rider landing on his head or a man being trampled by a bull. But nothing excites a rodeo crowd quite like a helmeted five-year-old kid holding on for dear life to a galloping sheep.

"Yes, ladies and gentlemen," Polhamus announced, "it's that time of the evening when we strap small children to farm animals and call it entertainment."

Suddenly, people sat up in their seats. Many yelled encouragement as, one by one, the mutton busters rode into the arena. The crowd groaned as one kid slipped to the side of the sheep, then rolled completely under and still made it another ten feet hanging onto the underbelly of the animal before falling off and getting run over by the back legs. Mutton busting drew the night's loudest ovations.

Next up was calf roping. Casey, with Luke standing by his side, sat atop his horse in the box, awaiting his calf. Casey gave a quick nod and rode into the arena swinging a rope. But his throw missed the calf's head and, just like that, Denver was a bust.

"That's a California Circuit champion right there," Polhamus announced. "I know we're a what-have-you-done-for-me-lately society, but that's a talented roper who has had some bad luck."

The crowd cheered politely as Casey rode from the arena. Ten minutes later, he was in his truck, driving alone through the night to Fort Worth, Texas.

Luke's good fortune ended the following night with his second steer. On the dismount, both he and his steer stumbled, and the animal ran off before Luke could recover. There was little time to lament the loss.

With the night's performance less than thirty minutes old, Luke hurried out of the arena, walked quickly through the snow, and climbed into Fields's idling rig. The two cowboys had about twelve hours to make the twelve-hour drive to northeast Texas. Luke sat in the passenger seat with a can of Red Bull and a can of Copenhagen, headed toward Fort Worth where he would win the average title and more than eight thousand dollars. But, as he looked out the window at the Colorado landscape that night, something was wrong. Something vague. It still didn't feel right being on the road without Travis.

CHAPTER 2

On the Comeback Trail

G o back thirty years to a Southern California desert town
and find a boy roping plastic horns strapped onto bales of
yellow hay in the dirt parking lot outside some shitty old
rodeo. Make the boy skinny. Dress him right, like a cowboy.
Give him an older brother. And a father for a hero. Teach him to
rope. Let him be crazy enough to jump off horses to wrestle
steers, but too smart to ride bulls. Give him a problem with authority. Make him at home on the road. Give him a dash of
Crash Davis. Saddle him with a Copenhagen habit. Give him
the foul mouth of a cowboy. Make him a gambler. Now give him
a dream. Make it the big one, the finals. Let him reach for it.
Have him destroy both knees and a shoulder. Let the best doctors put him back together. Have him marry a Cow Palace
rodeo queen. Give him a daughter, and a son. Slow down his
life, but not his spirit. Now let him reach for the dream again.
Give him a trip to the finals. Make him gamble on one moment
to win it all, and have him miss it by six inches at 30 mph. Let
that moment haunt him as he practices every day. Make him
relive it in the lonely grueling hours of rehabilitation that follow another knee surgery. Now let him come back. Let him
again be as good as there is on any given day here in the sunset
of his career.

Do all that, and you would have Travis Cadwell.

OAKDALE, CALIFORNIA

VALENTINE'S DAY

Travis climbed aboard an old blue Ford tractor and sat in its rusty seat. He fired the engine to life. He backed the tractor to a makeshift plow, and hooked the two together. Travis drove into the arena and began carving out large circles, watching behind him as crooked spikes molded the soil into tiny chocolate-colored rows. The plow kicked up an occasional tree root, a holdout from the apple orchard that stood there before Travis converted the land into a cowboy's field of dreams.

He built the arena on the northern end of a twenty-five-acre ranch located a few miles west of Oakdale, a Northern California rodeo town. The practice pad was created with one thing in mind: steer wrestling. It is eighty feet wide and three hundred feet long, giving galloping horses plenty of stopping room after their riders hop off. The chute was set at the southern end of the arena where a grove of majestic hundred-year oaks—the pride of the property—offers shade from the late-afternoon sun. At the northern end is a holding pen where nine Corriente steers crammed themselves into the corner.

As Travis worked the ground, the early signs of spring surrounded him. Knee-high weeds sprouted alongside muddy roads that snaked around the ranch. Birds tended to their nests in the high branches of the oaks. In a nearby almond orchard, honey bees moved about madly in the restless hum of February's popcorn trees.

Yet spring's arrival was not entirely good news: It also served as a reminder that Travis was missing out on some big winter rodeos. At that moment, eighteen hundred miles away in San Antonio, Luke and hundreds of other cowboys were taking their shots. Travis would have been there, too, but his left knee was not quite ready. It had been fifteen months since he had torn his anterior cruciate ligament at a rodeo in Rancho Murieta, California; everyone in the building heard the pop. Travis had reconstructive surgery, and missed the 2003 season rehabbing the knee. Now he was close, but he still did not have enough confidence in it. He figured another month of practice ought to do it.

Travis is a thin man in a big man's sport. He makes up for his lack of size with a solid technique and well-muscled arms and upper body. He looks the part of rodeo veteran: He walks with a slight stoop; creases of skin around his eyes deepen when he smiles; his neck has been tanned and hardened by decades of arena sun.

Like Luke, Travis is extremely polite in the company of strangers and rodeo fans, but his demeanor changes drastically when he's on the road. He's a constant source of noise, the loudest man in a poker game whether he's ahead or behind. His friends nicknamed him Donkey after the chattering ass in the *Shrek* movies.

Shortly after 1 P.M., Travis parked the tractor and climbed aboard his horse. He walked the horse around the arena to warm up. Down by the chutes, Vince Walker, another steer wrestler on the mend, fumbled with one of Travis's old knee braces, trying to put it on correctly. Once he did, he got on his horse and rode off to join Travis. A small group of family, friends, and neighbors, about a dozen in all, showed up to watch the day's practice session. They sat in lawn chairs and drank Coors Lights from ice chests. Several other people rode horses around the arena.

Travis backed his horse into the box, looking over the chute to make sure Vince was ready. Vince smiled. Then Travis looked at a friend manning the chute and nodded. The gates swung open and the steer charged out. Travis broke from the box, got his horse up to about 25 mph as he leaned right in the saddle, and jumped onto the ground with both hands on the steer. Travis skidded to a stop, grabbed the animal's nose, and slammed him into the dirt, kicking up a cloud of dust around them. The whole thing took about four seconds.

An older man, sitting at ground level just behind the box, nearly fell out of his lawn chair. "Jesus Christ!" he said to a woman sitting next to him. "You couldn't get me drunk enough to do that."

The man was no stranger to steer wrestling, but he'd never seen it up close before. Watching from the grandstands or on television, you can see the sport's speed, but not its power. People behind the box have their faces blasted by a spray of dirt when the animals burst for the arena. Those nearby feel the ground shake beneath the thunder of hooves. And, at ground level, they see what it's really like for a man to jump off a speeding horse and pounce on a charging steer with long sharp horns bouncing on every step.

After Travis finished the practice run, he and the steer slowly rose to their feet and headed their separate ways. The steer, having been through this daily exercise countless times, trotted off to its holding pen. Travis walked toward the chute, stopping at an ice chest next to the old man.

"You want a beer, Travis?" the man asked.

"No, no, I'm going to have a Gatorade," Travis said. "I try not to drink when I'm practicing."

He reached into the ice chest and pulled out a Coors Light, looked at the man, and smiled. Travis popped the top and took a drink.

"I'm sure glad they started putting Gatorade in these silver cans," Travis said.

"Me, too," the man said, taking a long drink.

Travis finished his beer and returned to practice. Throughout the afternoon, he threw steers to the ground with ease, looking like a man ready to return to competition. Of course, bulldogging with the best never has been his problem. Staying healthy has.

Travis, thirty-six, was born and raised on a 2.5-acre ranch in Nuevo, a town of about six thousand people and one of the last places in California that isn't growing. His father rode bulls and wrestled steers until knee injuries ended his career. Growing up, Travis spent most weekends at rodeos. His earliest memories are of sitting in a camper as his mom taught him to read, or sitting aboard his first horse, Chester, as his dad taught him how to rope. As a boy, Travis carried a rope around with him everywhere.

Before learning to compete, he and his brother worked for stock contractors, loading cattle and working the chutes. Joke is that was the last time Travis ever made money at rodeos. By the early 1980s, he and his brother had saved up a good portion of the money they had earned. His brother bought a pickup. Travis bought calves, steers, and ropes. He became a junior rodeo steer riding champion in his early teens, but decided not to graduate to bulls. Instead, he concentrated on calf roping and steer wrestling. He got his PRCA permit at age sixteen, and bought his first PRCA card four years later.

The following winter, at age twenty, he headed out on the big circuit for the first time with four thousand dollars he'd saved from a summer construction job. He won a go-round at Yuma, his first rodeo after turning pro. He came home and told his dad that maybe he was ready for this rodeo life. But he crashed back to earth the next week in San Antonio, choking on a couple of good steers, and he started questioning everything.

None of his traveling partners knew enough about winning to offer Travis much perspective. Reality is, like major league baseball hitters, even the best cowboys fail most of the time. By the time Travis hit Tucson, he didn't even want to rodeo anymore. He spent the next couple years learning hard lessons no one can teach. But as he got his mind right, his body began to let him down.

In 1991, he tore cartilage in his knee during practice, leading to his first knee surgery. He missed two months in rehabilitation. Shortly after he came back, a freak steer wrestling accident left him with gangrene in his toe. He spent eleven days in a hospital where doctors told him he'd lose the toe for sure. He looked beneath the covers and saw red streaks climbing his foot and lower leg. Eventually, the gangrene healed and he managed to keep his toe, but the year was shot. He went to a few rodeos the following year with little success, paying his bills by working construction.

In 1993, he made his first serious run at the NFR. By late August, he found himself in sixteenth place in the world standings. But then he tore up his shoulder practicing in Colorado Springs. After taking a month off to strengthen the shoulder, Travis returned to find the pain had worsened. Another season ended with a trip to the doctor, who told Travis he'd suffered a torn pectoral muscle, a torn rotator cuff, and a slight dislocation. The injuries required major surgery and five months of rehabilitation. Still, it couldn't be considered a bad year. He wound up in the top twenty-five, his best finish to that point.

Also that year, while Travis was wandering around the Cow Palace parking lot late one night, a young brunette woman named Tiffany Hunt drove past him. The two talked a little that night, then met up again four months later at the H-Bar-B, an Oakdale cowboy bar, and started dating.

In 1995, Travis was in the top fifteen in the PRCA's all-around standings and winning the California Circuit. But, in August, a steer fell on Travis's leg during a practice run, tearing the ACL and cartilage in his right knee. That led to another season-ending surgery. He threw some steers on weekends the next couple of years, but slowly he gave up his dream of making the finals. Except in that part of the mind where dreams don't die. He began to believe he didn't have whatever it took. He could match anyone in practice, but something always seemed to go wrong at the worst time.

At that time, a friend got Travis hired as a stuntman for TV shows and movies so he could get his Screen Actors Guild card and, more important, the medical benefits that came with it. He earned five hundred dollars a day plus extra money for performing more dangerous stunts. He fell down stairs during a fight scene. He got lit on fire and ran from a helicopter that had been shot down. He flipped a truck upside down at 40 mph for three thousand dollars.

He and Tiffany got married in 1998 and moved to Oakdale to start their family. That year, he won the steer wrestling title at Salinas worth nearly eight thousand dollars, and finished the season with about thirty thousand dollars in rodeo earnings. He never got on much of a roll the next season, but he remained healthy.

Then came 2000, the best year of his rodeo life. After a miserable winter where he earned just two thousand dollars, Travis won sixty-five hundred dollars in Cheyenne. That touched off a hot streak. He won fifteen hundred dollars here and two thousand dollars there, no fat checks but his name slowly rose in the standings. By the end of the month he'd won twenty thousand dollars, vaulting him from nowhere into the top fifteen. He stayed just hot enough the rest of the season, closing with twelve thousand dollars during the last three weeks to eek into the finals. There, a new brand of heartbreak awaited him.

Travis won the second round with a 3.9-second run that earned him more than thirteen thousand dollars and vaulted him from thirteenth to eighth in the world standings. He added to his total by placing well in the fourth and fifth rounds. More important, he strung together nine steady runs and was sitting second—four-tenths of a second behind the leader—in the aggregate standings that offered the winner more than thirty-three thousand dollars.

That set the stage for the final round of the NFR. Travis drew a good steer, one nobody had been longer than four seconds on at the finals. Travis rode into the arena that afternoon with an outside shot of winning a world title. He had two options: He could play it safe and make sure the steer got far enough into the arena, a strategy that likely would pay about twenty-seven thousand dollars for taking second in the average. Or, he could gamble everything and take a shot at winning the round and the average, and perhaps the title. The second strategy dangled the possibility of winning forty-seven thousand dollars, with a risk of winning nothing if Travis left too soon.

As Travis backed into the box, he was acutely aware of the stakes. It was a man and his moment, a scenario he had envisioned since he was a kid. It had taken thirty-two years for him to get to the finals and, as good as the season had been, he knew he might never make it back. The way Travis saw it, there was no choice; he pushed his chips to the center of the table and went all in.

He nodded, charged into the arena, and threw the steer to the ground as the crowd steadily grew louder. The scoreboard stopped on 3.5 seconds. Announcer Bob Tallman already had gone into his celebratory voice before the bad news came back:

a broken barrier. The steer had hesitated slightly before breaking from the chute, and Travis had ridden from the box too soon. Imagine this: After all the miles and years, it came down to about six inches at 30 mph in Round 10 of the finals.

There was no second-guessing the strategy, but there also was no way to stop lamenting the result. As the years passed, the run crept into Travis's head more and more. Four years later, he still thinks about it, often bitterly, sometimes fondly. The dream's tone slowly changed from galloping toward the future to righting a wrong from the past. It's a heavy thing, a man and his moment. Especially when the moment may be gone forever.

CHAPTER 3

A Tucson Hangover

Travis, tired from a late-night flight from Sacramento, stood in a cramped PRCA office and flipped through a stack of papers until he found his name. Next to it was the number of his first steer of the season. He set the papers down and headed outside.

Just outside the office, he pulled out a cell phone and called Luke to find out where he was. Luke didn't answer, so Travis left a message.

"Hey, I just saw a black horse and a bay horse running through downtown Tucson. They were being chased by a guy in a white pickup. I didn't know if that would be of any interest to you. Call me back."

Travis put the phone in his pocket and began making his way through a gravel parking lot brimming with trucks, trailers, and cowboys readying their horses for that morning's slack. Then something stopped him. He turned his head to look down a dirt driveway, and a warm smile flashed upon his face.

There was Brock Andrus, sitting atop a horse, silhouetted by the morning sunlight that crept above the mountains far behind him. Brock held on to the reins of another cowboy's horse, passing the time by acting disgusted at all the sponsors on the man's dress shirt. He didn't see Travis until he was just a couple feet away.

Brock twisted in his saddle to face Travis and smiled big and honest, the skin around his eyes crinkling from years of laughing in the sun. Brock, a man who friends call Shrek because his face bears a striking resemblance to the animated character, looked down and reached out a gloved hand that Travis grabbed firmly. The handshake lasted longer than normal as each man gave the other contented looks that said a million things at once.

It's been too long, friend. Oh the miles we've traveled together. Can you believe we're still out here?

But cowboys rarely talk that way, especially when the feelings are strong. Brock killed the moment's sincerity before Travis had a chance.

"Well," Brock said, "so you're a sellout whore, too, ain't ya?"

"Me?" Travis said.

"Look at all this shit," Brock said, pointing toward Travis's jacket from the 2002 California Circuit Finals. "Wrangler. Justin. Toyota. You're a human billboard, Cadwell."

"I didn't even go to this rodeo," Travis said.

"You didn't?" Brock said. "So, you're a charity case then."

"Hey what year is that finals jacket from?" Travis said, taking the offensive.

Brock started laughing, knowing he was caught. There it was, in enormous type across his back: National Finals Rodeo participant 2001. The black leather NFR jackets are badges of honor; they separate the best cowboys from the dreamers. Wearing a jacket from the previous year's finals means you're one of the world's reigning top fifteen stars in your sport, truly a man to beat. But, as time passes, the coats fade and begin to serve more as a reminder of how many years it's been since you accomplished something.

"I shouldn't even be wearing this thing anymore," Brock said, softly rubbing one of his sleeves like it was a decrepit pet. "Poor old relic. I oughta sell it on eBay is what I oughta do."

"I feel your pain, George," Travis said. "My jacket's even older than yours. Tiffany keeps trying to give it away to Goodwill. I have to hide it from her."

Travis laughed as he walked away. The morning's steer wrestling was about to begin, and he still hadn't found Luke. Travis made it about twenty feet before he stopped to tell Brock one last thing.

"I'll be ready for that coffee pretty soon," Travis said.

"Oh you will?" Brock said, looking amused as he twisted again in his saddle.

"Yeah, I'll be near the chutes in a minute."

"Oh, okay. You want me to bring it to you there?"

"Yeah. That'd be fine."

"You want a thermos or a cup?"

"Cup's fine," Travis said, walking away like a man in a hurry. "I already had some this morning. One more cup'll do it."

"Okay," Brock said, under his breath. "Yeah, I'll have something for you to suck on, cowboy."

At 8 A.M., Luke, Travis, Brock, and roughly seventy-five other steer wrestlers filled one end of the Tucson arena. The cowboys outnumbered the crowd by about fifty. This is to be expected. With limited slots available in the rodeo performances put on for large crowds, most cowboys compete in low-key slack competitions seen by hardly anyone. Frankly, most cowboys could not care less. Their concerns center on fast times and fat purses; crowds simply do not figure in the equation.

As Luke waited to make his run, he hopped up and down,

trying to keep warm in the cold desert air. The bottoms of his pants were bunched around the top of his boots. He looked like he'd just rolled out of bed and put his boots on, which is what had happened. Like many of the cowboys there that morning, Luke didn't get to sleep until the early-morning hours after competing in a steer wrestling jackpot at the house of a wealthy Tucson lumberman named Pat Manley. Unlike most of the others, Luke had pocketed fifty-four hundred dollars at the non-PRCA event. That came just two weeks after he'd won about six thousand dollars in San Angelo, raising him to third in the PRCA's world standings.

As the first bulldoggers made their runs, Luke and Travis stood next to each other, quietly laughing at wisecracks. Brock and Casey sat just behind them on horses. Travis took off a glove, slid an index finger inside his lower lip and dropped a gob of chew into the dirt, and then put his glove back on. He began getting his mind ready for his first bulldogging run in a long time. His season opener. Every so often, a cowboy came up and grabbed Travis's shoulders, telling him it was good to see him out again, whispering things that made both men laugh. Travis first entered Tucson in 1988. Now, seventeen years later, he looked around the arena and saw countless new faces. In fact, one of the only cowboys he remembered being at that first Tucson rodeo was Brock.

He thought of this as Brock backed his horse into the box. When Brock nodded to set the steer free, his horse reared and lunged forward, breaking the barrier before the steer had gone far enough. No time. Brock's second run didn't end up much better. Upon finally catching his steer deep in the arena, Brock fell to the ground, but still refused to let go. The steer dragged Brock a few feet. He clutched the animal's head as he fought back to his feet. Finally, he got the animal back in position for a takedown. At some point, it stopped being about making a good time and started being about putting that motherfucking steer on the ground. He ended with a time of 27.5 seconds, the kind of run that gives a man a lot to think about on a long drive back to St. George. Or gives him something to forget.

Travis's season opener fizzled as well. He caught up to his first steer fast enough, but both he and the animal fell down when Travis jumped from his horse. Travis stood, helped the animal to its feet, then slammed him back onto the dirt. By then, 11.1 seconds had passed, as had any hope of making the short round. His second run was a 7.3.

Luke's steer got a fast start, costing some time before he caught up, and he finished with a 6.8-second run. Though he came back with a 4.9 on his second run that won him fifteen hundred dollars, he fell just short of placing in the average. Casey found a little luck in Tucson, turning in a run of 5.5 seconds, good for seventeen hundred dollars and his first paycheck of the young season. But he had trouble catching up to his second steer in an 8.2-second run that also took him out of contention at Tucson.

After slack ended, some cowboys walked back to the vicinity of Luke's trailer. They hung around outside, wasting the late-morning hours with nowhere official to be until the next morning. Travis sat on a bale of straw, lazily flipping through a copy of *Playboy.* Luke opened his trailer door and began sweeping dirt outside.

The two longtime traveling partners had not rodeoed together much since Travis hurt his knee eighteen months earlier. At least one thing had changed significantly.

"So, you got a steady girl now?" Travis said.

"Yep," Luke said, sweeping, not looking up.

"Do I know her?" Travis said.

"Hope not," Luke said, stepping down to sweep off the step.

As he did, Brock walked up and began using Luke's step to scrape green globs of horseshit off the bottom of his boots.

"What the hell are you doing?" Luke said.

"I'm going in there," Brock said, trying to force his way into the trailer.

"No you're not," Luke said, holding him back. "I'm cleaning. See this? It's a broom."

Brock made another push inside, and finally made it in. Luke shook his head in disgust and went back to sweeping the step as Brock rummaged through the refrigerator. A minute later, Brock stepped out of the trailer empty-handed and walked to his truck. He rooted around through the detritus on the front seat, and emerged with a cold fast-food breakfast sandwich. He unwrapped it and took several bites as he looked over Travis's shoulder and examined the women in the magazine.

Levi rode up on a horse, stepped off, and tied the animal to a chain-link fence. He was getting hungry. He looked with great interest at the sandwich in Brock's hand.

"Where'd you get that?" Levi said.

"I just found it in my truck," Brock said, chewing a mouth full of food. "I bought three of these the other day. I just never got around to eatin' this one."

"How old is it?"

"Oh, I don't know," Brock said, in his standard drawl. "Two or three days, maybe. Somethin' like that."

Levi wrinkled his face and smiled, but no words came to mind. He looked over at Travis.

"Hey, you hungry?" Levi said.

"Yeah," Travis said, "I could stand to eat something. George, you wanna get some food?"

"Nah," Brock said, taking the last bite of his sandwich. "I'm good for now."

"All right," Travis said, standing and wiping the hay off his pants. "Let's go then. Fatty, we're taking your truck."

"Fine," Luke said, still trying to get all the shit off his step.

As Travis walked away, he turned to see Brock pick up the magazine and sit on the hay.

"George, you want us to get you anything while we're out?" said Travis, the only cowboy who addresses Brock by his real name. "Maybe a blow-up doll?"

"Sure, Travvie," Brock said, "I'd like to see you spend that much money on somethin'."

"Okay George," Travis said. "We'll drop her off at your truck after we eat."

"Sounds good," Brock said.

After lunch, a group of cowboys drove to a park near the rodeo grounds to play some basketball. It was mostly steer wrestlers like Luke, Travis, and Levi, but there were a few ropers as well.

As the cowboys played a full-court game against one another, a group of shady-looking Latino men gathered on the grass and discussed the situation at hand. They were the unmistakable embodiment of gang life. And, it was clear, they were used to dominating the park's court. Five of them came together on a patch of grass, waiting for the game to end so they could take over.

The vehicles in the parking lot told the story: It was the cowboys versus the gangbangers. On one side of the lot, there were four late-model diesel pickups, two of which held stacks of hay bales in their beds. Not far away were several four-door cars like Buicks and Cadillacs that dated back to the 1980s. The only thing the two groups had in common was that many of them were born into their current ways of life, and presumably they were living as their fathers had.

Just before game time, the cowboys agreed to go skins. As they peeled off their shirts, most of them looked like members of some strange cult: They had severely scarred tissue resembling hideous cigar burns on their lower stomachs. The marks come from years of steer horns gouging the belly during takedowns. The gang members also had their scars, mostly tattoos on their arms and legs. One of the young men had a large tattoo on his leg that read 187, the police code for murder.

He opened the game by scoring two quick layups as the gangbangers jumped out to an early lead. Their speed helped them build an early 5-0 advantage before the cowboys started making a concerted effort to play defense. After that, the cowboys came roaring back. Levi and roper Zane Bruce from Eldorado, Texas, helped bring the cowboys back quickly to tie it at 6-6. Travis, normally a decent player, missed every shot he attempted, though he simply was pleased his knee held up well in his first pickup game since the injury. Levi and Luke converted consecutive Travis misses into layups to force game point. Then Bruce made a short jumper for the game winner.

"That's game," Travis said, walking off the court.

"No," said the man with the murder tattoo. "That's only 10-7."

"No," Travis said, "that's 11-7."

"No," the man protested as his teammates left the court. "That's only 10."

Realizing he was the only one defending his case, he got pissed off, grabbed his basketball, and briskly walked to his car. Bruce decided to pour some gas on the simmering coals.

"Sorry the cowboys kicked your ass," Bruce yelled. "We'll be back in town next year if you want to try again."

Upon hearing that, the man's walk turned into a run. After informing someone that he'd be back to shoot the place up, he ducked into a car that sped out of the parking lot and disappeared into afternoon traffic.

The cowboys played one more full-court game against themselves. It was a listless affair marked by shoddy defense, uncontested layups, and distraction, the result of tired cowboys playing with a fair amount of concern about murder boy's whereabouts and intentions. Every car that pulled into the parking lot was given a good examination. While the game played out, each of the cowboys secretly planned an escape route in case a gunman returned.

Later, the cowboys sat around their trucks and laughed about the game. As the sun set, they tried to figure out what to do with the evening. Eventually, they settled on the usual plan: poker and Coors Light. They found a vacant warehouse on the rodeo grounds, and set up a long table and chairs near a roll-up door that gave a view of the grounds.

A group of rodeo boosters and fans, headquartered in RVs, partied just outside the warehouse door. The group emptied coolers of beer while standing around an open fire; drunken laughter grew louder as the night wore on. Other bonfires popped up around the grounds; scattered parties could be identified by smoke signals that let Tucson know the rodeo was back in town.

The poker game began with six cowboys sitting around two tables. Within an hour, it had grown to roughly fifteen gamblers who filled two tables. The night's game was Texas Hold'em, which is all anyone played since ESPN began showing the World Championship of Poker. Twenty dollars bought a small stack of poker chips. Stacks of empty beer cans littered the table, and fresh cases of Coors Light seemed to appear magically. At one point, a drunk cowboy wandered in through the open door, handed out a dozen flavored cigars, and, just as fast, disappeared into the night. The warehouse began to smell of spilled beer and cigar smoke, and the game was proper.

As Levi dealt a hand, steer wrestler Mike Garthwaite lit a cigarette. Travis looked over at him and wrinkled his nose.

"When'd you start smoking?" Travis said.

"I'm trying to quit chewing," Garthwaite said, studying his cards.

"Oh, that's smart," Travis said.

Travis looked at his cards, then looked at Garthwaite, smiled, and raised the bet. They were the last two left playing the hand. Garthwaite studied Travis's eyes, thought a bit, and then pushed all his chips into the stack.

"I'm all in," Garthwaite said.

"Are you now?" said Travis, thinking a few moments before matching Garthwaite's stack. "Well I'm with you. 'Cause I don't think you got shit. Let's see 'em, buddy."

"You first," Garthwaite said.

Travis set his cards down, showing off three kings. Garthwaite grinned. He turned his cards over to present three aces. Laughter erupted from all around the table, except where Travis was sitting.

"Fuck," said Travis. "That's the second time that's happened to me tonight."

"All right," Garthwaite said, standing up and pulling a mound of chips his way. "I don't care if I win another hand all night. I just wanted some of Travis's money."

"Hell, I'm no threat to you, kid," Travis said. "I haven't won a hand all night. You know, I haven't won shit all day. I might as well go back to the motel and sleep."

"Ah, you don't mean that, Trav," Casey said.

"No, I don't," Travis said. "But hell, I can't catch a break. My steer fell down on me. I couldn't make a single basket. Not one.

And I haven't pulled the chips in one time tonight. C'mon Levi, deal me some cards. I just want to reach out and pull the chips in once. I just gotta remember what that feels like."

"It feels pretty good," said Bruce, smiling as he looked over his cards. He'd won the first three games and was up nearly a hundred dollars.

But this was the night's big money game, and Brad McGilchrist was cleaning house. Sitting on the table in front of him were the towering stacks of both chips and empty cans. Most of those with steers in the morning were taking it easy, but McGilchrist chugged one beer after another. When someone suggested he slow down, he explained his rationale.

"Feel bad, do good," McGilchrist said, tossing chips into the pile. "Right Travvie?"

Travis, busy contemplating another shitty hand, answered without looking up.

"How old are you, kid?" Travis said.

"Twenty-three," McGilchrist said.

"Yeah," Travis said, nodding in thought. "Might work."

McGilchrist, holding yet another straight, pushed a large stack of chips into the pot. Travis tossed his cards onto the table. He leaned back in his seat, dropped a fresh chew into his mouth, and let out an exasperated sigh. Usually a bit of a card shark, on this night he was more of a guppy. Casey threw his cards in as well.

"I'm out," Casey said, rising from the table wearing a strange smile. "Guess I'll go stand over by that fire."

The maneuver deeply concerned McGilchrist, who had been making solid headway with an overly friendly drunk woman who had spent most of the night by that fire. She had average looks improved somewhat by the fact she left no doubt she wanted sex.

McGilchrist leaned his head to look outside, seeing if she still was there. She was. And now Casey, a playful, good-looking cowboy who has short brown hair and eyes that cast a warm sincerity, was walking away from the table toward her. McGilchrist sensed disaster.

"You're not going to' try and make it with her, are you?" McGilchrist said.

"Mmmm, I was thinking about it," Casey said. "It's cold tonight."

"Are you kidding?" McGilchrist said in disbelief.

"No," Casey said. "It's cold."

McGilchrist seethed at the table. But he couldn't leave. He was sitting behind a hundred dollars in chips, and he hadn't earned any rodeo money since Denver. His face grew red with naked anger. He picked up his cards and slumped into his seat. Then he heard Casey's voice.

"Braaaaaaaad," Casey said, smiling like a man who had just won the lottery. He held a secret weapon in his hands: his adorable puppy, Trot. The knife drove deeper into McGilchrist's back. Casey raised his hands near his face, and the puppy began licking his nose. Casey looked at McGilchrist and smiled fiendishly. The other gamblers all groaned in delight, loving the mounting tension. Casey laughed as he disappeared outside. McGilchrist wore the sad expression of a child whose scoop of ice cream has just fallen onto the dirt.

"Fuck, I can't believe that," McGilchrist said, again and again. He stood to go outside, but got stopped.

"Donk," Travis said, "you walk away now, you walk away from that money."

McGilchrist, a young Australian cowboy everyone calls Donk after a character in the *Crocodile Dundee* movies, sat back down. As he played his hand, he kept looking out the door to try to see the sinister events he imagined were playing out by the fire. Ten minutes later, Casey returned and grabbed his coat.

"Well guys," he said, "I'm heading off to bed. I'll see you tomorrow."

McGilchrist's head snapped up from his cards.

"You're not taking her back to your trailer, are you?" McGilchrist said.

"No, I'm not," Casey said.

McGilchrist relaxed in his seat, and nodded thankfully.

"No, she's got a motel room somewhere near here," Casey said. "She's gonna take me there."

"She's not," McGilchrist said.

"She is," Casey said with a victorious toothy grin.

Casey shook hands with everyone at the table while McGilchrist silently seethed. His face grew red. Casey let it go for a few minutes, as other cowboys warned him to wear a condom. As he headed out the door, he looked back at McGilchrist.

"Hey Donk," Casey said as McGilchrist looked up. "Don't get your panties wrinkled. I'm going to sleep in my trailer. Alone."

McGilchrist smiled and relaxed in obvious relief.

"You fucker," he said. "That wasn't funny."

Casey laughed heartily. Everyone at the table laughed. McGilchrist laughed, too, but his happiness was short lived.

A few minutes later, he caught a glimpse of a most disturbing scene: Carol and another man walking past the open door. She had her arm around him, and they were laughing easily as they headed toward the rows of parked horse trailers. McGilchrist, in the middle of a heated hand with Travis, called out to the woman as she walked away.

"Carol," McGilchrist said. "Carol."

She didn't seem to hear. He tried again.

"Carol, wait up," McGilchrist said. "I want to talk to you."

It was no use; she was gone. Pissed off and drunk, McGilchrist returned to his cards. He picked up a can of beer and emptied it with a long drink. He set the can down next to a stack of others. He went on to win the table and roughly eighty dollars on the night, but he felt anything but lucky. And Tucson had yet to deal him its worst hand.

The next morning came early. Looking extremely hung over, McGilchrist climbed atop his horse and slowly backed the animal into the box. When the steer broke free, McGilchrist chased it for a few seconds. But the animal veered to the right as McGilchrist was getting ready to take his shot. Watching the steer run away, McGilchrist slowed his horse and cursed his luck.

On this morning at least, the hangover experiment did not work: He never made it out of his saddle.

CHAPTER 4

This Is the Life

So, this is the life.

You're backed into a corner, sitting atop a quarter horse so pumped on adrenaline he's almost dancing in the dirt, snorting, ready to explode from the box the instant he feels your kick. It's like straddling a locomotive.

As you pat his neck to try to calm him, a judge stretches a breakaway rope barrier across the open end of the box, roughly even with your horse's chest; the rope is attached to your steer, giving it a head start that's next to nothing in tiny arenas and up to thirty feet in the largest one. When the steer reaches its advantage point, the barrier is released, opening the arena to you.

So you try to time the barrier, hoping to miss it by an inch or two at full gallop. Come out too soon and hit the rope, and a ten-second penalty dooms any hope of a paycheck. Come out too late, even half a second or less, and you'll waste an extra second or two you can't afford catching up to the steer. If the scouting report says your steer is slower, you'll plan your hesitation in tenths of a second. Timing is everything in the fastest event in rodeo; the world record is 2.4 seconds.

As you sit there, you try not to think about how much is riding on this run. But the fact is, without some money here, you have no idea how you'll get to the next rodeo. Your checking account balance flashes into your head, along with the memory of a friend, another cowboy, telling you he needs some of that money back soon. You glance in the stands and see a woman you met last night in a darkened bar. About now, you wish you still had that one hundred dollars you blew trying to impress her. Oh, you've sworn, too many times to count, that you're really going to quit this stupid scene for good. But deep inside, on some level, you know no one who loves rodeo ever chooses when to leave. No, cowboy, rodeo tells you when you're done. So you shrug it all away and get your mind right again. You look to the chute and see the gateman staring at you, waiting for your signal.

Now you're as ready as you're going to get. Once more, you go over a game plan that likely will be abandoned. As soon as that steer drops his head to take his first step, you're going, you tell yourself. Your horse is shaking beneath you. Everything is cranked to ten. The world outside disappears. You nod, the animals surge, and instinct takes over. Once it's on, there's barely time to react, much less think. Racing into the arena, you hear a chorus of cowboys behind you yelling, "You're out, you're out," meaning you cleared the barrier. You feel momentum growing by the hundredths of seconds as you close in on the steer. Suddenly, you like your chances.

Trouble is, your livelihood is anything but in your hands. The sport involves a bulldogger, hazer, gateman, judge, two timers, two horses, and a steer, meaning each outcome can be directly affected by six human brains and three animal brains. Factor in weather and ground conditions, injuries, luck, marital strife, road exhaustion, hangovers, and countless other variables, and it's easy to see why there hasn't been a repeat world-champion steer wrestler since Ote Berry won his second straight title in 1991.

Closing in on the steer, you lean to the right of the saddle, thankful nothing has gone wrong yet. Meanwhile, the hazer tries to force the action toward you, but it doesn't always work. Either way, you're on your own at this point. Your left foot leaves its stirrup as you bend your right knee until you're almost sitting on the right stirrup. You extend your right hand and touch the steer on the back. Stretching harder from the saddle, you slide your hand on up and reach for the steer's right horn, eventually hooking it with the crook of your elbow. Somewhere in there, you let go of the saddle horn and catch the steer's left horn. Now you are stretched and along for the ride—your lower body still riding your horse as your upper body holds onto the steer's horns. Here's where it gets dicey.

Steer wrestling is not an exact science. Techniques vary greatly from cowboy to cowboy, particularly recovery skills, but many runs devolve into dangerous games of improvisation where so many things can go terribly wrong: The barrier rope grabs you as it snaps through, yanking you off your horse. You miss the horns and crash hard into the dirt. You lose your grip on the saddle horn too soon and fall onto the steer. You grab the steer and his front legs buckle beneath your weight, and you both flip forward; cowboys have been paralyzed that way. One of the horses steps on you, breaking your leg, ankle, or foot. A steer horn gouges you in the eye. Your foot gets caught up in the stirrup, and you wind up on your back as your horse drags you to the end of the arena, the back of your head bouncing against the dirt and hooves; bulldoggers have been killed that way. Your horse trips, or your steer trips, or both. Your steer gets in front of the hazing horse and stumbles, causing a nasty collision of tumbling beasts; cowboys have been killed that way, too.

Injury is unavoidable. Blown knees are common, mostly from high-speed impact with the ground. Shoulders are torn out of cowboys trying to hang on to a steer's horns. Muscles are ripped from bone, teeth are knocked out, backs are destroyed, and testicles are sliced open. A cowboy can get hurt anywhere once he falls into a bad position.

But none of that's going to happen to you, not on this run. As your horse gallops off, your right foot slides from the stirrup and you prepare to land. You plant perfectly in the dirt, your right leg outstretched in front of you and your left leg bent a little, a good position to start your footwork. You muscle the steer to its left, quickly turning to slow it down, hoping to use the steer's momentum against it. Some call it cowboy karate. Otherwise, if the steer stops moving completely, it becomes a contest pitting your strength against his, and that's a time killer.

Still circling to the left, your left hand releases the horn and reaches out to grab the steer's slobbery nose. In one fluid motion, you lean your head back and push the nose hard to the right. The steer shoots into the air, landing in a heap on its left side, all four legs sticking out horizontally.

Noticing the crowd noise for the first time, you scramble to your feet. Your eyes search out the scoreboard, and there it is, written in lights: 3.4 seconds! You tip your hat to the crowd, showing off a big ole smile you don't care to contain. Slowly, you walk from the arena feeling a whole lot lighter than you did when you rode in. A great run fixes everything. An hour from now, you'll be at the beer stand, buying Coors Lights for all the cowboys whose luck ran out, and you won't care in the least because you just bought yourself another month on the road.

Yes, this is the life.

CHAPTER 5

Horses, Ponies, and Cash

K eep Austin Weird.

The city's unofficial slogan—embraced by some, loathed by others—appears on bumper stickers, T-shirts, and anywhere else normalcy easily can be fought. The city hosts an annual edible book festival, has a group that organizes flash mobs that assemble and quickly disperse for no other reason than to have fun and confuse people, and is home to a flamboyant homeless cross-dresser turned mayoral candidate named Leslie Cochran, who often can be spotted along Sixth Street where colorful characters hang out day and night. And some of Austin's weirdness extends to its rodeo, which is held each year in conjunction with a large carnival.

Luke, coming off an all-night drive from a rodeo in Montgomery, Alabama, knew he was getting close to the Travis County Expo Center when he saw the lights of a Ferris wheel. He pulled his rig into the parking lot at 6:30, an hour before the Rodeo Austin Finals started. As Luke unloaded horses beneath the neon glow of a vomit ride called The Freakout, Travis made a quick trip to the PRCA office to see the steers he and Luke had drawn. Travis returned fifteen minutes later feeling a bit giddy.

"Well?" Luke said.

"Well," Travis said. "You got lucky. But I got even luckier."

"You did?"

"Yep," Travis said. "Chancey Larson was 4.0 on yours. But mine's better. Bray Armes was 3.5 on him."

Luke listened and nodded. It was good news, indeed. Steers that fall quickly for one cowboy are likely to go down just as fast for another. And, at its essence, bulldogging is a combination of skill and luck of the draw. Luke and Travis, both of whom had qualified for the Austin finals earlier that week by finishing in the top twelve after two rounds, set off through the parking lot to gather intelligence; they had about thirty minutes to learn all they could about their steers.

Travis stopped at a group of men standing and talking outside a horse trailer. One of them was 1999 PRCA steer wrestling champion Mickey Gee, who saw Armes's 3.5-second run and gave Travis a scouting report on the steer.

"He leaves as good as any of them," Gee said.

"So take off when he does?" Travis said, formulating a game plan.

"Yeah," Gee said. "But then he stops."

Travis nodded with a serious expression on his face. That's the sort of behavior a rodeo man likes in a steer: The ones that stop running can be caught that much faster. As Travis milked Gee for every possible detail, Luke walked off in search of men who knew his steer. Luke and Travis met up again a few minutes later, and together they walked into the arena to look over their steers.

Once he reached the pen, Travis climbed onto a fence, holding a knee brace in one hand, and began scanning the cattle in search of number eighty-three. After he found his steer, Travis spent about five minutes examining the animal. Several rodeo fans sitting nearby watched with bemused expressions, not certain what Travis was doing. But before a run, every bull-dogger spends some quiet time getting acquainted with his steer du jour.

It took Luke a while to find his steer because someone had taken the number down wrong. Finally, he found it. Luke climbed up on the fence, looked the steer over for all of five seconds, then hopped back onto the arena dirt.

"Okay," Luke said, dusting off his hands. "Good enough then."

With that, the men headed back outside to finish getting ready. Travis dropped his Cinch jeans around his ankles, strapped on his knee brace, and pulled his pants back on. A soft warm wind moved through the air, carrying the scents of popcorn, cotton candy, and greasy food. The horizon held onto the soft remnants of a cloudless Texas sunset. One by one, stars emerged in the darkening sky. Luke and Travis, traveling together for the first time in eighteen months, hopped aboard horses and began riding in a large warmup circle. As they rode, an old Pink Floyd song blared from a nearby set of carnival speakers:

> "We're just two lost souls swimming in a fishbowl, year after
> year . . ."

At 7:30, the arena lights went out, bringing the first roar from the Expo Center crowd.

"Helloooooo Austin," an announcer bellowed as green lasers and heavy metal music filled the indoor arena. "A quarter of a million dollars. The cream of the crop. The top twelve in each event, taken from out of six hundred contestants. And tonight, we're gonna cut the checks."

Twenty minutes later, after the bareback bronc finals ended, the main arena gate swung open and the steer wrestlers paraded into the arena. Three of the first four bulldoggers missed their steers and the fourth put up a slow time that left the competition wide open. Ivan Teigen of Capitol, Montana, downed a steer in 5.3 seconds to take the early lead. After another no time, Todd Suhn of Brighton, Colorado, put down a 4.4-second run that moved him into first place in the average. His time of 13.5 seconds on three steers loomed large with Travis, Luke, and three others remaining.

Travis's name flashed onto the scoreboard as he rode into the box. He backed his horse into the corner, taking a few extra seconds to get settled. His face didn't show it, but he had a lot riding on this go-round. Eighteen months had passed since the last time he'd qualified for a short round. A little magic in Austin and he could announce to the rodeo world that, indeed, he was back.

He took a few deliberate breaths. His eyes studied the back of his steer's head for a couple seconds. Travis nodded. The chute snapped open. The steer charged into the arena followed closely by Travis, already leaning from the saddle. He grabbed the steer's horns and landed in the dirt, taking a couple steps left as he gained control. He reached and caught the animal's nose, pushed it right, and leaned back as hard as he could. He and the steer crashed onto the dirt. The scoreboard stopped on 3.8 seconds. The crowd erupted in applause.

"Oooooooooooohhhhhhhh," the announcer whispered in an ominous tone.

"Theeeeyyy'rrrrrre getting faaaaaasssttteeerrrrr."

Travis sat in the dirt for a moment with his legs stretched in front of him. He turned his head to get a look at the judges, to see if he had broken the barrier. The run was clean. He stood, brushed some loose dirt from his pants, and walked back to the group. He'd gone 12.9 seconds on three steers to move into first place.

After another bulldogger faltered, Luke backed his horse into the box. Travis stood next to them, his hand on the animal's hip to help keep it calm. As soon as the horse stopped moving, Luke nodded for the gateman and took off after his steer. He caught the animal and threw him down in 4.2 seconds. Travis clapped his hands together as he left the box. Luke moved into second place overall with 13.2 seconds. He and Travis stood together and watched the final two riders take their shots.

Bob Lummus's 5.2-second run was four-tenths of a second too slow to catch Luke. The last man to go was Armes, the average leader coming in who needed a time of 4.4 seconds to win the event. He raced out and caught his steer in plenty of time, but the animal clung to its feet for a few moments before Armes finally wrestled it down. He settled for a 4.9 and a three-round total of 13.3—one-tenth of a second behind Luke.

Travis and Luke, having finished first and second, walked through the arena, congratulating each other with put-downs. Travis stopped at the gate for a brief ceremony where he was awarded a pair of spurs. Someone handed him a horse, and he hopped aboard and galloped around the arena, nodding to the crowd, holding his cowboy hat in the air the entire way.

"Here's the big guy," the announcer said, drawing out more applause. "Trav Cadwell says, 'I'm so happy to have the money and the tour points that go with it, I'll even take the victory lap in a barrel racing saddle.'"

When he finished the ride, Travis hopped off the horse and headed out of the arena. He grabbed a Coke and walked around backstage, feeling a hand on his shoulder every minute or so as cowboys congratulated him. A few minutes later, Travis walked into the PRCA office for something worth a lot more than an ego boost and a pair of spurs: two checks totaling $5,080. He folded them neatly in half, stuffed them into his wallet, and made his way to Luke's trailer. Austin had been nearly as kind to Luke, who made off with $4,599.

But, as usually is the case, there was no time for celebration. It was Saturday night in Texas and the cowboys had to be one thousand miles away in Laughlin, Nevada, by eight o'clock Monday morning. Before the road trip began, Travis and Luke called their women. Travis got through first.

"Hello. . . . What's goin' on? . . . Still in Austin, but we're leaving now. . . . Well, we won the short round and the overall. . . . About $5,000. . . . Yeah. . . . Yeah, it's a relief. You bet it is. . . . Sure, let me talk to her. . . . Hi Kelsey. . . . You got a pony? . . . What's your pony's name? . . . All riiiiight! That's great Kelsey. . . . Have you rode your pony yet? . . . All riiiiight! . . . Hey Kelsey? Daddy can't wait to get home and ride with you. . . . I love you too, Kelsey. You give your little brother a kiss for me, too, okay? . . . Okay Kelsey. Good night."

Travis hung up the phone and dropped it into his shirt pocket. As he undressed in the trailer, a thought occurred to him. Something that couldn't wait. He walked up to the truck where Luke sat, leaning back in the passenger seat and talking to Lindsay on the phone.

"Hey, you remember when you said I ain't never won nothing in this hat?" Travis yelled through the open window.

"Yeah?" Luke said, looking up disgusted. "Good for you. I'm on the fucking phone, asshole!"

"So kiss my ass," Travis yelled as he walked back to the trailer. When he got there, he opened the door and flung the hat inside, muttering something to himself.

Anyone watching the exchange who didn't know Travis and Luke might have thought they were about to get into a fight. But that was hardly the case. Their friendship, over the years, has evolved to include a great deal of verbal abuse. It's dominated by it. They yell at each other anytime the mood feels right. They carefully craft the meanest put-downs, which often means Luke's weight and Travis's recent PRCA earnings. It has been this way since the day roughly seven years ago when a slimmer sixteen-year-old Fatty showed up at a bulldogging clinic Travis was teaching.

Exactly how it began is unclear. Travis says this spoiled rich kid came in acting like he was God's gift to steer wrestling, so the instructors took to cutting the boy down a little. Luke says he came in ready to learn, but Travis and the other teachers kept putting him down, so he started fighting back. The truth probably is in there somewhere. Regardless of its origin, the monster took root and now it shades out mostly everything else. Yet, far beneath the never-ending insult party, there is a solid friendship that manages to survive more than its share of backbiting, mood swings, and an overabundance of testosterone.

AUSTIN. JOHNSON CITY. FREDERICKSBURG.

As Luke pulled out of the Expo Center parking lot in search of an interstate, the mood inside the truck's cab was one of extreme lightness. He and Travis had spent all of ninety minutes in Austin that night, and they rode away with nearly ten thousand dollars between them. When it's good, it feels so easy. And when it's easy, it feels so good.

Luke drove as he looked through his CD case for something happy and upbeat. Finally he spotted the prize. He popped a disc into his stereo, cranked the volume, and looked in his rearview mirror at Travis.

"C'mon Trav," Luke yelled, bouncing his head to the beat, "you've got to sing the first part with me!"

"Sure thing kid," Travis said.

Luke paid no attention to the fact that Travis had blown him off. Truth was, Luke was too busy having a party of one to even notice. He began rocking from side to side and singing every word of the song along with Sir Mix-a-Lot:

"I like big butts and I cannot lie . . ."

Luke kept the rhythm going by banging his hands on the steering wheel. He looked in his rearview mirror again, and feigned frustration.

"C'mon Trav," Luke yelled. "I know you like this song."

"Sure thing kid."

Travis continued lazily flipping through the pages of a *Playboy* he'd found on the floorboard of Luke's truck. He nudged his elbow into the side of a bull rider named Russ Sanders, who was hitching a ride to Laughlin.

"Hey kid, look at that," Travis said. "Oh my, Rachel Hunter. Do you believe that body? And that's after a couple of kids, too."

The bull rider nodded in appreciation. Travis cocked his head slightly, wearing the expression of an art critic examining a painting. Luke gave up on the backseat. He just kept on driving and rapping, and banging the beat on the steering wheel.

BRADY. EDEN. SAN ANGELO.

Travis's cell phone, set on vibrate mode, began bouncing around the dashboard like a dying bug. Luke picked it up and saw that it was Brock calling. Luke looked in the rearview mirror at Travis.

"It's Brock, can I get it?"

"Sure," said Travis, still thumbing through the magazine.

"Hey Brock. . . . This is Luke, I'm answering Trav's phone. . . . Oh, you figured that out? . . . Yeah, you always were a smart one. How you doin'? . . . Where are you? . . . That's a good place to be. . . . Hell I don't know. Somewhere in Texas, close to New Mexico. . . . When you headin' to Laughlin? . . . I see. . . ."

Travis leaned up from the backseat.

"Did you tell him I finally beat you in a short round?" Travis said as he started yelling in triumph. "George, I broke the Fatty Curse! I broke the Fatty Curse!"

Luke, quickly growing disgusted, handed the phone back to Travis to shut him up. Travis put the phone to his ear.

"Hey, little George. Did you hear the news? . . . Little George?"

Travis looked at the phone to see the call had gone dead.

"Oh no, we lost little George," Travis said, sadly. "That's okay. I think he got the message."

Travis leaned back in the seat, dropped the phone into his shirt pocket, and picked up the magazine again, still mumbling something about the Fatty Curse. In addition to being a great steer wrestler, Luke also has benefited from a good deal of good fortune over the years; luck is one of the intangibles that makes him so hard to beat. In short rounds, when the stakes are highest, bad luck always seems to plague those competing against Luke. Some guys crash into the dirt empty-handed while others break barriers. Something always seems to go terribly wrong, and often it's freaky stuff. It's happened so many times that Travis gave it a name: the Fatty Curse.

Content to have prevailed over voodoo, for at least one night, Travis relaxed in his seat and continued flipping through the Rachel Hunter spread. After a while, he got bored.

"Fatty, are we there yet?" Travis said.

"You don't even want me to tell you how far we are," Luke said. "We're going to drive and drive and we won't even be there this time tomorrow night."

A few miles later, Luke looked in his rearview mirror at Travis.

"Hey, that's the first check you've cashed this year, isn't it Trav?"

There came no response from the backseat. Luke smiled and tried again.

"Man, that's probably more money than you've made in the last three years, huh Trav?"

"It hasn't been that bad," Travis said.

"Two years?" Luke said.

Travis didn't like the line of questioning. He changed the subject.

"Am I helping you drive to Logandale next week?"

"Yes asshole," Luke said, disgusted at the question. "You said you were. I'm sorta countin' on it."

"I changed my mind," Travis said. "I think I might fly."

"Well, you're gonna look pretty funny on that plane with a size double-E shoe up your ass."

"Fatty, are we there yet?"

"Trav, would you shut the fuck up for one minute? You act like you just won your first rodeo."

"It seems like it."

"No," Luke said. "You was at Huntsville the other day. I saw you there. And Houston, I saw you there, too. And Tucson. Oh, and Montgomery. You know, really, you've been to a lot of rodeos lately. Is that the first check you've cashed this year?"

"Yes it is."

"Well," Luke said, "the winter's over, buddy."

"Yeah, and I'm exactly where I wanted to be," Travis said. "I've got five thousand dollars heading into Oakdale."

"Yeah, I wanted twenty-five thousand but I came up about three thousand short," Luke said, trying his best to sound disappointed. "Oh well. That's the way it goes sometimes, I guess."

Travis smiled. Actually, he was right where he had wanted to be. He'd gone to five winter rodeos. He was gaining confidence in his knee. He'd even got the first win under his belt. Rodeo season truly doesn't get heated up until the summer. Even in 2000, the year Travis made the finals, he only won two thousand dollars during the winter.

"Hey, we got ourselves a new hazer," Travis said, looking up at Luke in the rearview mirror.

"We do?" Luke said.

"Yep," Travis said. "Kelsey got a new pony."

"Excellent," Luke said.

"You know, I'm actually very excited about that," Travis said. "I wish I was there to see it. I really didn't want to miss that one."

"Well, now you can afford that pony."

"Yes I can."

Travis got quiet. He looked out a side window and disappeared into thought, the neon of passing road signs occasionally lighting up his face. Being on the road so much, he missed out on seeing a lot of things his daughter did during her first three years. He was in Cheyenne when he heard his daughter say her first words over a cell phone. The call drove him nuts, leaving him feeling proud yet uncomfortably absent. And that's one of the high prices of being a rodeo cowboy.

BIG SPRING. BROWNFIELD. HEREFORD.

After driving a few hours, Luke turned the wheel over to Jeremy Unke, a twenty-year-old aspiring bronc rider who Luke paid $250 a week plus expenses to help out on the road. Jeremy exercises Luke's horses, cleans up stalls, and often drives the graveyard shift. Travis and Luke retired to the trailer. With no time for a sit-down dinner, the two rustled up what they could at a mini-mart during a fuel stop. Travis washed down a Snickers with a large bottle of Gatorade. Luke ate half a bag of fried pork skins and chased that with a couple miniature chocolate peanut butter cups. They talked for thirty minutes before finding their beds. The lights went out in the trailer sometime around midnight. Travis and Luke wound down by making cell phone calls to other cowboys scattered about the country. Everyone Luke called joined in the fun of trash-talking Travis's dry spell.

"Yeah, he finally beat me in a short round. . . . I know. . . . He's a lucky fucker. . . . No, I was happy for him."

Luke took the phone away from his face and shouted to Travis, whose bed was in the back of the trailer.

"He wants to know if that's the first check you've cashed since 1972."

Travis put his phone down to answer Luke.

"Who is that?" Travis asked.

"It's Ed."

"Tell Ed I'm still rodeoin', and where's he?" Travis said, returning to his phone call.

"Man, everyone's really giving it to me good. . . . Maybe I'm getting too old for this shit. Today when they saw the name Cadwell, they asked me if I was my son. . . . I know. It's terrible. . . . Hello? . . . Hello?"

The connection died. Travis dropped the phone onto the floor and rolled onto his side. He waited until Luke finished his calls before bidding his traveling partner a proper good night.

"Good night fat fucker," Travis said.

Luke waited a few moments, then answered in an overly sweet, high-pitched voice.

"Good job tonight buddeeee."

"Good job tonight too, buddeeee," Travis said.

"Good night Trav."

"Good night Luke."

Then the darkened trailer got as quiet as it gets at 80 mph, which isn't very quiet. The wind howled against the thin metal walls. The trailer rocked and creaked with every bump and turn in the road, sounding like a boxcar groaning on the tracks. Occasional flickers of light from roadside streetlights and neon signs flashed through the windows as the rig powered its way across rural Texas and New Mexico.

TUCUMCARI. ALBUQUERQUE. GALLUP.

Luke's trailer is divided into two living quarters: one for horses, one for people. The back half mostly is a tack room and stalls area with metal dividers that can separate up to four horses. Going down the road, the horses all face one direction with their mouths in reach of food and their eyes level with a window. Bales of hay are stored on top of the trailer.

The front half of the trailer is the closest thing Luke has to a house. It has three beds, closets, a shower, a toilet, a sink, cupboards, two ovens, and a flimsy table with bench seats. It also boasts a Playstation II, DVD player, VCR, and a decent collection of movies and pornos. Everything runs off a generator that needs refueling every couple of days. It is decidedly a bachelor pad. There are no plants. The refrigerator contains no vegetables. The reading material is dominated by magazines like *Maxim* and *Playboy*. The only attempt at decoration is a paper sign that Travis lifted from the Pendleton Round-Up. The sign, taped to a wall near the door, reads: KEEP YOUR CLOTHES ON. INDECENT EXPOSURE WILL NOT BE TOLERATED. ANYONE INVOLVED WILL BE BANNED FROM THE PREMISES. When anyone asks about it, Luke gestures to the sign proudly, grins, and says, "A little reverse psychology."

The trailer cost seventy thousand dollars. The tales of what's gone on inside are priceless.

Brock, one of Luke's past traveling partners, tells stories of opening the trailer, late for some faraway rodeo, to find Luke trying to talk naked women into getting dressed because he's got to get to work. There are countless drunken nights no one remembers. Cowboys who hitch a ride and sleep in the trailer must consider what could be on the sheets they are using for warmth. Luke's favorite trailer story happened a few years ago in Salinas. Oddly, it involves a night no one got laid.

Luke and a barrel racer hooked up while drinking whiskey in the Jack Daniel's booth long after the rodeo had ended. The two ended up in Luke's trailer, fooled around a little bit, but passed out before anything significant happened. At 3:30 A.M., Luke awoke when he felt someone tugging at his feet, whispering his name. Luke opened his eyes to find his girlfriend at the time standing at the foot of his bed. She didn't appear to be happy.

Understandably, she wanted to know what another woman was doing with him in his bed. Luke, now sober, sprung from his bed without saying a word and began acting inebriated. He struggled to his feet and banged into the trailer walls more than once while he fumbled his way to the door. Finally, the door swung free and Luke stumbled down the stair step onto the dirt outside.

He quickly unzipped his pants and starting taking a piss in the parking lot, pretending not to notice a nearby crowd of people standing by an open fire. Playing up the role of disoriented drunk, Luke even pissed all over one of his pant legs. Eventually, he told his girlfriend that a friend of his was trying to make it with the friend of the woman now sleeping in Luke's bed. Luke went on to explain that he only took the woman into the trailer as a diversion, so his buddy could work his mojo without interference. Luke said he and this woman simply had gotten drunk and fell asleep together. Somehow, the story worked, though

Luke and his girlfriend stopped seeing each other several months later for reasons that probably can be surmised.

WINSLOW. FLAGSTAFF. KINGMAN.

The drive from Austin to Laughlin proved long and rather uneventful, which is as good as can be expected. The only lengthy stop came at the Continental Divide when a tire blew out on the trailer. That cost about an hour. Still, Luke pulled his rig into Laughlin just after sundown.

Luke planned to meet Lindsay at the rodeo, which had become a regular occurrence as well as a recurring topic of conversation and concern among Fatty's friends. He was winning money at nearly every rodeo he entered. His pocketbook was flush. The updated PRCA standings showed him in third place after Austin. Everything seemed to be going his way. But that was about to change—for the time being, anyway.

LAUGHLIN

Later that night, Luke found out there would be no Jackpot in Laughlin. Or anywhere else anytime soon.

Jackpot is the name of Bryan Fields's quarter horse, a lightning-quick beast that Luke had been riding at rodeos since 2003. Fields, mired in an early-season slump, told Luke that his weight and riding habits were hurting the animal's performance, and teaching it bad habits. For one thing, Jackpot recently had developed a hop coming out of the box, a move that can cost a bull-dogger precious time. Fields felt Luke might be the cause.

The decision ranked as a significant development. Jackpot, a fourteen-year-old gelding that stands 14.3 hands, was named the American Quarter Horse Association's steer wrestling horse of the year in 2003, an honor voted on by the PRCA's top timed-event contestants.

Fields won roughly sixty-eight thousand dollars with Jackpot that year. Luke earned nearly forty-nine thousand dollars aboard Jackpot in the ten days of the 2003 NFR, in addition to much of the fifty-nine thousand that got him into the finals. And the twenty-two thousand he'd already racked up in the winter of 2004 came while riding Fields's horse. Luke's hot stretch also had been good to Fields, who got the customary 25 percent of those winnings—more than twenty-five thousand dollars—simply by putting his horse under Luke.

Luke, and a few other cowboys who also got kicked off Jackpot, didn't believe they were doing anything to hurt the horse, but Fields had made up his mind. Letting another cowboy make his run aboard your horse is a business decision. A good steer wrestling horse may last just a year or two on the circuit. Some stick around considerably longer, but every horse has only so many fast rides in its legs. For Fields, who weighs 185 pounds, the decision came down to the belief that his horse was being damaged by heavier riders. And a horse like Jackpot, who already was showing the signs of wear, was not easy to replace.

For Luke, losing Jackpot felt a lot like losing momentum. He had a good quarter horse named Roanie, but the animal hadn't been worked enough recently due to soreness.

Travis contemplated all this as he sat in a pickup the next morning with Tyler Holzum, another Oakdale cowboy. The two sat there, spitting Copenhagen juice into cups, taking a break from the weather. It was 8:30 A.M., half an hour before slack began, and already the temperature had risen into the eighties. A 25-mph wind blew dust everywhere. Every now and then, a cowboy could be seen running through the parking lot, chasing down his hat.

"So, what are you going to do?" Tyler said, looking over at Travis.

"I don't know," Travis said. "I think I'm going to ride Bryan's horse."

Tyler nodded. Travis repeatedly shook his head back and forth.

"Fuck man," Travis said. "Season's barely started and there's already drama."

"Yep."

With that, Travis stuck his finger in his mouth and pulled out a wad of tobacco, tossing it onto the dirt outside. He replaced it with a fresh one, stood, and walked over to Luke's rig.

The two men met outside the trailer. They made eye contact and nodded to each other. There clearly was some tension. Finally, Luke spoke.

"It's okay," he said, buttoning the top buttons of his dress shirt. "I was planning on riding Roanie here anyway."

Travis nodded, but he didn't say anything. He and Luke made eye contact again and Luke shook his head, wearing a frustrated expression. He had nothing funny to say. He walked around back to finish saddling his horse. Travis stepped inside Luke's trailer. A few minutes later, Travis walked outside, tightening his hat. He walked over to Luke, who was tightening a cinch. Travis spoke first.

"If you feel like I'm sticking it in your back, I'll get off him."

"No," Luke said, "if he'll let you on him, then fine. I just don't think I'm hurting his horse. If I had some proof that that was the problem, then fine. I just don't think that's the case."

"Look," Travis said, a serious look on his face, "if this is going to hurt our friendship or our traveling arrangement, I'll get off him right now."

"You know what? I'm here to see you win," Luke said. "I want to see you win as bad as I want to win."

"Thanks," Travis said, nodding. "I'm glad to hear that."

Luke put his foot in the stirrup and climbed aboard his horse. He tightened his hat in the wind, and looked down at Travis.

"Well," Luke said, "I'd just as soon go out and win first on this motherfucker now. Just to prove something, you know?"

"I hope you do," Travis said, looking up.

"I'll be all right," Luke said. "I'm going to go lope around."

"All right," Travis said. "I'll see you in there."

Luke grabbed the reins, nudged his horse, and started walking toward the arena. Travis watched him ride away.

The Laughlin rodeo grounds sit atop a flat lot of sand and pebbles. The grounds are bordered on one side by sand dunes and surrounded by a rim of treeless mountains. All that disturbs the desert scene is a row of gaudy casinos that rise from the edge of the Colorado River about half a mile away. Though the rodeo usually begins in late March, it's notoriously hot. Horses stand still, drops of sweat falling from beneath their saddles and disappearing into the dirt. A warm wind blows continuously, drying out lips, faces, and anything else with moisture. When the wind stops, it's even worse.

Any glow Luke and Travis had left over from Austin's theatrics wilted quickly that morning in the Laughlin sun.

Luke's turn came first. Fields remained Luke's choice as hazer, and the two men talked as they rode toward the box. If there were any hard feelings, it didn't show. When Luke nodded and the steer ran free, Roanie got a late break. Halfway through the arena, Luke still had not caught up to his steer, which drifted to the left. Luke finally gave up the chase and rode away.

Travis made a pretty run, downing his steer in 3.8 seconds, but a broken barrier killed any hopes of making back-to-back short rounds. The penalty proved dearly the next day when he threw down a steer in 5.0 seconds, which would have been plenty good enough for more money and tour points.

Casey found no kindness in Laughlin, either. He rode into the arena and lunged for his steer's head, but missed and disappeared into a cloud of dust. After landing on his back, he got up slowly, wiped his hands, and walked away hurting.

Tyler, who turned in a 4.5-second run on his first steer, caught his second steer in plenty of time. But the animal held strong to its feet, giving Tyler trouble before finally falling in 6.0 seconds. The delay cost Tyler a decent amount of money and an appearance in the short round. The only one in Luke and Travis's buddy group who put together a stellar run was Brock, whose 3.9-second run in the second round earned him about twelve hundred dollars.

Once the second-day slack had ended, Tyler and Travis simply wanted to get the hell out of hell. Tyler watered and loaded his horses, kicking the dirt and cursing his luck.

"Fuck," he said to himself again and again. "I can't believe that."

"You know what buddy?" Travis said, walking up and putting his hand on Tyler's shoulder. "You know what we get to do tomorrow? We get to wrestle some steers. And you know what we're gonna do Thursday and Friday? We're gonna wrestle some more steers. And then guess what we're going to do all weekend? That's right. It's just one rodeo. That's all it was. Let it go."

"I know," Tyler said, nodding in agreement. "But fuck!"

A few minutes later, Travis climbed into the passenger seat of

Tyler's pickup and slammed the door shut. Tyler drove through the parking lot, stopping at Fields's trailer to pick up a horse. After that, Tyler and Travis settled in for the nine-hour drive to their Oakdale homes. Both men wanted to put Laughlin in the rearview mirror as quickly as possible. As the sandy parking lot gave way to pavement, Tyler took one last look at the rodeo grounds and shook his head. The tirade resumed.

"Fuck!" he said, banging his fist lightly against the steering wheel. "I had that fucking steer caught in 3.5. Fuck."

Tyler ran through the names of chump bulldoggers who'd done better on his damned steer. He couldn't believe he wasted two precious seconds trying to wrestle the animal down. Now he was headed home with nothing but should-haves and could-haves.

"Fuck this rodeo," Tyler yelled, sounding far angrier than he really was. "Fuck. Fuck. Fuck."

He pounded the wheel one last time, then looked over at Travis and smiled. "Okay, I'm better now."

Now it was Travis's turn. His discontent centered on his first Laughlin steer.

"That motherfucking steer just stopped on me," he yelled. "He ran out the gate for everybody else. That little cocksucker."

"Little cocksucker," Tyler said, nodding, playing the straight man.

"If I don't break the barrier, I'm in the short round," Travis said. "That cost me some more tour points. That fucking steer is preventing me from making a living. He's taking food from my family."

"I know," Tyler said, nodding. "It's not right."

"Know what I oughta do?" Travis said, looking over at Tyler.
"What's that?"

"I oughta go shoot that fucking steer, that's what I oughta do. Shoot that motherfucker right between the eyes."

"Just go kill him," Tyler said.

"I'm going to kill him," Travis said, nodding to himself and looking out his window like a man devising a plan.

Tyler reached for the stereo and turned the volume up for White Stripes's "Seven Nation Army." He nodded his head in time with the kick drum. Travis reached down, grabbed his leg, and tried to work some of the pain from his knee. The entire way home, the two men never mentioned their steers again.

BULLHEAD CITY. NEEDLES. BARSTOW.

Tyler stopped in Needles to fill up on diesel, but saw a sign advertising $2.29 a gallon and settled for a cheeseburger and left town. He found little relief 145 miles later in Barstow where diesel prices reached into the $2.50s and $2.60s. It quickly became evident the desert probably was the nation's worst place to buy fuel.

It was late March, and daily newspaper articles kept predicting the real gas price crunch hadn't even started yet. Financially, the summer of 2004 was shaping up to hit especially hard on rodeo cowboys, who rarely sniff even ten miles per gallon pulling horses. Doubling the price of fuel puts a bad hurt on a cash-poor breed of man already known for keeping things together with baling wire and luck.

Tyler stood near a pump, dumping $150 worth of diesel into his tank, when his cell phone rang. He looked at the phone to see Brock was calling, and brought the phone to his ear. "Hello . . . Us? We're in Barstow. Why? . . . Oh. Where are you? . . . What are you doing in Kingman? . . . Hey, how much is gas there? . . . Fuck. . . . I know. We stopped in Needles to top off, but diesel was $2.29 a gallon."

Travis, who was standing nearby, interrupted.

"Hey, tell him what happened to my card," Travis said.

Tyler returned to the call.

"Yeah, Cadwell's card saw that price and the machine spit it right back out. Wouldn't even take it. . . . Yep. . . . You still planning on coming our way next week? . . . Good deal. . . . All right, Brock. . . . See you later."

Tyler sat in his truck, grabbed the wheel, and dropped a wad of Copenhagen onto his lower lip. He looked over at Travis.

"This is getting ridiculous," Tyler said. "I don't care who you are, you can't rodeo for $2.50 a gallon."

TEHACHAPI. BAKERSFIELD. TULARE.

Driving 70 mph in the fast lane into a blinding desert sunset, Travis and Tyler talked about all sorts of things: rodeo, music, what to do after retirement. Then the subject switched to Luke and the rocket speed with which he was settling down, a scenario that had seemed unimaginable just six months earlier.

"So, that's Fatty's good girl?" Tyler said.

"Yep."

"What's she like?"

"Don't know," Travis said. "That's the first time I've really been around her. She was pretty quiet."

"Well," Tyler said, "it's not like it's serious or anything. He's never been serious about anyone."

"This is different," Travis said.

"Really?"

"Yeah, this is different."

"You really think so?" Tyler said. "Well, it's not like he's going to marry her."

"Oh, I think that's a definite possibility," Travis said. "I've heard him saying that word more than once lately."

"Really?" Tyler said. "Man, he's so young."

"I know it," Travis said. "Can't tell him that though. Wouldn't even try."

"Would you have gotten married that young?"

"What, at twenty-three?" Travis said. "Hell no. I was anti-marriage until I was probably thirty years old."

Travis sat for a second and thought, quickly turning back to Tyler.

"You know," Travis said, "come to think of it, I still might be antimarriage."

Both men laughed. As they continued rolling toward home, they approached the ramshackle truck and camper driven by a team roper named Joe Shawnego. The chubby young cowboy, an immensely likeable American Indian, also was on his way from Laughlin to his Oakdale home. Shawnego had struggled most of his career before winning thirty thousand dollars in 2003. He'd used some of the money to buy a new traveling rig, as the old one literally left parts wherever it went. Still, even now, Shawnego looked like he was on his way to pick up the Joads.

Travis grabbed his cell phone and called Shawnego.

"Hello. . . . Do I know how to drive? . . . Kid, when you've driven a million miles, you don't have to drive no more. . . . You see, Tyler's been doing an amazing job behind the wheel. I don't want to interrupt his flow."

Shawnego had touched on a popular topic among anyone who has traveled with Travis. Cowboys are supposed to share the driving. However, that rarely applies to Travis, always quick to cite his veteran status and an obscure union rule that calls for twenty-four hours off anytime after he drives even a mile. He's continually promising to drive the next stretch, but it rarely works out. The fact that he'd done seventy miles between Austin to Laughlin was a rare feat worthy of celebration.

The phone call continued.

"What's that? . . . You did? In Houston? . . . Did you get yourself a whore in Houston? You got yourself a whore, didn't you? . . . You did? You didn't have to pay? . . . You pulled her right out of the beer stand? . . . Yeeeeaaaahhh! All right baby! . . . Excellent. Hey, just do me one favor, okay? Don't get married until after you've made the NFR. Got that? . . . All right buddy, that's what I want to hear. . . . Tyler's yelling at me here. He wants to hear more details. You got him all worked up. See us married guys are boring. We've got to live through you, kid. . . . Tell me more about Houston. Did you give it to her good?"

The phone went dead. Travis looked over at Tyler and started laughing.

"He got him some pussy in Houston," Travis said. "Pulled her out of the beer stand and gave her the old one-two."

Tyler reached over and took the phone from Travis's hand and called Shawnego, who had escaped a relationship that, by all accounts, had been terrible for everyone involved.

"Hey. . . . Tell me more about Houston. How'd the girl look? . . . Really? She said she'd fuck you next year? Oh that's good. . . . You get her phone number? . . . Did you put it into your phone? . . . Good job. You'll be fucking her for fifteen years buddy. . . . You stick it in her ass or anything exciting? . . . Just the old one-two, huh? Well, that's okay. . . . Well, did she lick your balls or anything exciting? . . . Did you horsefuck her? . . . Atta boy, that's good. That's how the West was won right there."

Travis leaned over and nudged Tyler.

"Hey, tell him next time he gets pussy, he's got to come report it to us old married guys."

FRESNO. MERCED. OAKDALE.

The tired cowboys reached Travis's home just after midnight. Tyler stopped his truck at the corral because Travis wanted to check out Kelsey's new pony before heading to bed.

"What time you want to practice tomorrow?" Tyler said.

"I don't know, one or two," Travis said. "That work?"

"Should be fine," Tyler said. "See you then, Trav."

Travis slammed his door closed and Tyler drove away. Travis walked to the pens beneath the oaks. There it was, his daughter's first pony, an absolute dwarf next to the quarter horses standing around. Travis laughed to himself as the pony walked up to the fence to smell his hand.

After a few minutes, he headed to the house. When he reached the front door, he kicked off his cowboy boots. He walked into the house, set his bag down, and headed upstairs.

Quietly, he walked into Kelsey's room. His daughter was sleeping. He bent down and kissed her on the cheek and walked out of the room. He made his way through the dark hallway into the master bedroom where his wife and son, T.C., slept. He leaned over his son's crib and watched him for a few moments.

Travis walked over and sat in his old green comfy chair, the one Tiffany has been trying unsuccessfully to throw away for years. There, he relaxed. For the moment, the two worlds that often pull at him—rodeo and family life—were at peace: His family was sleeping and he had fat rodeo checks in his wallet. As Travis took off his pants, Tiffany rolled over in bed and, still somewhat asleep, began mumbling with her eyes closed.

"Did you check the kids?" she said.

"Yeah," Travis whispered.

"Did you see Kelsey's pony?"

"Yeah, it's cute."

Tiffany rolled over again, and fell back asleep. Travis draped his pants across his green chair, peeled the sheets back, and slid into bed next to his wife. He closed his eyes, coming down from one world and landing softly in the other.

PRCA STEER WRESTLING WORLD STANDINGS

(Through March 31)

NAME (HOMETOWN)	MONEY WON	RODEOS
1. Jason Lahr (Emporia, KS)	$28,423.45	11
2. Steven Campbell (Midwest, WY)	$23,865.94	14
3. Luke Branquinho (Los Alamos, CA)	$22,939.91	10
4. Chancey Larson (Manhattan, KS)	$18,647.97	12
5. Bob Lummus (Folsom, LA)	$16,866.33	14
6. Joshua Peek (Pueblo, CO)	$16,464.38	10
7. Shawn Greenfield (Lakeview, OR)	$16,277.99	12
8. Lee Graves (Calgary, AB)	$15,666.83	9
9. Chad Biesemeyer (Stephenville, TX)	$14,969.77	12
10. Curtis Cassidy (Donalda, AB)	$14,856.81	8
11. Cash Myers (Athens, TX)	$14,522.71	14
12. Trevor Knowles (Mt. Vernon, OR)	$14,193.67	10
13. Matt Gilbert (Ludlow, SD)	$13,955.10	8
14. Baillie Milan (Cochrane, AB)	$13,276.76	8
15. Stockton Graves (Newkirk, OK)	$13,107.45	11

OTHER NOTABLES

22. Clyde Himes (Stanton, TX)	$10,020.50	13
46. Frank Thompson (Cheyenne, WY)	$5,664.14	8
48. Brad McGilchrist (Sheridan, CA)	$5,521.23	13
53. Travis Cadwell (Oakdale, CA)	$5,079.58	5
68. Bryan Fields (Conroe, TX)	$3,635.38	11
94. Casey Branquinho (Los Alamos, CA)	$2,380.72	4
207. Levi Rosser (Wheatland, CA)	$573.42	8
224. Ron Schenk (Moorpark, CA)	$436.50	4
233. Austin Manning (Las Vegas, NV)	$381.53	5
—Tyler Holzum (Oakdale, CA)	$0	—
—Brock Andrus (St. George, Utah)	$0	—

CHAPTER 6

The Legendary H-Bar-B

OAKDALE, CALIFORNIA

SATURDAY, APRIL 10

It's rodeo weekend and you're standing on East F Street, watching the madness play out in the old brick building across the road. Through the large foggy glass windows, you see people crammed inside and you sense their careless abandon. Someone yips wildly every few minutes. Three bartenders work like men possessed, pouring drinks as fast as they can, occasionally grabbing hand towels to wipe sweat from their faces. There's a cowboy telling loud stories to a small crowd, gesturing wildly with his arms, yelling out a drink order as he tosses an empty can onto the floor. Every time the front doors swing open, a few crushed beer cans spill out onto the sidewalk. Small groups of people fight their way outside, breathing relief in the fresh air away from the mob. They always head back in, like fighters answering the bell. It's 11:30 P.M. and the crazies are out, and you're wondering if this is the place for you. You're thinking a fella could get hurt in there if he says the wrong thing. And you're absolutely right.

Every rodeo town worth a damn has a cowboy bar, a place where cowboys and cowgirls know to meet without having to make plans. In Pendleton, it's Crabby's. In Calgary, it's the Ranchman's. And in Oakdale, it's the H-Bar-B.

Against your better judgment, you decide to head on over for a closer look. As you near the bar, the front doors burst apart and an inebriated man staggers onto the sidewalk and heads directly into the street, pulled back to safety at the last moment by one of his friends. Everyone laughs. The scene plays out again an hour later, yet somehow no one ever seems to get run over. Traffic is dominated by patrol cars and taxicabs, vehicles whose sole mission on this night is to haul drunk people. A young woman tries to hail a taxi, but it moves swiftly past her and all that can be made out in the yellow blur are four cowboy hats inside the cab.

Now you push your way through the front door because that's the only way you're getting in. The next thing you feel is the rush of warmth as you take your first breath inside. The stench of flat beer and sweat hits you shortly after that. People are sticky in here, and you have to rub against them to go any-where; everyone on the move is always touching someone, no way around it. You begin to take carefully measured steps be-cause every inch of the hardwood floor is wet with spilled beer. Short people lift their chins in search of the good air, and tall people are blinded by cowboy hats. Cowboy attire is not re-quired, but it is advised.

Screwed deep into the walls are hundreds and hundreds of framed photos, mostly black and whites, depicting cowboys working rodeos and ranches. There are cowboy hats hanging off the horns of a bull's skull, mounted behind the bar next to old pieces of wood and iron farm equipment. A huge banner that covers the top of one wall announces: WELCOME RODEO FANS! CROWN ROYAL. Nearby, another sign proudly states: THERE ARE MORE OLD DRUNKARDS THAN OLD DOCTORS.

The opening riff of John Cougar's "Hurts So Good" pours

through the speakers, and small pockets of dancers spring to life. But it's far too crowded to dance, so people mostly jump up and down to the beat, bouncing off people caught in the way. Moving through the crowd, a man nudges his friend and lifts his eyebrows toward a big-chested woman squeezing her way past them. She's still well within earshot when he yells,

"Christ, did you see those?"

"Yeah, they're fake," his friend says. "I used to date her. She's a bitch."

A couple feet away, a sloppy drunk man tries to formulate a weak pickup line as his target smiles politely and tries to move away. There's nowhere to go, and she's trapped. But he wastes the opportunity standing there trying to explain how he got too drunk to speak, and, eventually, she is able to slip away.

The bar has an air of impending danger. Unruliness seems encouraged. The place has that vaguely chaotic feel like the area near the stage at a rock concert just before the mosh pit breaks out. A bartender takes the small hose used to water drinks and begins spraying it into the crowd to cool people down. This touches off another round of whooping and hollering by the masses, pissing off only the few who still care how they look tonight. A few women sit with their butts on the bar, turned with their legs straddling their men as they talk face-to-face. The animated conversations drown out the music blaring from the stereo speakers. So someone turns the stereo louder. So everyone yells to be heard and the whole thing spins out of control until the party can be heard several blocks down East F Street.

Beer cans are everywhere. They line every ledge and cover every flat spot. They are left in a pyramid atop a video game. They are scattered along the walls and they collect in the corners, literally thousands of them. You can't go anywhere without crunching them beneath your feet. But no one cares, especially the man everyone calls Bachi: bar owner Mike Bacigalupi. That's because the H-Bar-B does more business during the four-day rodeo weekend than any month of the year outside of April. The 320 cases of beer delivered Wednesday were gone by Monday morning. At $2 each, that's $15,360 worth of mostly Coors and Budweiser. Bartenders also served fifty bottles of Crown Royal and a case of Jack Daniel's. And very little wine.

Surprisingly, there only was one fight this year. A steer wrestler named Marc Jensen, a good friend of Luke's, got into a bit of a shoving match with another man inside the bar. The two headed outside and Jensen punched the man in the face, knocking him out cold.

Of course, the H-Bar-B wasn't always so tame.

Its Wild West days came during the 1980s, not long after it became a cowboy hangout. On a busy night, it was unusual not to see a bar fight. Sometimes the brawls would grow to involve more than a dozen cowboys, some of whom had no idea or interest in what the fight was about.

Once, in the early 1980s, a melee broke out inside the bar. At some point, a man got knocked out the front door and he rolled into the street. The man who punched him ran into the street to give him some more, trailed by some of the punched cowboy's friends. As the story goes, before long there were fifteen to twenty cowboys trading blows in the street as traffic stood still for ten minutes. A few of the fighters left in patrol cars. Those who weren't hauled away went back inside the bar and, within a few minutes, were laughing and drinking again like nothing had happened.

In the mid-1980s, a bullfighter was walking up the street toward the bar when three men approached him. One of the men said something the bullfighter didn't like, and he knocked the man out cold with two face punches. As the man lay unconscious by the railroad tracks half a block from the bar, his two friends ran away. The bullfighter calmly walked into the H-Bar-B, sat down at the bar, and ordered a beer. No one there knew anything had happened until an ambulance pulled up a few minutes later and drove the injured man away.

The Saturday morning rodeo parade route always passes in front of the H-Bar-B. For years, a colorful shaggy-bearded rodeo clown named "Wild" Bill Lane rode his pet donkey in the parade. Whenever he reached the bar, he made an abrupt right turn onto the sidewalk into the crowds that lined the street. He worked his way to the bar's front door and yelled in his raspy voice until someone let him in. When the door opened, he made his way in and took a drink from the bartender. He chugged the drink as he rode through and, not breaking stride, set the empty glass down at the other end of the bar. Then he rode out the side door onto the sidewalk, worked his way through another crowd of people, and rejoined the parade, not even losing his place in line.

There has been no shortage of animals inside the H-Bar-B over the years. And not all of them have been people. After several folks rode through the bar on horseback, people began to compliment Bachi on having a real cowboy bar where a rider could bring his horse in one door and out the other. A couple years ago, someone tried to fit a Budweiser Clydesdale through the front door: The animal actually got its head and front feet inside, but had to back out after its withers got stuck against the top of the door frame. That probably was a good thing considering the basement beneath the old wooden floor.

One late Sunday afternoon in 1984, former PRCA world champion team roper Jerold Camarillo and his partner, Doyle Gellerman, were driving back to Oakdale after a roping competition in Danville. They decided to stop at the H-Bar-B for a beer.

Or, more beer, to be exact. Jerold, who spent a good deal of time at the Branquinho family ranch in Los Alamos while Casey and Luke were growing up, had tried out a new horse that day. He liked him so much he paid seventy-five hundred dollars for him, a hell of a lot of money at the time. It was the nicest horse Jerold had owned. As the ropers parked, Jerold decided there was no better way to christen a new horse than to ride him into the H-Bar-B.

A few minutes later, a drunk man walked out the bar's front double doors to find Jerold sitting atop his horse, awaiting assistance. Jerold asked the man to hold the door open as he rode inside. He rode across the floor to the bar, climbed off his horse, and looked at bartender John Brennan.

"I'll have a couple beers and some water for my horse," Jerold said.

Brennan got a weird look on his face and walked to the back to find Bachi, who was working in the kitchen.

"Hey," Brennan said, "Jerold's in here with his horse."

Bachi looked up and nodded.

"What's he want?" he said.

"He wants some water for his horse," Brennan said.

"Well give him some," Bachi said. "There's a bucket over there."

Brennan did as he was told. He filled the bucket with water and placed it on the bar. The horse took a drink. As the ropers sat at the bar, drinking their beers next to the horse, Jerold noticed a couple guys playing pool.

"I'll take the winner," Jerold said. "Loser buys a round of drinks for the house. And I'll play from my horse."

"I'll take that bet," one of the pool players said.

As the game began, Bachi grabbed the phone behind the bar and called Jerold's wife, Liz.

"Jerold get a new horse today?" Bachi said.

"I don't know," Liz said. "He was trying one out in Danville."

"Well, I think he bought him," Bachi said. "He's in here with Doyle and the horse right now."

"What? You mean he's got the horse inside the bar?"

"Yep."

"Shit," Liz said, knowing her husband probably was drunk. "I'll be right over."

Meanwhile, Jerold began sinking one shot after another. Being a high-stakes pool shark until he saw what happened to Paul Newman in *The Hustler*, Jerold made quick work of his challenger, who ended up buying drinks for the ten or so people in the bar that day.

Liz showed up a while later with a lead rope in her hand. Without saying a word, she walked into the bar, grabbed the horse, and led him outside.

Of course, the H-Bar-B isn't always so wild.

The bar has an entirely different feel in the easy morning hours. At 8 A.M., shortly after Bachi opens for business, the dimly lit bar is somber and subdued: The place almost feels like it has a hangover.

As a bartender refilled cherries, olives, and lemon slices in the condiments tray, Bachi sat at the bar reading the morning newspaper. No one else was there. Then the front doors swung open, and a burst of sunlight shot through the place as Jerold walked in trailed by his cow dog, Reba. The dog found her usual spot beneath a table, curled up, and quickly fell asleep like she's been doing for more than a decade.

"Mornin' Flappy," Bachi said.

"Mornin'," Jerold said as he walked around behind the bar.

Jerold poured himself a cup of coffee. He turned, grabbed a bottle of brandy off the shelf, and gave his coffee a little jolt.

Then he returned the bottle to its place. People started calling him Flappy during his early rodeo days when he subsisted mostly on flapjacks, and Bachi is one of the last people who still calls the fifty-seven-year-old cowboy by his nickname.

"Man, it's chilly this morning," Jerold said, rubbing his hands together.

Bachi nodded as he continued reading his newspaper. A beer man walked up behind him, and stood there until Bachi noticed.

"I was just reading through the obituaries looking for your name," Bachi said, turning his head to look at the man. "You're not in here. That's good. I don't talk to dead people."

The man laughed and set an invoice on the bar. Bachi looked it over, signed it, and handed it back, and the man left. Bachi returned his attention to the newspaper.

"Looks good Flappy," Bachi said.

"What's that?"

"You're not in here either."

"That's good to hear," Jerold said. "That means I can go help Ace find his cattle."

"He lose some?"

"Yeah, he's got about ten head that wandered off into the mountains. I told him I'd ride out and help him find 'em today."

The phone rang. Jerold reached over and grabbed the receiver.

"H-Bar-B, Jerold. . . . Mikey? . . . Yeah, he's right here. Let me get him."

Jerold handed the phone to Bachi and filled another cup of coffee. He added another shot of brandy and took a long sip. As he stood there, he took a long slow breath of air in through his nose.

"God, I love the smell here," he said, exhaling.

He took another drink of his coffee, put an elbow on the bar, and watched the morning traffic pass by the front window. The H-Bar-B has been his second home for decades. Before cell phones, anyone trying to reach Jerold started by calling the bar. He begins most of his mornings with coffee here.

Years ago, Jerold's wife tried to figure out why her husband wasn't much interested in having coffee at home. She figured there must be something special about it. One day she called Bachi and asked him what kind of coffee he used. Farmers Brothers, he told her. She said she wanted to duplicate Bachi's coffee, so he agreed to order her a twenty-five-pound sack.

A few weeks later, Liz called Bachi again. Jerold still wasn't drinking her coffee. She began asking about Bachi's brewing technique, and finally he leveled with her.

"Liz, you ain't never gonna make coffee like I do," Bachi said.

"Why's that?"

"Because here there's a little brandy in it."

The front door swung open and a white-haired veterinarian walked in. His name is Lowell Douris, but everyone calls him Doc. The door on his truck was being repaired nearby and he had a couple hours to kill. He came to the H-Bar-B to pass the time, taking up a spot next to Bachi at the bar.

A few minutes later, two more cowboys walked in: Jim Charles and Bill Martinelli. The two men, both in their late six-ties, logged sixteen trips to the NFR between them. Martinelli went eight times as a saddle bronc rider, and Charles made it eight times riding bulls.

As they walked up to the bar, Charles moved around pretty good, but Martinelli hobbled up with a profound hunch. He was a month away from major back surgery, the result of decades of wild rides and hard landings.

The two sat at the bar for coffee. Charles poured himself a

cup and added a shot of brandy. Martinelli drank his black. Bachi, a week away from a hip replacement surgery brought on by a freak team-roping accident, looked up from his paper and greeted the men. Anyone wondering where cowboys go after rodeo life needed to look no further than the bar that day. Or any day really.

"Hey Doc," Martinelli said. "I need to get me some of that West Nile."

"How much you need?" Doc said.

"I got five horses."

"All right," Doc said. "It's sixteen dollars apiece."

Martinelli stood and pulled an assortment of crumpled bills from his pocket. He straightened them a bit, counted out eighty dollars, and handed it over the bar. Doc took the money and put it in his pocket.

"I don't have my truck right now," Doc said. "It's being worked on. I'll leave them in the refrigerator and you can pick 'em up this afternoon."

"Okay," Martinelli said. "Thanks Doc."

The H-Bar-B is the kind of place where you can open the refrigerator behind the bar and find Budweiser next to syringes full of animal vaccination. Martinelli and Charles finished their coffee, stood, and said their good-byes. Then the two rodeo legends headed out the door, bound for a day of shoeing horses.

A few minutes later, the bar phone rang. Bachi answered it, then handed it over to Jerold. It was his wife. She wanted to know how Jerold was progressing on the list she gave him earlier that morning. As he picked up the phone, Jerold winked at Bachi and smiled.

"Hi honey. . . . I'm getting there. . . . Yeah, I can do that. . . . Okay dear, I'll get right on it. . . . All right then. . . . I'll see you later. . . . Good-bye."

Jerold sat with Bachi and Doc and had one more cup of coffee. Then he stood, woke Reba from her nap, and the two headed out the door together to get started on the day's chores.

Rodeo cowboys don't ride off into the sunset. They play forever in the dirt of arenas, the little boy inside them alive and well. They always hang out in second homes like the H-Bar-B, passing time in the company of men who will never forget what it was like up there at the top.

And, long after they have returned to dust, the cowboys live on in the photographs that hang as tributes on the storied walls of the H-Bar-B. In the pictures, they are riding. They are laughing. And they are alive.

Hey, isn't that Harley May? You know, he was one of the great ones. Look, there's "Wild" Bill Lane. God, he was a crazy fucker. Hey, you remember that time Jerold rode his horse in here?

And, in those fleeting moments, what was is again.

CHAPTER 7

A Chute-Out at the Orleans

LAS VEGAS, NEVADA

THURSDAY, MAY 13

As the sun set behind the desert mountains outside Las Vegas, the city's neon skyline began to glow. From a distance, the casinos flashed to life one by one. Throughout Vegas, the night's gamblers began filling seats behind tables and slot machines, clinging to chips and hope. At the same time, across I-15 from the Strip, the first of roughly forty-one hundred rodeo fans took their seats in the arena at the Orleans Hotel and Casino. For the hottest cowboys and cowgirls in the world, that night's rodeo held all the action they could want.

The Orleans was home of the Pace Picante ProRodeo Chute-out, a high-stakes rodeo that marks the end of the winter season. The three-day show features the top twelve from the Wrangler ProRodeo Tour winter series in a championship showdown that often gives its big winners something in the neighborhood of twenty thousand dollars. Considering that's more money than a lot of the Chute-out contestants win during the season's first five months, it's about as big a rodeo as there is outside the NFR.

At about 6:30 P.M., Bryan Fields and Jeremy Unke stood on the blacktop behind the Orleans Arena, talking and waiting for Luke to finish meeting his steer. A few minutes later, Luke rounded a corner of the horse stalls wearing a pleasant expression on his face. He obviously liked his steer.

"Well," Bryan said, "how's he look?"

"Real pretty," Luke said as he walked up. "Blue steer with long horns."

As the men stood there, Luke finished buttoning his black U.S. Army dress shirt. It was the first time he had worn it since being named one of eight cowboys on the Army of One team. The Army had agreed to pay Luke tens of thousands of dollars during the next two years, the first major sponsorship of his career. Before that, Luke's biggest sponsors were Platinum Performance, which gave him five hundred dollars a month, and WL Trailers and Classic Conversions, which gave a nice discount on his traveling trailer.

Bryan reached out and felt the collar on Luke's shirt. He nodded in appreciation at the sturdy fabric. There was only one problem: the color.

"Man, that's going to be hot in the summer," Bryan said.

"I know it," Luke said. "When they showed us the outfit, it was black hat, black shirt, and black pants. I was like, 'Hey, have you guys considered something a little cooler? How about a straw hat, white shirt, and blue jeans?'"

"You know," Bryan said, looking down at Luke's belly, "on second thought, black might be a good color for you."

"You think it makes me look thinner?"

"Yeah," Bryan said, "I think those slimming qualities are really gonna help you."

Bryan and Jeremy started laughing. Luke sucked in his stomach, then exhaled. As the men talked, Rope Myers walked up and joined them. They moved the conversation to the tailgates of a couple pickups parked nearby. Rope looked out at the towering casinos, then turned back to Luke.

"Wasn't this where you were with Anna Nicole Smith?" Rope said.

"No, that was in Laughlin," Luke said.

"That woman's got some big titties," Jeremy said.

"Man, they was huge," Luke said with a look of amazement on his face. "Each one of them probably weighed twenty pounds. They were bigger than your head, Rope. And you've got a big old head."

"I do have a big head," Rope said, laughing and nodding.

"Someone said she lost a lot of weight since then," Luke said. "Well, that night we were all excited to meet her and we went up to her room. And then we saw her. It was like, 'Whoa, where's the woman who was in your poster?'"

"Yeah, but she wasn't too big for you to stay the night with her," Rope said.

Luke got an honest expression on his face.

"I didn't sleep with her," he said. "That was Mike. But I was trying."

Everyone laughed as Luke filled in the details of the story. It was a sunny afternoon in Laughlin, and Luke and several other cowboys who had qualified for the short round were waiting for the performance to begin. Anna Nicole Smith was in Laughlin that weekend, filming a segment for her TV show. She was sort of with a trucker from Los Angeles who had won some competition that offered a date with Anna. At some point, the two showed up at the rodeo grounds where Anna struck up a conversation with some of the cowboys in the stands. Before long, she had ditched the trucker and invited a group of steer wrestlers and team ropers to party in her room. Luke, Mike Fletcher,

Kenny Coppini, and a few others went to the hotel and spent a good deal of the night downing Budweiser longnecks.

"Man, I'm not kidding," Luke said, finishing the story. "She'd gotten big. She sat on my lap and she was hanging over on both sides."

Everyone laughed. Rope clapped his hands once, shook hands with everyone, and walked off to get ready for the rodeo. It was almost showtime. Luke stood, stretched his back, and walked over to a nearby stall. He opened the door, walked inside, and grabbed Jackpot's reins for the first time in six weeks. Rodeo wounds heal fast.

In early April, after Jackpot's leg injury had worsened, Bryan took the horse to a vet in Oakdale. The vet discovered some swelling in the sciatic nerve; a simple touch to the nerve could make the horse crumble in pain. The vet treated Jackpot, and the horse was up and running again a month later. The timing couldn't have been better for Luke: Roanie was nursing an injury, and his other horse wasn't ready for something as big as the Chute-out. Though chronic injuries were numbering Jackpot's days as a great steer wrestling horse, there still weren't many better in a small arena like the Orleans.

Bryan had another reason for wanting Luke to ride Jackpot: money. After winning nearly sixty-nine thousand dollars in 2003, Bryan suffered through a miserable winter season. Coming into May, he still hadn't won five thousand dollars. His cash situation had deteriorated to epidemic proportions. Putting your horse under the world's hottest steer wrestler is always a good bet, considering the horse owner takes 25 percent. And heading into the Chute-out, no steer wrestler was hotter than Luke, who simply took over the sport in April.

He finished sixth in the average to win $3,100 at Logandale,

Nevada. A week later, he won a round in Oakdale for another $1,600. His April highlight came in Red Bluff, California, where he won the average and took third in the short round en route to a $6,000 paycheck. He finished the month on April 30 by winning Bakersfield and another $1,500. Heading into the Chute-out, he had taken over the lead in the world standings with more than $33,000.

However, his good fortune was not rubbing off on his traveling partner. Travis struck out in Logandale, and never caught either of his steers in Oakdale. He broke barriers in Red Bluff and Clovis. He did manage a two-thousand-dollar check for winning the average at a rodeo in Lakeside near San Diego, but by then he had fallen far from contention. As Luke and Bryan finished getting ready for the Chute-out that night, Travis was on his way to Southern California for a couple more rodeos that would prove fruitless.

At 7:15 P.M., Luke and Bryan led their horses toward the Orleans Arena. Their spurs jangled every time their boots clacked on the pavement, sounds mostly drowned out by the loud clopping of hooves behind them. Jeremy walked a few feet behind. No one spoke. A serious expression already had taken over Luke's face. As the men reached the warm-up arena, an enormous roll-up door rose at the south end of the Orleans Arena and a few dozen contestants rode inside. Luke trotted Jackpot around the outside arena for a few minutes, stopping to look inside when the crowd roared to life for the first time. Now he felt the pang of nervous anticipation.

Inside, the arena went dark. Fireworks exploded. Rock and roll music blared from the speakers. Machines blew thick smoke from all corners of the arena. The announcers spoke in loud, excited tones.

"Ladies and gentlemen," one announcer yelled. "It's show-time in Las Vegas."

That set the stage for the bareback bronc riders to start things off. As the opening event unfolded, Luke continued to warm Jackpot. Then the call came for the bulldoggers.

Two by two, steer wrestlers and their hazers navigated a hall-way that led them through the concrete underbelly of the Or-leans Arena. Luke and Bryan guided their horses onto long rectangles of dark carpet set between short steel barriers that formed a makeshift fence. The riders passed by large stacks of Pace Picante sauce and pallets of Budweiser and Coors Light, moving beneath a maze of enormous silver air conditioning pipes. At the end of the hallway, Luke and Bryan ducked their heads beneath an overhang and rode into the north end of the arena. Together, they watched the competition unfold. Luke, who was second in the winter points standings, was set to go eleventh out of twelve bulldoggers.

Casey McMillan got things started off with a 5.7-second run. Next up was Rope Myers. "Here's the number five man in the world," the announcer said. "A third-generation rodeo man. He owns the NFR arena record."

Rope's run looked pretty good until his steer rolled over back-ward on the takedown. By the time he got a legal takedown, 10.2 seconds had passed. He walked away, cursing his luck, knowing that run had probably doomed him.

Chancey Larson followed with a 5.8-second run. Birch Ne-gaard provided the event's first real fireworks, throwing his steer down in 4.9 seconds, but a broken barrier took him out of the pic-ture. After that, things started heating up. Ronnie Fields, a young cowboy on the rise, took over first with a run of 5.2 seconds, but that lead was short-lived as Josh Peek answered with a 5.1.

After Sean Mulligan missed his steer, Steven Campbell (8.8 seconds) and Randy Suhn (5.7) turned in runs that weren't fast enough. That brought up one of the sport's elder statesmen: forty-five-year-old Ivan Teigen, the oldest bulldogger in the Chute-out.

"For those with gray on top of your heads, I want you to cheer for this man," an announcer said. "He's got a lot of gray on his head. He's a rancher from South Dakota."

With that, Teigen charged from the box to try to catch his steer. But he had drawn a runner. In fact, the steer ran so hard to get away that it crashed hard into the fence on the far side of the arena, bringing a loud groan from the crowd. Then a gate swung open, and Luke and Bryan rode into the arena.

"This man should be feeling A-OK," an announcer said. "The Babyface, Luke Branquinho. The three-time NFR veteran. I'm telling you guys, he'll win his share of the money."

Luke settled Jackpot back into the box. A video screen showed the crowd the cowboy's face, devoid of expression. He nodded, exploded into the arena, and caught his steer, which hopped as Luke reached for him. He hung on, then whipped the animal into the ground. The crowd roared. Luke looked up to find the scoreboard, and waited those excruciating moments for his time to appear.

"Number one man in the world," the announcer yelled. "Did he do it? Did he do it?"

The crowd roared again as his time flashed onto the scoreboard: 4.9 seconds. That knocked Peek out of the lead.

"YES!" the announcer yelled. "And we have the audacity to call him Babyface."

"Boy, that kid is awesome," the other announcer said. "He could win it all."

Luke rode out of the arena and found a spot along the fence to watch the night's final rider, Bob Lummus, take his shot. Lummus got off to a decent start, but his steer held to its feet on the throw-down, forcing Lummus to settle for a 5.3.

With that, Luke walked into the arena, $3,916 richer, and gave a live interview to Jennifer Douglas of the Outdoor Life Network that was shown over the video screen. When he finished, Luke looked directly into the camera and stood there expressionless for a couple seconds, wearing a look that seemed to say, "I'm not done here." Then he smiled big, turned, and walked away, waving to the crowd as he left the arena.

The Chute-out's second-night crowd was much smaller. The stands were half-full when Luke and the other event leaders took turns riding through the arena before the competition began. When the winner parade finished, the arena lights went out again and green laser beams lit up the smoke from a pyrotechnics show. The speakers played the opening chords of Steppenwolf's "Born to Be Wild." Throughout the night, the crowd got pumped on snippets of music by the likes of the Rolling Stones, AC/DC, and The White Stripes. For decades, rodeo has been associated with country music, and that union still exists. But these days, when rodeo wants to whip a crowd into a frenzy, it turns to rock and roll.

"Get your motor running!" an announcer bellowed, and the crowd responded. "It's party time in Las Vegas."

At 7:45 P.M., the bulldoggers collected in the north end of the arena, ready to take their shots at making the semifinals. The Chute-out uses a tournament-style format, with each of the twelve contestants competing in the first two rounds during the first two days. The top eight in the average move on to the final day's semifinal round; previous times are thrown out. The top four from the semifinal move on to the final round, where big money awaits the top two finishers.

Mulligan opened the second night strong with a 4.4-second run. After Teigen failed to catch his steer, Myers took the suspense out of the evening with a brilliant 4.1-second run. As he rose from the dirt, he smiled broadly, kissed his finger, and pointed to the cheering crowd. The run would earn him $3,916, and it would prove to be the fastest bulldogging time of the entire Chute-out.

The next seven steer wrestlers turned in times that wouldn't be good enough for any second-round money. Then Peek bolted into the arena and threw down his steer in 4.8 seconds, shooting into the lead in the average with one bulldogger to go.

Luke backed into the box and got settled quickly. He looked over to his hazer, Bryan, to make sure he was ready. Then Luke's eyes focused on the back of his steer's head.

"Here's Babyface," an announcer said. "Now, I was on the elevator with a couple of Luke's friends today. And they asked me, 'Why do you keep calling him Baby Branquinho?' I said, 'Because he's got a baby face.'"

"He may look like a teddy," the other announcer said, "but he bulldogs like a grizzly."

Luke nodded for his steer. The chute swung open.

"Watch out!" an announcer yelled as Luke rode into the arena after his steer. "The number one gunner from last night. California here he comes!"

The steer ran far into the arena before Luke caught up, which usually spells doom. But Luke recovered well, catching the steer and throwing him down in a flash.

"Whoa!" an announcer yelled. "Halfway across the arena and he still got it done in 5.2 seconds."

As Luke walked back to catch Jackpot, a song rarely heard at rodeos played from the speakers:

"Baby face, you've got the cutest little baby face . . ."

The 5.2-second run didn't earn any round money, but it was good enough to help Luke pocket another $3,000 for placing second in the two-day average. That gave him about $6,850 heading into the last day. Through two days, Peek was the big winner with $8,300.

After the rodeo, most of the ninety-six Chute-out contestants sat at tables outside the Orleans and signed autographs. Luke, Suhn, and Lummus sat next to one another, laughing, sipping beers, and making small talk with rodeo fans.

A father and his six-year-old daughter walked up to Luke's table. The girl held a sweatshirt marked up with dozens of scribbles from Sharpie pens. She chewed on her finger, too shy to talk. Her father nudged her gently, but she turned and hugged his leg. Finally, Luke leaned forward and looked the girl in the eye.

"Hi," he said, "how are you?"

The girl smiled, and turned away, shyly.

"Did you have fun at the rodeo?" Luke said.

"Yes," she said in a soft voice. "Can you sign my sweatshirt?"

"Sure, I'd love to."

As Luke took the sweatshirt, the girl's father leaned down to his daughter's ear and said, "Honey, this man is leading the world right now."

Luke smiled as he finished signing his name, and handed the shirt back to the girl. She took it, thanked him, and moved on to another table.

Next, a pleasant-looking woman in her early twenties walked up and asked if she could take a picture with the three cowboys. When they agreed, the woman handed her camera to her friend and climbed onto the table. Lummus looked at Suhn, raised his eyebrows, and smiled. The woman spread herself across the table, lying on her side, striking a seductive pose. Behind her, the three cowboys all moved closer together and smiled for the camera.

After the picture, she hopped up from the table, thanked the men and adjusted her shirt. She and her friend laughed together. After some more small talk, she said good-bye. The men watched her walk away.

A few minutes later, Lindsay's father, Mark, made his way to Luke's table to congratulate him. Luke stood and walked around the table, taking Mark aside.

"I know this probably isn't the right place for this," Luke said. "But I really think the world of your daughter. And I wanted to get your blessing for you to marry me."

In all the nervousness, the words didn't come out quite right. The man laughed and bailed Luke out.

"Give me a call and we'll talk about it," Mark said.

"Okay, sir," Luke said. "I'll do that. Thanks for coming tonight."

Luke rejoined Suhn and Lummus at the table. The mood was light, not just because they all had won checks during the Chute-out's first two days. More because each of them had earned a spot in the final night where someone was about to take a giant leap forward in the overall standings. A crowd of more than forty-three hundred rodeo fans turned out the next night to see who that would be.

Myers opened the semifinal with an 8.1-second run that all but eliminated him. Then Ronnie Fields electrified the crowd, manhandling his steer in 4.6 seconds.

"That's smokin'," an announcer said. "That's going to set the standard for sure."

Lummus answered with a 4.9 that moved him into second. After Larson settled for a 7.2, Suhn made a great run, downing his steer in 4.7, dropping Lummus to third.

Next, Luke rode into the box. As he got himself and Jackpot ready, the announcers had more fun with him.

"The baby face of California," an announcer said. "He's number one in the world and he's already won sixty-eight hundred dollars here in Vegas."

"When he grabs ahold of a set of horns, the steer has absolutely no choice," the other announcer said. "A 4.5 would make you the new sheriff in town."

Luke nodded for the gateman. The chute opened and the steer broke into a run. As Jackpot closed the gap hard, Luke leaned over and took hold of the horns, came to a skidding stop, and slammed the steer into the dirt. The crowd went wild. When he looked up for the scoreboard, his hat moved to reveal a big smile on his face. He already knew.

A couple seconds later, 4.5 flashed onto the scoreboard. The crowd rose to give him a standing ovation. As he walked back toward Jackpot, Luke looked over at Bryan, who smiled in disbelief and shook his head from side to side. Just like that, Luke had won another forty-seven hundred dollars. And the night wasn't over yet.

An hour later, Luke, Suhn, Lummus, and Ronnie Fields climbed aboard their horses for the final showdown. The fastest of the four would earn $10,575. The second-place man would take home $7,050. Third and fourth paid nothing.

Lummus, who finished fourth in the semis, took his shot first. He got his steer to the ground in 6.4 seconds, but a broken barrier eliminated him. Next up was Suhn, whose steer rolled over on the wrong side. By the time he got the animal back onto his feet and threw it down again, 9.3 seconds had ticked away.

That left Ronnie and Luke. Ronnie sat in the box awhile, having some trouble getting his horse set. He took a couple of deep breaths as the announcers filled the air.

"This is the kid," an announcer said. "Oklahoma City is his home. He won Guymon a couple weeks back with a 3.9 final."

Ronnie nodded for his steer. He rode out and caught the animal, throwing the steer onto its back in 5.4 seconds. The crowd cheered the new leader, who was guaranteed at least second place.

"There's one more man, and it's Baby Branquinho," an announcer said. "Las Vegas, this dude can do it."

Luke gave his steer a menacing glare as he rode into the box. As he got Jackpot settled, Luke looked over at Bryan, who was focused on the steer, ready to go; Bryan had a lot on the line as well. Satisfied all was in place, Luke turned his attention back toward his steer.

He took a deep breath and exhaled forcefully, puffing out his cheeks. He tightened his grip on the reins. Then he nodded.

There are moments in a man's life where everything comes together in a rush so clean, and so slow-motion pure, that it feels like he's swinging through the sweet spot of the universe. Call it luck, or fate, or the work of the gods. Or maybe there really is a Fatty Curse. Whatever it was, it visited Luke Branquinho that night in Las Vegas.

He caught the animal quickly enough. He got him stopped pretty fast, too. But when he reached his left hand to grab the steer's nose, Luke caught a fistful of snot and lost his grip. That left him off balance, with his right hand on the animal's right horn. Often in that scenario, the steer gets away. But somehow, Luke held on and managed to throw the steer to the ground with one hand—"off-horning one" is how bulldoggers put it. The scoreboard read: 4.8 seconds. That meant $10,575.

The announcers went wild, yelling into their microphones to be heard over the roar of the crowd. Luke stood in the middle of the arena, holding his hat in the air and laughing. He laughed because it's always better to be lucky than good, but the two together are a powerful combination. As he walked out of the arena, he continued to laugh as he waved to the crowd, which was showering him with yet another standing ovation. And he laughed all the way to the bank. The final-round money kicked his three-day Chute-out total up to $22,129, more than any other competitor in any event. Not bad for 19.4 seconds worth of work.

After the winners' ceremony, where Luke and the other event champions were awarded large crystal cups, Luke walked off the stage and into a hallway where Jeremy was waiting for him. Jeremy couldn't contain his excitement, and Luke didn't try. They both jumped into the air and slapped hands. Cowboys aren't normally a high-fivin' bunch, but the moment was spontaneous and pure.

After giving a couple of interviews to newspaper reporters, Luke propped himself against a wall near a men's bathroom. His heart was still racing. He pulled a cell phone out of his pocket. He tried to get through to Travis, but settled for leaving a message on his voice mail.

"Hey Trav, I wanted you to know I just off-horned one for ten thousand dollars. Call me back."

Luke and Jeremy walked together through the underbelly of the Orleans Arena. When they got outside, Luke asked Jeremy to go to the truck and retrieve his checkbook. Luke, the crystal cup still tucked beneath his arm, waded through the crowd, shaking hands with congratulators as he made his way to the autograph table.

When he finally sat down, he retrieved his cell phone again. This time, he used the calculator function to figure out 25 percent of $22,129. The total came to $5,532.25, which was to be Bryan's cut. Jeremy returned and handed the checkbook to

Luke, who started writing Bryan's check. As he did, Bryan came up behind Luke and tickled him behind the ear. Luke looked up and smiled.

"Good run, huh?" he said.

Bryan laughed.

"I missed the barrier by a foot," Luke said. "Then I missed the nose."

Bryan nodded. Luke shook his head in disbelief. His Vegas theatrics pushed his season money total to nearly fifty-six thousand dollars, giving him a twenty-thousand-dollar lead over second-placed Ronnie Fields and assuring Luke of making it back to the NFR even though it still was only May, a remarkable feat for a steer wrestler. Even scarier for the rest of the field was the fact that Luke had accomplished all that in just seventeen of a maximum seventy-five rodeos.

When Luke finished writing the check, he ripped it from the checkbook and held it in the air. Bryan took the check, folded it neatly in half, and tucked it into his wallet. It was more money than he'd made all season.

CHAPTER 8

Cowboys in Love and Pain

SANTA MARIA, CALIFORNIA

THURSDAY, JUNE 3

As the Santa Maria Elks Rodeo began its four-day run with a night performance, a few dozen cowboys stood around a beer stand telling stories, laughing, and downing three-dollar Coors Lights. Three men poured the beers from an old horse trailer that someone long ago converted into a beer dispenser. A cool breeze moved through the air as the sky faded from blue to black. In the distance, a soft haze covered the miles of coastal mountains that separate the rodeo grounds from the ocean. The atmosphere was a welcome break from the scorching afternoons of the summer rodeo season.

Casey and his team roping partner, Chance Johnson, stood and drank a few beers before switching to whiskey and Cokes. They'd been at it awhile and both men had gotten pretty drunk. A few young cowboys gathered around, laughing and listening as the ropers told stories about this night's subject: snakes.

A couple days before, a cowboy friend had left Casey a dead, coiled-up rattlesnake on his truck's floorboard. Casey said he felt his heart jump when he saw the snake. But he got his revenge the next day when he spotted the prankster cowboy's truck and trailer rig parked at a truck stop, its owner nowhere around. Casey unhooked the man's trailer from the truck and hid. The man came out, got in his truck, and drove away, until he realized he had left his trailer behind. As Casey finished the story, everyone laughed and drank.

That reminded Chance of the time he and Marc Jensen were riding with Luke back to the Branquinho family ranch. Luke spotted a rattler crossing the pavement and abruptly parked his truck in the road. He got out, grabbed the snake behind the head, and brought it back into the cab before Chance or Jensen had time to flee. Luke has no fear of snakes. Spiders yes; snakes no. He took great delight in waving the angry snake's head around the cab, feigning strikes within inches of the men's faces as they cowered in genuine fear. As Chance finished the story, everyone laughed and drank some more.

A few feet away, Travis and Tyler stood, drinking beers and talking about the weekend itinerary. Both men had steers to run in Santa Maria and Palmdale, as well as a suspicious-sounding jackpot event at the Branquinho arena.

"So let me get this straight," Travis said. "He's the hottest man in the world. And we're going over to his house tomorrow to try and beat him on his steers?"

"That's about the size of it," Tyler said. "Pretty stupid, huh?"

Travis just shook his head, laughed, and spit a stream of tobacco juice onto the dirt. Tyler finished his beer and took a cell phone from his pocket. He called Brock to see if he'd reached California yet.

"Hey, what's going on? . . . Really? . . . You on your way out here? . . . Yeah, we're at the rodeo. I'm standing here having beers with Cadwell. . . . What? . . . Your back? . . . Shit, when did that happen? . . . (Long pause) . . . Fuck Brock, you're crippled. . . . (Laughter) . . . The doctor? What'd he say? . . . Did you tell him what you do for a fucking living? You gotta pay bills. . . . No shit. That's terrible. . . . I know. . . . All right. Hey, when you up in Palmdale? . . . Okay, we'll be over there in the afternoon sometime. . . . Yeah. Well, we'll see you then. . . . All right Brock. . . . Talk to you later."

Tyler put the phone in his pocket, took another drink of his beer, and thought of the plight of his closest friend. As Tyler puts it, Brock suffers from a common ailment: He just don't give a fuck.

Brock and his wife, Bell, lived in a converted garage at Brock's parents' house many years after Bell gave birth to their three children. He bought a house in 2002, the down payment mostly coming from his earnings at the previous year's NFR. Through 2003, he had earned roughly $450,000 during his eighteen-year career. But very little of that had come during the past season as a mysterious injury shrank his left forearm, robbing him of the strength needed to throw down steers. That's not to mention the severe pain the injury causes him. To stem the pain, he grasps his left hand on a fold in his jeans for about fifteen minutes after a bulldogging run. Even worse, he's unwilling to rest when he's hurt. All that creates significant problems for a man who pays bills with rodeo earnings and occasional horseshoeing gigs. If Brock has a long-term plan for the future, he hasn't told anyone.

Tyler took another drink of his beer and looked at Travis.

"What time is that jackpot, anyway?" Tyler said.

"Don't know," Travis said. "Whenever slack gets done. Brock say he's coming?"

"Yeah," Tyler said. "He's coming."

Rancho San Juan is a fourteen-thousand-acre cattle ranch surrounded by sprawling grape vineyards in the rolling hills of Los Alamos. It has been in the Branquinho family for five generations. But, like many of the nation's great cattle ranches, Rancho San Juan's days were numbered; the family corporation had begun selling the ranch in pieces. Friday afternoon's jackpot event was to be the final one held there. That was a source of great sadness for Casey and Luke, who had known no other home. Other than the road.

Around 1 P.M., steer wrestlers and calf ropers began leaving the Santa Maria rodeo grounds and heading for the ranch twenty minutes away. The pavement shrank from six lanes of freeway to a windy stretch of two-lane blacktop. Getting closer, the endless rows of grapevines gave way to barren graze lands surrounded by rusty barbed-wire fences.

Alongside the road, just before the ranch entrance, the carcass of a bloated cow was being ravaged by flies and a dozen or so lounging buzzards. As cowboys turned onto a gravel road to enter the ranch, a sign hanging on a rusty gate greeted them: A GOOD RAIN AND A BABY CALF ARE ALWAYS WELCOME. The dusty road wound past lopsided stacks of sun-bleached hay and decayed wooden fences holding in cattle and horses, and rose into the hills to a clearing that is home to the Branquinho arena.

By 2 P.M., a group of about forty people had gathered around picnic tables beneath the shade of an ancient oak tree that stood just south of the arena. A man used tongs to turn enormous slabs of meat—pork and venison killed on the ranch—over an open-pit barbecue. Coors Lights and Cokes disappeared rapidly. But Santa Maria's slack was dragging on, and Luke, Travis, Brock, and several other steer wrestlers still had not arrived. After everyone had eaten, there was little to do but talk and drink. As the hours passed, the jackpot looked in peril.

Finally, at 4 P.M., steer wrestler Robbin Peterson stood and announced, "Hell, if we're not gonna bulldog, I'm switching from beer to whiskey."

He stood up, wearing a specially designed belt that could hold six cans of beer at once.

He began whipping out beers, pretending to be quick on the draw, and passing them around. He was particularly proud of his belt.

"Isn't that nice?" said his wife, Carrie, who was several months pregnant. "And I reproduced with him. We're pretty sure the sperm that made the gig was drunk."

Her husband smiled as he walked to his truck to retrieve a bottle of whiskey. Just then, a caravan of cowboys came charging toward the arena. Luke flew up in a beaten-up farm truck. He slid to a stop, pushing a cloud of dust across the picnic tables.

"What the hell took you so long?" someone shouted.

"Fucking barrel racers," he said, shaking his head in exasperation.

Everyone laughed, particularly because Luke now was dating a barrel racer. With that, the shade tree was abandoned and roughly fifty cowboys made their way into the arena.

Each man put in $150. Money would be paid out to the top four in each round as well as the overall average; a first paid $254, second was $191, third got $127, and fourth was worth $63.

Luke and a couple other cowboys rounded Luke's steers into a pen that led to the chute. After everyone had warmed up, Luke's mother, Brandy, sat in a raised press box and announced the event over a loudspeaker. Upon hearing Luke would go first, Travis and Bryan Fields, standing near the chute, looked at each other, smiled curiously, and shook their heads. Indeed, something smelled fishy.

"Is he really going first?" Bryan said.

"Yeah, I guess he is."

"Are you serious?" Bryan said.

"Yep."

"Did he load 'em, too?"

"Yep," Travis said, looking at a jet black steer moving around in the chute. "I'm sure that's a good one."

"Man," Bryan said, "this is a sucker's bet."

"Hey," Travis said, "someone's got to help pay for his new rig."

A few minutes later, the black steer broke from the chute. Luke quickly stopped him and slammed him into the ground. As he walked back, his mother announced the time of 5.3.

Travis and Bryan looked at each other again and grinned. But Travis would overcome the odds as both he and Tyler scored 4.2-second runs in the first round.

Awaiting his run, Brock sat atop a horse with his arms folded and a trademark sour look on his face. When it was his turn, he rode into the box and looked at Tyler with a quick question.

"Is it two?"

"No," Tyler said, "it's three steers for $150."

"Straight three? There's no short round or anything, is there?"

"Nope."

"All right," Brock said dryly, "sounds just fabulous."

Brock nodded and his steer ran from the gate. He rode halfway into the arena before catching up to the steer. Once on the ground, Brock tried to wrestle the animal down, but the steer held strong. Eventually, the animal slipped away. Brock grimaced in pain as he calmly walked to his horse. He tightened the cinch and groaned a little as he climbed back in the saddle. Then he resumed his perch, again sitting with his arms folded and a sour look on his face.

His second run didn't go any better. When he caught the steer, Brock landed hard in the dirt, and simply let go of the horns and watched the animal trot away. It had been that kind of year.

Travis ran a 4.8 in the second round to finish second, one-tenth of a second ahead of Tyler, who was one-tenth of a second faster than Luke. The three cowboys had nearly identical runs in the third round, and Travis won the overall title while Tyler took second. Despite the favored conditions, Luke finished third.

Brock's final run was magnificent and sad. As he sat in the box, he gathered his thoughts and stared at the back of the steer's head. He nodded, taking off shortly after the animal broke from the chute. He caught the steer and threw him into the dirt. But, as the steer climbed to his feet and ran off, Brock remained on the ground for a few seconds in obvious pain. Travis ran a few steps toward Brock, clapping his hands together.

"That was a hell of a run, George," Travis said as Brock worked his way to a sitting position. The run was good for second place in the round and $191—a whopping $41 profit on the day. Slowly, he made it back to his feet. He grabbed his pant leg with his left hand, not saying a word to anyone.

Travis watched his friend with a helplessly concerned look on his face. Repeatedly, he had urged Brock to see a doctor or at least rest the injury, but the man is as hardheaded as he is strong. Travis had seen the strength proven countless times since he met Brock at a Barstow rodeo during the summer of 1986. He'd seen the flat-ass broke man, faced with winning in Cheyenne or going home, answer with a beautiful run worth more than six thousand dollars. He'd seen the 260-pound cowboy turn cartwheels inside bars for free drinks. He'd seen a drunken Brock, pinned to the ground by five police officers beating him with batons, somehow manage to keep his hands from being cuffed. But, in all those years, he'd never seen the man lie in the dirt.

After the jackpot ended, Travis, Brock, and Clyde Himes leaned against a fence beneath a shade tree and talked.

"That was a hell of a run, George," Travis said again.

"Yeah, it really was," Clyde said.

"Yeah," said Brock, still gripping his pants. "Hey, you think I could haul that steer around with me for a while? That's the first one I threw down in three years."

Travis and Clyde laughed.

"I've been getting fucked by everything I've drawn all year," Brock said. "Right now, I'm pretty much a big vagina."

"I'd try you, George," Travis said. "What about you, Clyde?"

Clyde nodded politely, trying hard not to picture the scene Travis was painting.

"See?" Travis said. "Me and Clyde here would try you."

"That's comforting," Brock said as he started to walk away.

"Hey George, you going to the pay window?" Travis said.

"I was thinking about it."

Travis trotted to catch up, and he and Brock walked through the dirt together as the sun began to set behind the mountains. Their long shadows stretched across the arena. Brock put his hand on Travis's shoulder.

"You know, Cadwell," Brock said, "someone oughta take a picture of this. It's probably the last time we'll go to the pay window together."

"Maybe so, George."

SANTA MARIA. CUYAMA. MARICOPA.

Later that night, Travis sat behind the wheel of Luke's truck and headed east to a morning rodeo in Palmdale. Luke, Lindsay, and Jensen slept in the trailer, leaving Travis the cab to himself. He drove the first hour mostly in silence, accompanied by the whining sound of the diesel engine and spitting Copenhagen juice into an empty coffee cup. Just past midnight, a nearly full yellow moon peeked over the eastern horizon, softly lighting the Sierra Madre Mountains. Tired of the quiet, Travis flipped through Luke's CD folder until he found Afroman. And all was right with the world.

"I was gonna go to work, but then I got high . . ."

Afroman, the hip-hop artist who lives in and often raps about Palmdale, struck it big with the 2001 hit "Because I Got High," an ode to the procrastinative powers of marijuana. The song played exhaustingly in Luke's rig during the time he, Brock, and Travis traveled together. Now, anytime the cowboys get anywhere near Palmdale, all humor revolves around Afroman. Among the cowboys, the rapper has morphed into a mythic Santa Claus–like figure who can summon magical powers to solve any problem in the vicinity of Palmdale.

Feeling Afroman's spirit growing, Travis reached for his cell phone and called Brock, who was an hour ahead and driving with Austin Manning. While Travis waited for someone to answer the phone, he readied his black man impression—a shtick that, though heartfelt, needs considerable work.

"What's up niggah? . . . Where you be? . . . So, where the fuck is this rodeo? . . . You need to find Afroman. He'll know where the rodeo grounds are . . . Don't worry. He'll be there. He's probably on the street somewhere right now. . . . Thanks buddy. . . . Well, I'm just sitting here driving around Mr. Luke Branquinho. . . . I know. I was thinking about pulling off to the side of the road, unhitching the trailer, and driving away. That way we'd have a chance. . . . That's right, niggah! . . . All right! Well go find Afroman. He can help. . . . Okay, George. . . . Peace out, niggah!"

METTLER. WHEELER RIDGE. LEBEC.
Once he reached Interstate 5, Travis pulled into a truck stop to take a piss and buy another can of Copenhagen. It was a little

after 2 A.M. He drove the rig back onto the freeway and called Brock again, shrieking in hysterical tones.

"You get there yet? . . . What?! You dumb redheaded niggah! Palmdale ain't that big a place, George. . . . (Laughter) . . . You can't find the parking lot? Forget the parking lot, George. You need to find Afroman. . . . He's there, I know it. . . . What? . . . Hello? . . . Hello? . . . Who's this? Austin? . . . What, is that red-headed niggah too busy to talk to me? . . . Fine then. How do I get there? . . . Fourteen south, Okay. . . . Right on Tenth and a left on Technology. . . . Okay. . . . I've got Mr. Luke Branquinho with me. Can you save us a spot? . . . Well make it a big one because he's got a big rig. . . . All right Austin, thanks. Peace out, niggah!"

GORMAN. LANCASTER. PALMDALE.

Luke climbed out of his bed at 7 A.M. and walked into the kitchen wearing tired eyes and a pair of underwear. As Lindsay, Travis, and Jensen slept, Luke started the morning by sweeping a couple days' dirt outside. He opened a cupboard and grabbed a can of Folgers coffee. He opened it, digging his fingers around with no luck.

"Those fuckers," he said to no one, "they forgot my little yel-low scooper."

He poured the grounds into a paper filter, then started to remove the old filter from the coffeemaker.

"Whoa!" he said, quickly realizing how long it had been since anyone made coffee. The old filter had grown green and furry. Chasing off some flies from the sink, he cleaned the filter and added fresh coffee grinds. As it brewed, Luke decided it was time to address the fly situation: Dozens of flies, stowaways from the ranch, had taken over the trailer. One bugger kept buzzing around Luke's face. He threw the door open and a flash of sun-light bleached the inside of the trailer.

"All right flies," he said, pointing his finger to the door, "this is your last chance."

A couple of them left, but most remained inside. He opened a drawer and removed a fly strip. Ready for battle, he shut the trailer door and looked around at the walls.

"Okay, then," he said, surveying the ceiling, "the rest of you are gonna die."

He unwrapped and unfurled the strip, carefully trying not to touch the sticky surface. He tried several times to hang the strip from the ceiling, but the cheap thumbtack kept bending. With each failed effort, tiny strands of yellow goo webbed onto his fingers and forearm. He began to resemble Brer Rabbit fighting the Tar-Baby. The flies quickly sank to priority number two.

In the back, Travis rolled over in his bunk and spoke in a groggy voice.

"Fatty, you got my breakfast ready yet?"

"I'm sorta busy here, Trav," Luke said, still trying to free himself. "There's coffee though."

Finally, Luke opened the air conditioner vent, jammed the top of the strip inside, and closed the vent. He watched for a while as the dangling trap caught no flies. Losing steam, he poured himself a cup of coffee and choked down the first gulp. It tasted like mold. He set the cup on the counter and didn't take another drink.

Finally, he said to hell with it all, dressed, and headed outside to saddle his horse. On his way out, he peeked in the back bunks where the other cowboys still slept, twenty minutes before slack was to begin.

"Hey, you guys thinking of doing any bulldoggin' today?"

A few minutes later, Travis climbed down from the top bunk. He got dressed, grabbed his cowboy hat, and headed out the door. Jensen still was waking up.

"Okay Jensen," Travis said, "let's go make us some fucking money."

But there would be no earning on this day. Travis's run was doomed from the outset. His steer stalled coming out of the chute, forcing Travis to pull back on his horse's reins. By the time he recovered, any hope of a good run was lost.

Luke didn't make it out of the saddle, either. He rode out hard and reached for his steer, but the animal veered to the right as Ron Schenk, Luke's hazer, failed to help much. With visions of his face crashing into the dirt at 30 mph, Luke pulled the saddle horn and climbed back atop his horse, yelling "Whoo-hoo" as he rode off, knowing how close he'd come to disaster.

Jensen, an extremely likeable cowboy who always seems to find hard luck in the arena, caught his steer in enough time, but the animal pushed him on a long skidding slide through the dirt. Eventually, the run ended with Jensen on his back, looking up at the steer's face and still holding on to the horns. The steer nearly had him pinned against the dirt. As he was about to get trampled, Jensen let go of the horns and the steer ran away.

Brock caught his steer and got him stopped. But his hurting left arm slowed the takedown. The two rolled around on the ground for a few seconds before Brock finally muscled the animal flat on his side. The run lasted 10.6 seconds. When it ended, the steer hopped up to his feet and trotted away. Brock remained on his side for a few more seconds. He rolled over, pushed himself up with his right arm, and slowly walked over to catch his horse. His immediate future was looking worse with each run.

So Brock packed up and limped home. Travis and Jensen caught rides back to Santa Maria. Luke and Lindsay hung around Palmdale that afternoon. Mostly, they sat on the trailer's couch and hugged and kissed, passing the time before Lindsay competed in the barrel racing at the night's performance. Her run didn't go well at all. But there was no sign of disappointment as she rode with Luke back to his family's ranch. The couple held hands the entire five-hour trip. As Luke drove, Lindsay put her feet on the dashboard and read questions from a cell phone Jeopardy game. Occasionally, she leaned down and kissed Luke's hand. He kissed hers in return. When she got tired, she lay down and rested her head on his arm, using it as a pillow she touched gently until she fell asleep.

The love fest continued through the next afternoon at the finale of the Santa Maria rodeo. As Luke and Travis milled around the box, waiting for steer wrestling to begin, Lindsay rode up on a horse and stopped alongside the fence. Luke hopped up on the fence and kissed her as she leaned down from her horse. This prompted another round of eye rolling from some of the cowboys' wives, who sat in the grandstands and talked about the couple's nonstop touching with tempered disgust the way those not feeling swept away by love speak about those who are. And, on this day, the man who long had been known for tramping around rodeo grounds, flirting endlessly with barrel racers and other young women, clearly cemented his about-face: Luke asked Travis's wife to help him pick out an engagement ring later in the week. The move came as little surprise. The couple had grown inseparable over the previous few months, and everyone knew where it was heading.

Travis paid little attention to the kiss. He was focused more on his own issues, primarily trying to build confidence and get a little momentum started. He had won nearly two thousand dollars in Redding a few weeks back that moved him up to ninety-five hundred dollars and thirty-seventh in the world standings, but he still hadn't managed much success outside Austin. And Santa Maria offered no help. He made a good run of 5.4 seconds, but a broken barrier killed his hopes.

As Luke settled his horse into the box and got ready to nod, Casey stopped him.

"He's not right, Luke," Casey said. "He's not right."

The horse's hind legs were out of position for the takeoff. Casey, standing in the box with his hand on the horse's side, pushed the horse until it adjusted. As Luke got himself situated, the announcer worked the crowd.

"Anybody here want to see the number-one-ranked cowboy in the world?" he said, drawing a big applause. "Here we are on June fourth and he's already won fifty-seven-thousand dollars. Wouldn't that be something? Somebody from our own central coast coming home in six months with that world championship buckle?"

Luke nodded for the gateman. The steer broke from the chute and Luke charged after it. He reached for the horns and dug his heels into the dirt, sliding to a hard stop. He whipped his arms and the steer flopped onto its side. The crowd erupted in a roar as 5.5 seconds flashed on the scoreboard. As Luke walked off, he smiled and tipped his hat to the crowd. He'd finished in the money in both rounds and also placed second in the average behind Schenk. Another weekend, another two thousand dollars.

A few minutes later, Travis and Tiffany told Luke good-bye and walked to the parking lot. They loaded their kids into the Excursion and settled in for the eight-hour drive to Oakdale. They hadn't been home in two weeks, traveling around California hitting rodeos, Disneyland, and clothing stores to check on inventories. Tiffany, a sales rep for Cinch Jeans, is one of the only rodeo cowboys' wives who actually travels more miles a year than her husband. As Travis pulled out of the parking lot, he dialed Brock's number on a cell phone.

"Hey. . . . Oh, we're heading home. How'd you do in Palmdale? . . . Oh. . . . No, I broke a barrier. . . . Fatty? Well, Fatty put on a show for the hometown crowd. After his ride, they stopped the rodeo, paraded him around the arena in a covered wagon. . . . Yeah, the mayor came out and gave him a key. Marching band played. They released some birds in the air. It was touching. . . . Exactly. . . . Well, you know, Fatty just don't miss right now. . . . All right, go back to sleep. . . . We'll talk at you later, George."

CHAPTER 9

A Drunken Christmas

RENO, NEVADA

SATURDAY, JUNE 26

Travis walked across the dirt behind the grandstands of the Reno Rodeo until he came to a group of pickups parked by a chain-link fence. He looked over the tailgate into the bed of one of the trucks and spotted the treasure: an unguarded ice chest. He opened the lid, raised a wicked eyebrow, and smiled at Ron Schenk, who was standing a few feet away.

The ice chest was brimming with Coors Lights and ice.

At that moment, a roper rode his horse past the truck.

"Hey Trav," the man said, "can you spare one of those?"

"Sure thing, buddy," Travis said, reaching up and handing the man two beers as he rode past.

Travis dug into the ice chest and pulled out two more. He walked back to Schenk and handed him a beer. Schenk said thanks, popped the top, and took a long drink. Neither man had made that night's short round, so there was no good reason not to stand around getting drunk. Even though it was only 8 P.M., they were off to a pretty good start.

The two mostly laughed at everything; free beer will do that to men. But, at one point, Schenk looked at Travis in a moment of drunken sincerity.

"You know, I don't want to quit rodeoin' this year after Cheyenne," Schenk said.

Travis looked at his friend.

"No one does, Schenk."

"I don't think I'm going to stop this time," said Schenk, who normally goes back to work after July. "I'm staying out."

Travis nodded and considered his own future. He knew if he didn't turn his season around soon, he might not even make it to Cheyenne, the biggest regular-season rodeo used by many cowboys as the season's make-or-break point. More and more, Travis had come to view his last shot as Cowboy Christmas—the period roughly between the end of the Reno rodeo and the Fourth of July where big-money rodeo purses abound throughout the West. For Travis, it was becoming increasingly harder to justify the time and money demands of rodeo, especially now that he wasn't winning and his wife was busy juggling her own job travel and two young children.

When their beers were gone, Travis walked over to the truck and got a couple more. And a couple more. It progressed that way for more than an hour. Then trouble came.

Tony Amaral, a heavyset man who works the bulldogging chute for Cotton Rosser's Flying U Rodeo Company, walked over to the truck and lifted the lid on the ice chest. He cussed and shook his head in disgust. He began scanning the area for culprits. His eyes fixed on Travis and Schenk, who were laughing together at some cowboy story. Amaral noticed cans of Coors Lights in their hands. He looked around, and everyone else was holding cups of draft from the beer stand.

Travis looked over at Tony, nodded, and smiled.

"How's it goin' Tony?" Travis said.

Tony glared in anger. He didn't say a word. Schenk looked away so he wouldn't laugh.

"We weren't drinking out of your truck," Travis said. "We were drinking out of that white truck over there."

Tony looked into his cooler again and did a quick tally. He picked up his ice chest, opened the front door, and set the chest on the seat. Then he locked the door.

"Hey, Tony, could we get a beer?" Travis said.

"I'm out," Amaral said.

"Can't be," Travis said. "I saw a couple in there."

"I'm out!" Amaral said, getting more upset.

"C'mon," Travis said, "can't a fella get just one beer?"

"I've got six left," Amaral said. "There were forty-two in here when I left."

"Well, I don't know what happened," Travis said. "Like I said, we've been drinking from that white truck, not yours."

Amaral turned and started walking back to the rodeo.

"Tony?" Travis said.

Amaral ignored him and kept walking away.

"Tony?" Travis said louder.

Travis and Schenk both started laughing uncontrollably. Amaral turned once more, gave an angry look, and disappeared around the corner of the grandstands. Travis and Schenk laughed and laughed, then set about finding a new beer source.

A while later, Casey rode past Travis and Schenk after roping a calf in the short round. He'd broken a barrier, turning a magnificent 8.3-second run into a bloated 18.3. The broken barrier cost him thousands of dollars and what would have been his first career victory in a short round.

As Casey rode back to his trailer, Travis and Schenk followed, hoping for a change in plans. Luke and Lindsay already were in Greeley, Colorado. Travis, Casey, and Jensen had planned on driving Luke's rig to Greeley as soon as the short round ended in Reno. But now, that didn't sound nearly as fun as a night in the casinos.

As Casey unsaddled his horse, Travis and Schenk caught up to him. Jensen stood a couple feet behind them.

"So what do you want to do, Casey?" Travis said.

"Doesn't matter to me."

"It's your call," Travis said. "You're the one with a calf in Greeley on Monday morning. We don't go until Monday night."

"Trav, I really don't care. We could leave tonight or in the morning. I'm with you and Jensen, so it's up to you guys."

"No, it's a Branquinho rig. It's up to you."

"Well," Casey said, "if you didn't have to stick around and wait for me tonight, what would you have done?"

"We would have left after the steer wrestling," Travis said.

"Then load the horses and we'll go."

"But that was two hours and a twelve-pack ago," Travis said.

"Well, we'd have to find pens for the horses," Casey said. "Or we can load them in the trailer and get out of here."

"Oh, we got pens for the horses," Schenk said, smiling.

Casey looked at Travis. They both smiled, too.

"That's fine," Casey said. "Let's stay then."

"You're sure now?" Travis said, a serious look on his face. "That's what you want to do?"

"Yeah, it's cool," Casey said.

"That's good," Travis said, grabbing the reins of two horses and walking toward the barns. "Then Casey, could you grab that bale of hay and bring it over to the stalls?"

"Sure thing, Trav," Casey said, laughing.

As Travis walked away, he emptied another beer and burped loudly.

"All right boys," he said. "Let's go make us some fucking money."

A few hours later, loud cowboys had taken over a bar at the

Silver Legacy Casino. Coors Light and Crown Royal flowed like water. Casey and Scott Sparrow, a young bronc rider, talked with a group of young women—buckle bunnies—who travel from rodeo to rodeo lusting after cowboys. Casey first met the women after a rodeo in Clovis, and he'd seen them several times since. Nearby, Jensen and a blond woman drank, talked, and laughed together. Jensen, a tough, husky twenty-seven-year-old with short cropped hair and a wildness in his eyes, seemed particularly happy as it looked like his two-month slump was about to end.

Over in the casino, Travis and Schenk weren't having as much luck. Travis lost $60 and decided that was enough. Schenk dropped about $200 in an hour. Whiskey and Cokes were the only thing disappearing faster than their chips. Schenk, having hit the casinos earlier that day, had to wait until midnight to pull another $400 from the ATM. So, just after midnight, he sat before another dealer and spread four crisp $100 bills on the table. He proceeded to lose four consecutive $50 bets. So he switched to $100 bets and lost two of those. Just like that, he was broke again.

Disgusted, the two men walked outside and found a cab waiting in front of the casino. Schenk climbed into the passenger side and Travis got in back. A large black man with a big shaved head sat behind the wheel, looked at Schenk, and asked where he wanted to go.

"Take me to a strip club!" Schenk demanded as he reached over and shifted the cab into drive. The man glared at Schenk.

"Don't you ever do that again," he said in a rich deep voice.

"Am I not supposed to do that?" Schenk said, innocently. "Oh, sorry."

Travis leaned up from the backseat.

"You'll have to excuse my friend," Travis said. "He's a little drunk."

The cabbie pulled out of the parking lot and drove the cab

toward a strip club. Schenk looked the man over, occasionally looking back and smiling at Travis. The cabbie appeared both nervous and angry.

"Where you from?" Schenk said.

"Bangladesh," the cabbie answered.

"Where the hell is that?" Schenk said. "Is that in Africa?"

"It's in east Asia," the cabbie said. "Over by Thailand."

Travis leaned up again.

"So you're not African-American?"

"No," the cabbie said. "I'm Asian-American."

"Hmm," Travis said, leaning back in his seat.

The man pulled the cab in front of a strip club and stopped the car. It was about 1:30 A.M. Schenk looked at the marquee and suddenly changed his mind.

"Never mind," he told the cabbie. "Take us to the rodeo grounds."

Undaunted, the cabbie shifted into gear, drove to the horse trailers, and dropped off the two cowboys. Travis and Schenk paid the man and disappeared into their trailers. Travis had nearly fallen asleep when Jensen ripped open the door, drunk and cussing.

"Motherfucker," he yelled, throwing his hat off the trailer wall. "I don't fucking believe that."

"What's wrong Jensen?" Travis said.

"I just got rat fucked," Jensen said. "That's what's wrong."

Travis laughed. Jensen was always getting rat fucked, which is his way of describing a plan that goes terribly awry. If a steer walks all over him, Jensen got rat fucked. If a horse bucks him off, again, rat fucked.

"You know that woman I was talking to?" Jensen said.

"Yeah," Travis said. "I thought that was looking like a done deal."

"Well, she was about to come back to the trailer with me," Jensen said. "She wanted to. But her friend wouldn't let her because they didn't know me. I just got rat fucked by her fucking friend!"

"That's too bad, Jensen," Travis said. "It's been a while since you got some, hasn't it?"

"Two fucking months," Jensen said, shaking his head. "Two fucking months."

"Damn Jensen, maybe you're gay."

"Fuck you. I'm not fucking gay."

"Okay, buddy, okay. I'm just saying a fella goes that long without getting laid, maybe he's gay."

"I'm not fucking gay," Jensen said. "I just got rat fucked is all."

"Hey, whatever you say, Jensen," Travis said.

Travis rolled over in his bunk and fell back to sleep. Jensen pulled a frozen pizza from the freezer and stuck it in the microwave. He ate it quickly and, within a couple minutes, the sound of heavy snoring filled the trailer.

Seven A.M. came like a dagger. Travis rose slowly and stood in his underwear in the trailer's bathroom, rummaging through the medicine cabinet for some Advil. He had a blinding headache, and he squinted just enough to see. Once he'd swallowed the pain relievers, he sat on a bench, wrapped in a sleeping bag, wearing a pained, disoriented expression on his face. He stared, thoughtless.

"Where the fuck is Casey?" Jensen said as he got out of bed. "We gotta get going."

Time crawled. An hour passed. Casey never showed. No one had seen him leave the casino, but he had disappeared pretty early into the night.

"That motherfucker," Travis said. "Hell, I'm going back to bed."

Luke
Branquinho

Travis Cadwell

Casey
Branquinho

Brock Andrus

Marc Jensen

Frank
Thompson

Levi Rosser

Tyler Holzum

Luke, Travis, Brock, and two other cowboys pose during a Wyoming lightning storm.
(Courtesy of *The Modesto Bee*)

Luke throws a steer in the dust at Salinas. (Courtesy of *The Modesto Bee*)

TOP Travis grinds to a halt in the Salinas dirt. (Courtesy of *The Modesto Bee*)

LEFT Moments before hitting the road again, Travis gets ready to hand his daughter, Kelsey, to his wife. (Courtesy of *The Modesto Bee*)

Brock drives through a Utah sunrise, trying to make a rodeo in Ogden. (Courtesy of *The Modesto Bee*)

Travis and Kenny Coppini (right) play a game of 85-mph Hold'em. (Courtesy of *The Modesto Bee*)

TOP Luke and Lindsay share a soft moment, waiting on a rodeo.

BELOW A cowboy silhouetted in the sunset at an Ogden rodeo

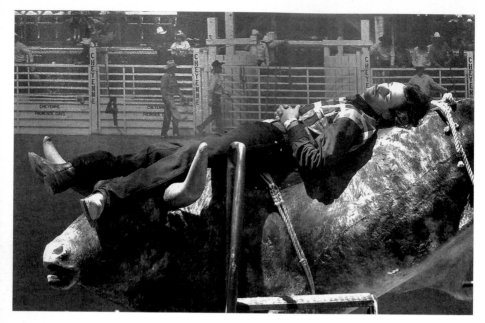

A concessionaire takes a nap during downtime at Cheyenne.

A cowboy gets ready for a mud bath in Cheyenne.

A steer-wrestling run as it appears from the rafters of Utah's Salt Palace

Travis, Ron Schenk (center), and Robbin Peterson (right) talking dirty and having beers in Salinas a few minutes after Travis's latest "retirement"

Luke demonstrates his technique to Ronnie Fields in Spanish Fork, Utah.

Marc Jensen waters the horses in a creek outside rodeo grounds in Ogden.

Frank Thompson slows a steer in the mud at Cheyenne, then cozies up to the animal after the run.

TOP Lasers beam through the Thomas & Mack Center at the opening of the National Finals Rodeo.

RIGHT Luke signs autographs for fans in Las Vegas.

All photography by Bart Ah You

TOP Luke tips his hat to the crowd after winning some NFR cash.

INSET Luke hugs his father, John, moments after securing a world title.

"Fuck it then," Jensen said. "Me, too."

The two fell back to sleep. A little after 8 A.M., Casey opened the trailer and peeked his head inside.

"Hey, you guys ready to go?" he said, sounding refreshed.

Travis rolled over on the couch, squinting in a searing blast of awful Reno sunlight.

"Yeah," Travis said in a whisper. "You driving?"

"I can," Casey said. "I gotta load the horses first."

"Okay," Travis said, before falling back to sleep.

A few minutes later, Casey pulled the rig through the city streets into a truck stop. He loaded Luke's truck with diesel, bought a big cup of coffee, and merged into light morning traffic on I-80 east.

RENO. SPARKS. WADSWORTH.

As Casey pushed east on I-80, the unofficial freeway of summer rodeo, he studied an atlas, occasionally glancing up at the road. He figured out how far it was to Greeley and dropped the atlas on the passenger seat. It wasn't good news.

"One thousand fifty miles," he said to himself.

He reached onto the dashboard and grabbed a pair of sunglasses. The sun's glare was making his head pound worse. He drank the coffee quickly, trying to chase away the whiskey headache. It was a low-grade hangover, really. Nothing like the one that hung with him for two days following that lost night the year before at San Juan Capistrano.

Casey had won twenty-five hundred dollars at the rodeo. Coming off a month on the road, it had felt great to be drinking with his California buddies again. And, in a VIP bar behind the arena, bartenders began pouring contestants unlimited free drinks. It was a recipe for disaster.

Casey ordered gin and tonics two at a time, fearing the bar

gods would come to their senses and stop serving up freebies. He drank and drank, telling animated Wild West stories with loose groups of cowboys that included Luke, Travis, Cash Myers, and Tim and Doug Pharr. Casey figures he had twelve or fourteen strong gin and tonics, but that's not the sort of thing a cowboy usually keeps track of.

At some point, Casey was talking to a couple friends, and seemed fine. But moments later when one of the Pharr brothers turned around to ask Casey a question, he was lying facedown on a table, out cold. He remained that way for quite a while. Finally, Doug and Tim lifted Casey, each brother ducking beneath an arm, and they began carrying him through the parking lot toward the trailers. Casey woke every few seconds, saying he was okay and managing a few drunken steps before passing out again, his boots once again dragging across the pavement. Here there is a black spot in Casey's memory.

A while later, Casey woke up in the parking lot. His shirt was gone and he tasted vomit. He looked up to find Doug yanking on Casey's boots, pulling him across the blacktop. The maneuver tore a good deal of skin off Casey's shoulders, bloodying him a little. Problem was, those now in charge of helping Casey also were shit faced. The Pharr brothers decided it would be funny to remove Casey's pants and leave him sleeping outside the trailer, naked. Casey woke up again just after the attempt had started.

"You stupid bastards," Casey said, slurring every word. "You wanna see my bare ass? I'll get naked."

Lying on the pavement, he fought to take off his boxers and pants. He got them to his ankles, but they got stuck on his boots. He staggered to his feet, naked from the ankles up, and began running in tiny steps through the parking lot, cussing and laughing. The Pharrs chased after him, laughing like hyenas. People driving past slowed their cars to study the scene.

Eventually, the brothers got Casey into a new trailer owned by Justin Davis, another steer wrestler. Casey threw up all over Davis's bed and floor. He fell asleep, waking up every now and then to puke some more. At 4:30 A.M., roper Brad Goodrich began searching for Casey and finally found him in Luke's trailer. No one knew how he had gotten there. Goodrich woke Casey, and helped him to a car because they had a plane to catch. Goodrich drove to a hotel to pick up the Pharrs. Casey threw up there, too.

An hour later, the four cowboys boarded an airplane at John Wayne Airport for a flight to Seattle. Casey, still somewhat drunk, collapsed into his seat. He immediately grabbed a vomit bag, leaned back, and fell asleep, clutching the bag with both hands. He awoke to hear the pilot saying Lake Tahoe could be seen out the windows. Then Casey felt the hot sweats. His mouth watered. He turned a vent on, trying to cool himself down. He began taking deep measured breaths. Then he tried to hold his breath altogether. It was no use; he knew what was coming. Before long, he was filling the vomit bag. The other cowboys roared every time he puked, rooting him on. Each painful heave clearly was heard by the hundred or so people on the plane, and most of them did not find the episode amusing.

After they landed, the cowboys made their way through the terminal at Seattle. Casey walked slowly, always falling a few feet behind the others. His head pounded and his stomach muscles ached. Sunglasses hid his tired eyes, but his slumping body language told the story. He carried his clothes bag over one shoulder and held on to a leather strap from his rope can that was dragging along the floor behind him. His other hand held a fresh vomit bag he had taken from the plane.

He slept the next two days; he hasn't had a drink of gin since.

LOVELOCK. WINNEMUCCA. BATTLE MOUNTAIN.

Casey pulled off the freeway to get some food. But there was no time for that, so he stopped at McDonald's. He and Jensen ordered meals and carried them into the truck's cab. Travis kept on sleeping. As they rode toward Utah, Jensen and Casey mostly ate in silence.

Once Jensen had finished, he stared out the window at the unyielding Nevada landscape. A big grin overtook his face. No longer upset about the previous night's missed opportunity, Jensen now was content simply knowing he lived in a world that included buckle bunnies. He looked over at Casey.

"Man," he said, "I can't believe those girls go around from rodeo to rodeo like that."

"Those girls go to more rodeos than I do," Casey said. "That one woman was at Clovis. Then I saw her at Santa Maria and Livermore, and now Reno. I'm sure she'll be at Salinas, too."

As Jensen listened, another casino bar memory popped into his head. He grinned in amusement and looked over at Casey.

"You know that girl who was hanging all over Scott?"

"Yeah, the little blonde?"

"Yeah," Jensen said. "She kept telling Scott she wanted to get married to him."

"What'd he say?"

"Not much," Jensen said. "He just got awful quiet."

Casey looked at Jensen and laughed. Casey was about to say something, but his cell phone rang. He picked it up off the dashboard.

"Hello. . . . What? . . . (Laughter) . . . Um, I don't know what you're talking about. I slept in my buddy's room last night. . . . I did. . . . (Laughter) . . . Again, I don't know what you're talking about. . . . Hello? Hello? . . . The reception is terrible here in Nevada. I'm going through a bad spot. I'll have to talk to you later."

Casey hung up the phone and set it on his lap.

"Hey, you need to clear off your voice mail," Jensen said. "I tried to get ahold of you last night, but it won't let you leave a message."

"It won't?" Casey said. "Well, that's no good."

Casey picked up his cell phone, pushed a couple of buttons until he found the right menu. He held the phone in front of him. Each time he could hear a voice, he pushed a button to delete the message.

"You know, buddy," Jensen said, "I think people probably wanted you to listen to those."

Casey smiled as he continued clearing his messages. When he finished, he tossed the phone onto the dashboard, looked at Jensen, and smiled.

"There," he said, proudly. "Now you can leave me a message, Jensen."

"Thanks Casey."

ELKO. DEETH. OASIS.

The rig charged up a hill at 80 mph and disappeared into the soft golden glow of a long mountain tunnel. Through the front windshield, a small hole of light grew larger in the distance until the vague darkness vanished with a brilliant flash of daylight that exposed the ugly beauty of the eastern Nevada landscape and beamed off the nose of the truck as it rumbled along on a journey that, through the side windows, always seems to be another endless drive through a life-size painting of the new American West.

Empty fast-food cups and cigarette butts collect in the

shadow of a fallen freeway sign that rests upon the dark gravel shoulder separating the skid-stained pavement from the road-side shrubs that push out in all directions in a vast sea of mottled greens, rolling like waves across the countryside.

Men from a prison work crew wearing orange reflector vests meander alongside the road; occasionally, one reaches down, picks up a piece of trash, and stuffs it into a white garbage bag blown full by a soft desert wind.

Miles and miles of rusty barbed-wire fences stretch alongside the road, hugging the terrain. Wooden power poles, linked by thick sagging lines, tower above the countryside in a winding row. A two-tire dirt path starts at the edge of a frontage road and winds across the landscape and into the hills in a lost trail that seems to lead nowhere.

Dozens of black, red, and brown cattle stand with lowered heads, picking through scraps of grass that come up between the shrubs, while a handful of cows cool heels in shallow ponds that slowly disappear in the heat. Farther off the road, a Union Pacific freight train pulls a line of graffiti-stained black tankers loaded with half a mile of corn syrup bound for the West.

High above it all, majestic flat-bottom clouds, floating like grand explosions planed on the wind, pass before a sunny blue sky, throwing bloated shadows that move in slow motion across the hills and disappear beyond a ridge of snow-capped mountains.

But there were no sightseers inside the truck. Jensen reclined in the passenger seat, sleeping with his mouth open and his left leg propped on the dashboard. His body shook every time the tires rolled over a bump in the road. Casey leaned forward and stretched his back for a minute, groaning quietly. He sank back into his seat, keeping his right foot heavy on the gas and his left arm gripping the top of the steering wheel. As the road's dotted white line flickered in the reflection of his sunglasses, Casey kept his eyes fixed straight ahead on the unforgiving black snake of pavement that rises over hills, sinks into valleys, bends around rivers, pulls restless men farther, and always disappears into a point on the horizon no one ever seems to reach.

SALT LAKE CITY. EVANSTON. GREEN RIVER.

Casey made it through eastern Nevada and Utah's salt flats before exhaustion took over. He pulled into a Flying J truck stop and fueled up as an orange-and-purple sunset lit up the desert skyline. The trailer door swung open and Travis slowly stepped outside.

Having slept for most of eighteen consecutive hours, he took a series of small painful steps. He moved around the parking lot stretching his arms and legs, looking like a man trying to shake off rigor mortis. And he had become so bored, a rare thing happened: He actually felt the urge to drive. As Casey and Jensen retired to the trailer, Travis climbed behind the wheel for a solo drive through eastern Utah and into the badlands of Wyoming.

Travis reached into his pocket for his cell phone and called Brock, whose arm injury had degenerated to the point where he had taken the extreme step of visiting a doctor. The clincher had come in Reno, where he caught two steers but could not summon the strength to throw them down.

"Hello George. . . . Just driving, buddy. You? . . . You go to the doctor yet? . . . You did? . . . What'd he say? . . . Did he give you an MRI? . . . When are you gonna do that? . . . Don't get all excited George. We were just checking on you, seein' how you're doing. . . . No, your health is important to me, buddy. . . . You're feeling better huh? You entered anywhere coming up? . . . What day you team roping in Cheyenne? . . . Really? . . . I think we're up there on the twenty-fifth. . . . What? . . . Hello? . . . Hello?"

Travis looked at his phone. The signal was weak and fading with every mile. Giving up on conversations to get him through the night, Travis settled in for a long, quiet drive through the Rocky Mountains. He pulled into Greeley a little after 3:30 A.M. and steered the rig through city and rural streets for half an hour, trying to find the rodeo grounds with no luck. He wasn't lost, because cowboys are never lost: They simply are checking out real estate. Once he'd seen enough of Greeley's real estate market, he stopped the rig and woke Casey, who knew where the rodeo was. The cowboys finally pulled onto the grounds at about 4:30 A.M.

RAWLINS. LARAMIE. GREELEY.

At 7:30 A.M., Casey woke and started getting dressed for the morning's calf roping slack. After he got dressed, he splashed some water on his face. He opened a Red Bull, took a few big gulps, and sat down on the couch to put on his boots. Despite hardly any sleep, Travis also was up early to watch the steer wrestling slack and get a fix on the steers he would be drawing from.

As Casey and Travis finished getting ready, they did what veterans do best: They made fun of the rookie. In this rig, that meant Jensen, who was lying in bed fending off hard comments about his sex life.

"Jensen, there's a rodeo this morning," Travis said. "Might be a good idea to have a look at the steers."

"I know, Trav. I'm getting up. I didn't sleep for shit last night."

"Well, I tried to drive nice and smooth for you, buddy."

"Oh, was that smooth driving? How many times did you run over the fucking rumble strip?"

"Why's he so testy?" Casey said.

"Ol' Jensen hasn't been laid in a while," Travis said.

"Really?" Casey said. "That's too bad. How long is a while?"

"Two fucking months," Jensen said, sitting up in bed. "Are you happy?"

"Wow," Casey said. "That's a long time to play with yourself."

After enduring five minutes of verbal assaults, Jensen finally climbed out of his bunk, rubbing his eyes. The previous day's hangover had been whiskey, but this morning it was the road. And, in some ways, a road hangover is worse.

"Fuck," Jensen said, stretching his back. "I never felt so tired. I can't seem to wake up."

"Well, if you want, I can whip out my dick and slap it on your forehead a couple times," Casey said.

"No, that won't be necessary. But thanks for thinking of me, Casey."

"Suit yourself," Casey said as he headed out the door. "Poor rookie. Everybody treats him so bad."

An hour later, Casey walked his horse to the warm-up area, tied him to a fence, and began trying to work the miles out of his arms and legs. Once he'd stretched, he made his way into the arena and spent the next hour awaiting his turn.

When his name was called, he rode into the box, rubbing his hands together for warmth. He pulled a pigging string off his arm and stuck it in his mouth. He nodded for the gateman, and rode into the arena after his calf. He swung the rope through the air and it landed around the calf's neck and tightened. Casey hopped off his horse, ran over and tied up the calf, then looked up at the scoreboard to see his time: 9.6 seconds. It seemed pretty good at the time, but as other ropers took their turns, Casey's time slowly dropped out of the money. His second run didn't win him any cash, either, and his 1,050-mile gamble didn't pay off.

After Casey's second run, Travis drove Casey to Denver to catch a flight back to the Pacific Northwest where he would spend Cowboy Christmas team roping with Chance. Casey wasn't having his best year, but it was a decent season, one that saw him hover in the top thirty of the all-around standings most of the summer.

Travis, Luke, and Jensen all made their first Greeley rides at a performance later that night. And, with Bryan Fields in town, everyone got a chance to ride Jackpot. That didn't help Jensen, who drew a runner and never was able to catch up to the animal. Travis settled for a 5.2-second run, worthless except that it kept him alive in the quest for the short round. Luke dropped his steer in 4.3 seconds, the quickest run of the night that earned him eighteen hundred dollars.

Two days later, on a cool Colorado morning, a couple dozen steer wrestlers readied themselves in the arena. Jensen's dry spell continued with a 7.8-second run worsened by a broken barrier. Luke got a good break on his steer, but the animal stopped abruptly as Luke leaned in the saddle, forcing him to pull up at the last second and ride away. Travis had trouble catching up to his steer, and he reached out for a moment but pulled back when he realized he had no shot of making the short round. He was beginning to wonder if he'd ever make a short round again; his win in Austin felt like years ago.

After slack ended, Travis and Luke walked to the trailer. Jensen sat on a couch eating a nectarine and talking on his cell phone. Jeremy sat next to him, playing a handheld video game. Travis walked into the trailer and threw himself on the bottom bunk.

"Fuck!" he yelled, punching the bottom of the top bunk. "God, I hate rodeo. Dumbest fucking sport ever invented. I hate it. Hate!"

He shook his head in frustration, and thought of throwing more punches. But he held back.

"I hate rodeo," he said, the tone of his tantrum calming. "At least until we get to Cody."

He rolled over and closed his eyes, still muttering about the dumbest sport on the planet. Luke walked into the trailer, laughing.

"I can't believe you didn't get off your horse on that one," he said. "That was the perfect haze."

"Is that right?" Travis said, rising from his bed. "Is that what you'd call that?"

"Hey," Luke said, "it couldn't have gone more wrong. I almost fell off. My rope fell out of my hands. Then I lost the reins. And my feet came out of the stirrups. You know what that feels like when you're just floating along in the saddle?"

"No, actually Luke, I don't know what that feels like."

"Yes you do, Trav. You know exactly."

Travis looked at Jeremy and Jensen, who were listening to the exchange and laughing quietly.

"You know what that reminds me of, guys?" Travis said. "Me and Fatty were practicing one day. As I'm about to catch my steer, I look up and there goes a hazing horse running by me with no rider. I look back and there's Fatty, sitting on the ground in the middle of the arena. Until then, I'd always thought it was the other guy who's supposed to get off his horse."

As everyone laughed, Luke defended what had happened the day his hazing horse bucked him off, but everyone kept laughing until he said the hell with it and walked back outside.

He and Lindsay fed and watered horses, and loaded them into the trailers. Later that afternoon, two rigs pulled out of the rodeo grounds, Luke and Lindsay in hers, and Jeremy, Jensen, and Travis in Luke's. Greeley had been a complete bust, and the group was more than ready for the seven-hour trip to Cody, Wyoming.

EATON. PIERCE. CHEYENNE.

A sea of dark gray clouds filled the front windshield scene as Jeremy drove across the northern Colorado border into Wyoming. Three hours before sunset, the last hint of sunlight disappeared into a dark, eerie calm. The first raindrops came, hitting the windshield harder and harder as the force of the deluge grew. Before long, each raindrop pelted the glass like the thud of a giant insect, rising into a clack that sounded like the hooves of horses galloping across hard dirt.

Jeremy leaned forward in his seat, straining to see the road.

"Damn," he said. "I can't see a fucking thing."

He slowed the rig to 25 mph. Torrents broke across the pavement of Interstate 25. Jensen and Travis took a break from their poker game to watch the storm.

"Man, I've never seen it rain like this," Jensen said, looking out the window. "This is supposed to be the middle of summer."

"It's Wyoming, dude," Travis said.

Ten minutes later, the rig's wheels parted the parking lot lake outside a Flying J truck stop. Everyone got soaked as they ran inside. As Travis, Luke, and Lindsay walked through the store aisles looking for dinner, they came across a shelf of western artwork. Travis nodded to a small statue of a bronc rider floating over the hindquarters of a bucking horse.

"Hey look," he said. "There's one of Fatty hazing."

Lindsay smiled. Luke shook his head at Travis.

"You're an idiot," Luke said as he walked past.

Travis smiled on his way to the checkout line. He bought a bag of chili cheese Fritos and a Gatorade. Jeremy grabbed a heat-lamp burrito. Jensen stuck with his routine of Copenhagen and sunflower seeds.

A few minutes later, three wet cowboys headed north on I-25, eating what would prove to be dinner. Jensen and Travis resumed their game of Hold'em, using the truck's center console as a makeshift poker table. The rain had let up. Then Jeremy spotted it first.

"There's the Daddy," he said, nodding to a sign along the freeway that read THE DADDY OF 'EM ALL.

Jensen and Travis abruptly stopped gambling, and the cab fell silent. The cowboys all stared out the side windows as Cheyenne's rodeo grounds came into view. It is a scene that always stirs strong emotions in the belly of a cowboy: the birthplace of rodeo; the death place of Lane Frost; the century of legends who have graced the arena dirt; a million dollars in prize money given away each year. Cheyenne is a mecca for cowboys.

The three continued to watch as they passed the empty grounds. The rodeo still was a month away. Miles beyond the arena, brilliant beams of light had broken through holes in the purple clouds and were shining onto the prairie. It was as close to a religious moment as these particular cowboys come. And Travis prayed.

"Hello Daddy," he said aloud, clutching a deck of cards near his heart. "I hope I make it to you. You've pulled me through before. I know you can pull me through again."

As the rig passed by the white overhang that towers above the grandstands, Travis turned his head slowly, like a flower following the sun. When the moment passed and Cheyenne was behind him, his attention returned to the table. He shuffled the cards, looked to the backseat, and raised his eyebrows at Jensen.

"All right, cocksucker," he said, "you ready to lose your ass?"

WHEATLAND. DOUGLAS. CASPER.

Riding through the city of Casper, Travis looked off to the right and pointed to a large red-roofed building on a hill: the Casper Events Center.

"God, me and Luke flew into here one time in a snowstorm," Travis said. "That was scary."

"How is that rodeo?" Jensen said.

"Don't know," Travis said. "We were only there for five minutes."

"Really?" Jensen said.

"Yeah," Travis said. "They were already bulldoggin' when we got there. Barely made it. We ran our steers and walked outside and got into the rig and drove to South Dakota."

It was 2000, Luke's rookie year. With one week left in the season, Travis was in thirteenth place and Luke was sixteenth. The two embarked upon a hellish adventure that shows the lengths cowboys are willing to travel to try to make the finals.

Travis and Luke competed in a rodeo in San Francisco on a Tuesday night. The next morning, they flew to Kansas City for an afternoon performance there. After that, they rushed to an airport and boarded another plane to get to the rodeo in Casper at eight o'clock that night. But a delay made them late getting into Denver and they missed their connecting flight.

Desperate, they chartered a small Cessna for seven hundred dollars apiece. The pilot tossed them blankets and said they would need them. Luke looked out the window at the snow-covered ground, then nervously asked Travis what was on the wings. Travis gave a grim smile, and told Fatty it was ice. A friend picked the two up at the airport and sped to the rodeo. Even though steer wrestling already had started, those in charge held back Luke and Travis's steers, something that isn't done much anymore.

Someone had driven Luke's rig to Casper for him. After the rodeo, Luke and Travis drove to Brookings, South Dakota, for a Thursday night performance. When that ended, they moved on to Detroit for a Friday night rodeo. Later that night, they boarded a red-eye flight to Sacramento, rented a car, and drove to Rancho Murietta for a Saturday morning rodeo.

At that point, Travis had won enough to assure himself a spot in the finals, but Luke still needed six hundred dollars to move into fifteenth. They drove back to the Sacramento airport to catch a plane to Alamogordo, New Mexico, for that night's rodeo. When Luke reached the airport curb, he stopped, looked at Travis, and said forget it. He finished sixteenth that year—the loneliest spot in the standings.

As Travis finished telling the story, he thought of how grueling it had been. "I slept for three straight days after that," he said.

NATRONA. POWDER RIVER. HILAND.

As the wheels rolled, Travis and Jensen divided their concentration between the Hold'em game and the bleak quest for a place to buy beer in the wide-open spaces of Wyoming.

The two men had met about a year before, but this was their first time traveling together. They went together well. Travis is a man always stalking a good time. And Jensen is game for anything, be it drinking beer, chasing women, or just sitting around and moaning about rodeo. They liked one another immensely.

At sunset, Jeremy drove past a green sign announcing the community of Hiland. The sign stated the population of ten, which seemed to be a gross exaggeration. There wasn't much in sight besides the combination bar/café/gas station.

"What about there?" Travis said.

"Where?" Jeremy said.

"That place," Travis said. "Let's try it."

Jeremy stopped the rig in the middle of the highway. He shifted into reverse and began backing about two hundred feet to a darkened roadside bar. There was little danger of being hit by another car because the road basically was deserted. Jeremy backed into the bar's parking lot and stopped. No lights were on. Travis walked up to the bar and knocked, and a friendly old man answered the door. He was the only person in the place.

"You open?" Travis said.

"No," the old man said. "But I can't really afford to be closed."

"Well, we could really use some beer."

"I can probably help you there," the old man said.

The man had two beer choices: a cold twelve-pack, or a warm eighteen-pack. And that was all the beer in the entire bar, which obviously did not deal in quantity.

Travis bought the twelve-pack, and he and Jensen moved the Hold'em game to the trailer. They gambled and drank the night away as Jeremy drove at 75 mph through the hinterlands of Wyoming.

SHOSHONI. THERMOPOLIS. CODY.

Cowboys will gamble on anything.

Waking up in Cody with an entire day to waste, Travis and Jensen embarked on a marathon gambling session, beginning with a game of Hold'em that ate up the late morning and early afternoon. The scene shifted to the Whisky River Discount Liquor & Saloon in downtown Cody where the two challenged Luke and bulldogger Joe Butterfield to games of pool for rounds of tomato juice and beer. The Hold'em game resumed once Travis and Jensen returned to the trailer. That ended only when the duo, full of a day's beer, wandered over to the opening night of the Cody Stampede Rodeo feeling pretty good.

Cody's rodeo grounds were built just outside of town on a flat patch of ground near a winding cliff overlooking the Shoshone River. Wind, water, and time pick at the cliff's rocky walls, which crumble into a thick red dirt that melts into the river. That night, a full yellow moon rose among darkened horizon clouds lined with silver. A cool breeze blew the strong scent of sulfur through the air. Steady lightning flashes lit up the distant mountains, completing the Halloween moonrise scene.

A big crowd gathered for the Stampede opener, but that's no surprise. Whereas many places claim the title of Rodeo Capital of the World, Cody actually earns it: The town hosts a rodeo every night during June, July, and August. Like other Wyoming rodeo crowds, Cody draws a smart bunch that seems to prefer good drama and competition over the shock of a spectacular cowboy crash.

The exception on this night were Travis and Jensen, who perched themselves atop a white wooden fence near the roping chute, far from the crowded grandstands. Taking great delight in mocking one rider after another, the two men resembled drunken versions of Statler and Waldorf, the incorrigible duo who sat in the balcony and heckled Muppets performances. Travis and Jensen bet beers on each event. For rough stock, they waged how long a rider could stay aboard, either in seconds or animal hops. For team ropers, the over/under line usually was drawn at five seconds. By the time the bull riding had started, a decent pile of crushed cans had collected beneath them. Jensen's belly was full of free beer and Travis was getting pissed—in more ways than one.

"Okay, Jensen," Travis said, "your choice."

Jensen looked up at the scoreboard, but didn't recognize the next bull rider's name. He thought for a moment, studying the faraway chute for a sign.

"I say five hops."

"Five hops you say?" Travis said, intently considering the ride. "This guy won't last five hops. I say lower."

Both men quickly turned their attention to the chute. It opened and a little black bull emerged with a series of harmless hops across the arena. The bell sounded, the rider jumped off with ease, and the crowd groaned in disappointment. Jensen laughed and took a long drink. Travis shook his head in disgust.

"You see that Jensen?" Travis said, throwing an empty beer can into the fence. "I could have ridden that motherfucker."

"That's 3-0 Trav," Jensen said. "Man, you're a sore loser."

"Well, fuck, did you see that?" Travis said. "That little bull comes hopping through the arena in a straight line. If my steer runs like that tomorrow, I'm winning some money."

The name of the next rider came over the loudspeaker: Blue Stone.

"Well, all right," Travis said, wringing his hands and smiling confidently. "This man's a world champ. Jensen, he's gonna ride this bull."

"Full eight seconds then?" Jensen said.

"Yep," Travis said. "Blue'll make it eight seconds."

Travis looked to the chute and began yelling encouragement.

"C'mon Blue," Travis shouted. "Show us how you won that buckle."

The gate swung open and the crowd cheered the former champ. But Blue lasted all of two hops before the bull tossed him high into the air. He landed in a heap, got up, and ran away.

"Fuck me," Travis yelled. "I can't fucking believe that shit. You see that? I can't even win on a world champ. Ol' Blue really let me down there."

Jensen laughed as Travis stormed off to take a piss. He returned a couple minutes later with two more beers. He handed one to Jensen.

"That's 4-0 Trav," Jensen said.

"Just shut the fuck up and pick the next one."

"Okay, buddy," Jensen said, studying the chute once again before setting the bet at four hops.

"Four, huh?" Travis said. "This guy'll last four. I'll take the over."

When the gate opened, Travis and Jensen simultaneously counted the hops aloud. One. Two. Three. Then the bull flipped the rider off his back. Jensen looked at Travis and smiled, needing no words. Travis jumped down from the fence and began pacing like a gambler who had just lost a fortune.

"You no-trying motherfucker!" Travis said. "What a little fucking pussy! You see the size of that bull?"

"Yep," Jensen said, laughing. "Wasn't much of a fucking bull, was it?"

"That's because it was a steer," Travis said. "I feel bad for all these people here. They waited around all night for this. And what'd they get? Steer riding. These ain't fucking bulls."

"It's 5-0 Trav," Jensen said. "Man, this beer tastes really good. Thanks buddy."

Travis ignored Jensen and focused on predicting the next bull rider's fate. Without giving it much thought, Travis announced the man would make it eight seconds. When the gate opened, a black monster of a bull blew out of the chute, its rider hanging on for dear life. He made it about six seconds before the bull shifted directions and flipped the rider into the air. He landed hard on his head and lay motionless in the dirt as bullfighters worked madly to prevent the bull from doing the man more harm. Travis and Jensen both winced.

"Whoa!" Travis said, a serious look on his face. "Well, at least he tried."

"Yeah, that guy was a trying motherfucker," Jensen said.

"You know how you can tell he was trying?" Travis said. "When you land on your head, you were trying."

Jensen nodded. Both men took the last drinks of their beers, crushed the cans, and dropped them with the others. Travis walked off and came back a couple minutes later with two more beers. It was a little past eleven o'clock as the crowd filed out. Jensen and Travis remained on the fence and talked some more.

"You know," Jensen said, sounding disappointed, "I was hoping Fatty'd come drinking with us tonight."

Instead, Luke had caught a ride to Red Lodge, Montana, to spend the night with Lindsay in her trailer. Travis nodded as he finished his last beer of the night. He crushed it in his hand and beer soaked into his sleeve. He dropped the can onto the dirt with a dozen or so others and wiped his mouth.

"Fatty's in love right now, Jensen," Travis said. "He can't stand for them to be apart for two minutes. But let me tell you something. That's gonna change someday. I don't know when, but someday."

Jensen smiled and drank his beer as Travis continued his rant.

"There will come a day when Fatty's gonna say, 'You know, I think I'm gonna go hang out with my old buddy Travis tonight.' She'll say, 'What are you guys gonna do?' And he'll say, 'I think me and my old buddy Travis are gonna go to a rodeo and throw down some steers.'

"And she'll say, 'But I thought he retired.' And he'll say, 'Nope, I entered him.' Now I don't know when, Jensen, but I promise you that day is gonna come. And it'll be just like old times."

Jensen jumped down from the fence and dropped an empty can. As he and Travis walked slowly back to the trailer, the full moon had moved directly overhead. The two got to bed after midnight, giving them about four hours' sleep before the start of a busy morning.

At 4:30 A.M., the rows of horse trailers were dark and quiet. A light came on inside Luke's trailer and revealed, through a window, the shadows of cowboys stirring in the darkness before dawn. The side door swung open, and Jensen emerged fitting a cowboy hat on his head. He climbed behind the wheel of Luke's truck and started the engine. A couple minutes later, Travis stepped out of the trailer and saw Jensen behind the wheel. A huge smile appeared on Travis's face as he sat in the passenger seat. He looked over at Jensen with a giddy expression of surprise.

"Jensen," Travis said, shaking his head in amazement, "you are one hell of a guy."

Jensen smiled. "You're just happy 'cause I'm driving."

"No, I mean it Jensen," Travis said. "Motherfucker. I just want to hug you right now. Here it is, I might have been a little grumpy getting up this early. But who could be grumpy around a fella like you? You never stop, do you Jensen? You're just open twenty-four hours a day, ain't you?"

Jensen laughed quietly as he pulled out of the rodeo grounds onto a two-lane highway headed to Red Lodge. The two stopped for some coffee, then resumed the trip with just enough time to make the seven o'clock slack.

CODY. SHOSHONE RIVER. BELFRY.

As Jensen drove into a blinding sunrise, a confused expression appeared on his face. The sun rose in the east. The highway signs indicated he was traveling west. And Red Lodge was due north. Unable to make much sense of things, he turned to Travis, who was busy reading a sports page.

"You know Trav, I know Red Lodge is sixty miles north on I-20. But the sun is rising there [pointing toward Travis's side window], and the signs say we're heading west. I know the sun ain't gonna set here [pointing toward front window], it's gonna set way over there [pointing out Jensen's side window]. So, how the hell are we going to get to Red Lodge by going west?"

Travis closed his newspaper and looked at Jensen with an expression of amusement and bemusement. Not sure quite what to say at first, he nodded and said, "Um, all right."

"I was just putting that out there for you, buddy," Jensen said. "You know, just something for you to think about. That's all."

Travis continued to nod as if deep in thought. His mouth formed a subtle smile. Finally, he could hold back no longer.

"I'll tell you what I know, Jensen," he said. "I know if the sun ain't up, then a fella ought to still be in bed. We're not farmers, we're cowboys."

Jensen nodded as Travis continued.

"Tell you what else I know, Jensen. Those guys who build roads for a living, well we'll let them decide where the roads go. And guys like you and me, we just drive where the roads are. That's just something I'm putting back at you buddy."

Travis stared at Jensen, and they both smiled.

"Is any of that getting through?" Travis said.

"Oh yeah," Jensen said. "Thanks for clearing all that up for me."

"Now don't get me wrong, Jensen," Travis said. "I think it's great that you're trying to think and stuff, I just don't want you to hurt yourself."

Travis opened his newspaper again and resumed his reading.

Jensen continued to ponder direction. He looked at the compass above Luke's mirror: It still read north.

BEARCREEK. WASHOE. RED LODGE.

Red Lodge is a quaint tourist town tucked near the foothills of the snowcapped Beartooth Mountains in southern Montana. Once a thriving coal-mining community, Red Lodge's population reached 1,180 by 1892 and grew by just 700 during the next century. The rodeo grounds were built on lush green acreage just outside town, bordered by tall trees on one end and a narrow asphalt airstrip on the other. The dark wooden bleachers are covered with hints of paint long worn away by years of harsh weather.

A heavy rain the night before had turned the arena dirt into a thick soup. As slack began, Travis muttered to himself as he walked over to join Jensen and Luke at the chute.

"Goddamn it," he said, shaking clumps of mud off his boots. "I told Fatty not to enter me in this motherfucker."

Travis's mood suddenly fell sour, and the mud was but a small factor. Red Lodge, which offered a couple thousand dollars to the winner, held little allure for him. As his summer spiraled toward hell, he now needed big money to move back into contention. Trouble was, his rides were looking worse all the time and he didn't know why.

As the first few steer wrestlers made their runs, Travis stretched his arms and legs mostly in silence. Someone turned in a 4.1-second run to set the pace. Then, at 7:15 A.M., the rope on the barrier came apart. As several men worked to put it back together, the competition stalled. Luke and Travis looked at each other in disbelief. Their morning's schedule already was tight. They needed to leave Red Lodge by 7:30 A.M. to have enough time to get back to Cody by 9 A.M. to run their steers.

And Cody promised its winning steer wrestler a prize of more than eleven thousand dollars.

The men got the chute fixed after a ten-minute delay. Jensen rode into the box at 7:36 A.M. He was late catching up to his steer, but wrestled him down in 6.8 seconds.

Travis backed into the box at 7:42. His steer was a runner that made it far into the arena before Travis caught up. He grabbed the horns and skidded to a stop. But he never got his feet set and the steer took off again, taking Travis for a ride. Finally, he let go and the steer ran free. Another no time.

Luke's summer couldn't have been playing out more differently. At 7:46, he backed into the box and got his horse settled. He nodded, caught his steer in a flash, and slammed him into mud. He waited for the announcer to call out his time. A couple seconds later, a 4.0 came over the loudspeaker. That shot him into the lead, but ultimately he settled for third and about twenty-five hundred dollars.

Luke, Travis, and Jensen walked briskly back toward the truck. Luke stopped and gave a quick good-bye kiss to Lindsay, who had a run at Red Lodge later in the day. Travis and Jensen already sat in the truck when Luke climbed inside, started the engine, and shifted into gear. It was 7:58—sixty-two minutes until slack began in Cody. That meant a 90-mph drive through winding rural roads where mule deer commonly stand alongside, or sometimes in the middle of, the road. As he sped through downtown Red Lodge, Luke pulled on his seat belt, an extremely rare occurrence. Jensen, sitting in the backseat, noticed the move with some concern, and quickly pulled his seat belt on as well. Travis did not. Instead, he reached into his pocket and retrieved his cell phone. He called Tiffany and left her a quick message.

"Hi honey. I didn't do any good in Red Lodge. The fat guy's

winning it. We're headed to Cody now. I don't know if you can hear any of this, but I'll call you later."

RED LODGE. WASHOE. BEARCREEK.

As Luke sped out of town into the foothills, he looked over at Travis in the passenger seat. Their moods and fortunes couldn't have been more different.

"Kind of a neat little town though," Luke said, with mock sweetness.

"Yeah, it's real fucking neat," Travis said.

"Well, it's a cute little rodeo."

"Yeah, real fucking cute."

Luke reached over and tickled Travis behind the ear. Travis ignored it and stared out his window.

"C'mon Trav, rodeo is fun."

"Yeah, it's real fucking fun, kid."

"Ah, what's wrong, buddy? You need a hug?"

"Nope."

"You sure?"

"I'm sure."

"All right, I was just trying to help."

As Luke drove, he continued to pepper Travis with questions, speaking with the enthusiasm and soft tone of a little boy.

"Did you think I got a good start, Trav?"

"Yeah, you got a good start. And you looked real pretty in your hat. Showed us all how it's done."

"Really?"

"Yeah, the army would be proud of you, kid."

"What, 'cause of all that mud and shit?"

"Yep," Travis said. "When the conditions are bad, a soldier will rise. Improvise."

"Man, why do you think no one else was able to do any

good on my steer?" Luke said, pretending to be dumbfounded.

" 'Cause you're the best there is, kid," Travis said. "The number one man in the world."

"Thanks Travvie. Do you really mean it?"

"Oh yeah, buddy. The best there is."

Satisfied, Luke nodded to himself and turned back toward the road. As Luke drove near the site of an abandoned coal mine, Travis leaned forward in his seat to get a good look. He saw the scene earlier that morning and could tell something big had happened there. He wanted to know what it was. Outside of rodeo and football, perhaps his deepest interest is American history. When he spotted a large wooden marker along the roadside, he pointed to it.

"Pull over," he told Luke.

"What?" Luke said, gasping. "Are you serious?"

Luke, wearing an absolutely horrified expression, whipped his neck to look over at Travis. Luke was completely stunned, and knocked momentarily speechless: Cody's a big money rodeo.

"C'mon," Travis said. "Just pull over."

Luke looked down at the clock. Still wearing his horrified expression, he looked back at Travis.

"We got time," Travis said. "C'mon, I want to know what happened here."

Luke shook his head in utter disbelief. Finally, some words came to mind.

"You're a complete fucking idiot!" he yelled. "You know that?"

"I know," Travis said. "C'mon, there's a good chance I'll never be on this road again."

"I take it back," Luke yelled. "You're a nerd! That's what you are, a nerd!"

"I know," Travis said. "C'mon, just pull over."

"You're serious?" Luke said, still having trouble believing it. "Fine."

Luke slowed his truck, pulled into a turnout, and parked alongside the large wooden sign.

The top line read, in big letters: SMITH MINE DISASTER. Luke looked at Travis in amazement.

"Hey buddy," Luke said, throwing his hands into the air, "would you like me to read it to you?"

"Sure thing, kid."

Luke looked at Travis and shook his head. Then Luke turned and began reading the entire sign aloud in a mock scholarly tone:

Smoke pouring from the mine entrance about ten o'clock the morning of February 27, 1943, was the first indication of trouble. "There's something wrong down here. I'm getting out," the hoist operator called up. He and two nearby miners were the last men to leave the mine alive.

Rescue crews from as far away as Butte and Cascade County worked around the clock in six-hour shifts to clear debris and search for possible survivors. There were none. The night of March 4, workers reached the first bodies. More followed until the toll mounted to 74. Some died as a result of a violent explosion in No. 3 vein, the remainder fell victim to the deadly methane gasses released by the blast.

The tragedy at Smith Mine became Montana's worst coal mine disaster, sparking investigations at the state and national level. Montana Governor Sam C. Ford visited the scene, offered state assistance, and pushed through a thorough inquiry into the incident.

Today's marker of the Smith Mine Disaster follows a simpler one left by two of the miners trapped underground

*after the explosion, waiting for the poisonous gas they knew
would come.*

*Walter and Johnny. Good-bye. Wives and daughters. We
died an easy death. Love from us both. Be good.*

When Luke finished reading, he looked over at Travis and
smiled.

"Hey buddy?" he said.

"Yeah buddy."

"Think we could go to that rodeo now?"

"Sure thing, buddy," Travis said. "Hey, thanks for stopping."

Luke reached out and gave Travis several hard pats on the
chest.

"Anything for you, good buddy," Luke said.

Soon the speedometer needle moved to between 85 and
90 mph as Luke raced past the freshly cut hay fields of southern Montana and the wide-open cattle ranges of northern
Wyoming. He slowed to 55 mph as he weaved his way through
traffic in downtown Cody, pulling into the rodeo grounds at
9:10 A.M. Slack already had started, but they made it with ten
minutes to spare.

Travis, Luke, and Jensen hurried to the arena and sat atop a
fence near the roping chute as they awaited their turns. Each
had visions of what a first-place run in Cody could do. For Luke,
it could significantly pad his lead on the pack. For Travis, it literally could erase months of coming up empty and move him
near the PRCA's top fifteen. For Jensen, it could take him from
nowhere to atop the Rookie of the Year standings.

Jensen got his chance first. He had drawn one of the best
steers in the lot. Not too big. Not too fast. Goes down easy. Rid-

ing into the box, he took a long look into the animal's eyes. Once he got his horse settled, he nodded for his steer. He caught the animal and got it turned, but spent a few costly seconds bringing him to the ground. As Jensen stood, a 7.0 flashed onto the scoreboard. That wasn't nearly good enough in Cody, where the winning time would be 3.9 seconds. He walked away, muttering and cussing to himself.

Next up was Luke. As he backed his horse into the box, he looked over to see if Travis was ready to haze. He was. Joey Bell, Jr., a fellow steer wrestler from Salem, New Jersey, climbed into the chute behind the steer, wrapping the animal's tail around one hand before placing both hands on the steer's rump. He got ready to give the steer a little push when the chute opened. Jensen moved to the front of the chute, reached inside, and held one of the steer's horns so the animal's head wouldn't get stuck on the release. In steer wrestling, one man is on the line, but many team up in small ways to help him. Luke nodded and his steer charged ahead. It took a few seconds for the cowboy to catch up, and Luke had to settle for a 5.0-second run, which wouldn't earn a penny in Cody.

Finally, it was Travis's turn. He took the horse from Luke and climbed into the saddle. As he rode into the box, Travis gave his steer a long sideways glance. He nodded and raced out to catch his steer. Once Travis hit the ground, he and the steer fell over the wrong way. Travis got the animal back to its feet and tried to wrestle him down as the 10-second mark passed on the scoreboard. Travis continued attempts to muscle the animal down, but it held to its feet. Frustrated, Travis threw his hands up and stood as the steer ran away.

After he'd walked back to the fence, Travis stood with his hands on his hips, trying to catch his breath. A few seconds later, he climbed up on the fence and sat down next to Luke.

"Sorry," Luke said.

"About what?" Travis said.

"That haze."

"Not your fault," Travis said.

Travis shook his head as he thought about the morning. During his slump, and most of the slumps over his career, the problem often had been a quick trigger finger: costly broken barriers on runs that would have made money had he waited a split second longer. But now, both in Red Lodge and Cody, things had changed: He felt like he was embarrassing himself in the arena. And, for a proud man and an NFR-caliber steer wrestler, it was a new and entirely ugly feeling.

After slack ended, Travis and Jensen took a long slow walk back to the trailer. They were both tired. And particularly tired of losing. At the moment, neither man gave a shit about the promise of July, perhaps rodeo's biggest month of the season. They spent the rest of the morning in their beds, sleeping like cats. Occasionally, one would wake up, stretch, maybe get a drink or nibble on some food. But, for the most part, they just slept. And slept.

By 4 P.M., their exhaustion had morphed into utter boredom. It was wet outside, leaving them little choice but to stay inside the trailer. Neither felt much like gambling. So Travis lay in his bunk, staring out a small window at the Shoshone River canyon with a blank expression on his face. Jensen sat on a couch, staring straight ahead at a cabinet.

Sometimes, he looked up to monitor the progress of a fly that slowly was walking across the ceiling. The trailer was silent except for the generator's hushed hum and the soft dreary sound of a light rain falling on the roof.

"Jensen?" Travis said.

"Yeah."

"What are you doing?"

"Sitting here."

With that, one of history's most uninspired conversations began. Two homesick rodeo haters spoke in monotone, like bored robots. Thoughtlessly they stared, hardly ever blinking. All that moved was their mouths, and just enough to get the words out.

"Why?" Jensen said.

"Oh, just wondering."

Another minute of silence followed.

"Trav?"

"Yeah Jensen."

"What are you doing?"

"Lying here, staring out the window."

"How's it look?"

"It don't look like Oakdale, Jensen."

"Kinda looks like Coalinga."

"I meant it doesn't look like I'm staring out a window at home."

"I knew what you meant, Trav."

More silence.

"Of course," Travis said, "if I was home, my boy would be crying and my girl would be cussing."

"She cussin' already? She's only three, isn't she?"

"Yeah. Tiffany told me a couple nights ago that Kelsey came up to her and said she had a fucking headache. Ten minutes later, she blew some gas and said, 'What do you think about that?'"

"That's really sweet, Trav. She's daddy's little girl."

Another ten minutes passed. Finally, Travis couldn't take any more staring out the window.

"Fuck this Jensen," Travis said, groaning as he got out of bed and grabbed his boots. "I'm gonna go eat another cheeseburger."

"Okay," Jensen said, still staring at the cabinet. "Hey, while you're out there Trav, would you bring me back a hammer?"

"Okay," Travis said, looking confused. "Why you want a hammer?"

"So I can smash up my fucking leg. Then I could go home."

"Yeah, I'm pretty sure there's a plane flying from here to Sacramento tomorrow," Travis said. "I've thought about making that call several times today."

Travis opened the trailer door and stepped outside. He buttoned his coat and looked back one last time at Jensen.

"You know what Jensen?"

"What's that, buddy?"

"I still might make that call."

With that, Travis put on his cowboy hat and closed the door. Jensen listened as the crunching sound of boots on gravel faded away. He looked up and resumed his stare. Now the fly was walking down the wall. Outside, the rain kept falling.

PRCA STEER WRESTLING WORLD STANDINGS
(Through July 31)

NAME (HOMETOWN)	MONEY WON	RODEOS
1. Luke Branquinho (Los Alamos, CA)	$82,539.71	37
2. Teddy Johnson (Checotah, OK)	$62,965.03	41
3. Ronnie Fields (Oklahoma City, OK)	$57,365.45	39
4. Stockton Graves (Newkirk, OK)	$51,823.03	43
5. Jason Lahr (Emporia, KS)	$50,550.53	40
6. Sean Mulligan (Aurora, SD)	$43,117.76	38
7. K. C. Jones (Las Animas, CO)	$42,204.95	34
8. Rope Myers (Van, TX)	$38,232.32	37
9. Shawn Greenfield (Lakeview, OR)	$38,113.24	40
10. Spud Duvall (Checotah, OK)	$37,986.46	42
11. Trevor Knowles (Mount Vernon, OR)	$37,863.97	35
12. Lee Graves (Calgary, AB)	$36,135.63	35
13. Bob Lummus (Folsom, LA)	$33,539.99	37
14. Birch Negaard (Buffalo, SD)	$33,156.15	33
15. Chad Biesemeyer (Stephenville, TX)	$32,564.72	38
OTHER NOTABLES		
18. Joshua Peek (Pueblo, CO)	$29,746.39	39
25. Bryan Fields (Conroe, TX)	$24,652.62	41
32. Frank Thompson (Cheyenne, WY)	$22,051.73	31
46. Clyde Himes (Stanton, TX)	$17,900.21	39
48. Ron Schenk (Moorpark, CA)	$17,125.19	32
53. Brad McGilchrist (Sheridan, CA)	$12,509.53	39
73. Travis Cadwell (Oakdale, CA)	$9,977.51	28
97. Levi Rosser (Wheatland, CA)	$8,186.36	34
104. Austin Manning (Las Vegas, NV)	$7,740.92	20
117. Tyler Holzum (Oakdale, CA)	$6,842.01	31
120. Robbin Peterson (Mira Loma, CA)	$6,663.65	29
158. Casey Branquinho (Los Alamos, CA)	$4,502.51	17
245. Brock Andrus (St. George, UT)	$2,635.81	28
424. Marc Jensen (Coalinga, CA)	$972.18	29

CHAPTER 10

On the Top and the Bottom of the World

NAMPA, IDAHO

TUESDAY, JULY 20

Winning is hard. Losing is harder.

The summer of 2004 stuck that principle into Jensen's face, day after day. He had gone more than three months without earning a paycheck, spending thousands of dollars a month in the process. But now, as he stood near a fence inside the Idaho Center Arena, hunched over and sweating profusely, the summer dry spell was the least of his concerns: Instead, he simply was trying not to throw up or pass out.

As cowboys took their shots during the morning's slack, Jensen looked like a man trying to hold off death. He propped himself against a horse, his lowered head resting against the saddle. A fever raged inside him. His mouth watered, and sweat beads collected on his forehead. The hot flashes came every few minutes, leaving a glazed, lifeless look in his eyes. And, bad as it was, the flu was just one of his many ailments.

A few days earlier in Salinas, Jensen fell into a bad position during his second-round run. He wound up on his stomach as a steer ran amok all over his back, leaving a trail of yellow-and-purple hoofprints on his skin. That night, while he was out at a

154

cowboy bar drinking off the back pain, someone sucker punched Jensen in the face. Jensen had gotten into what seemed like a mild disagreement with the man's friend, and never saw the punch coming. The blow swelled one side of Jensen's face and ravaged his jaw. Now every time he opened his mouth, his jaw made a peculiar popping sound. The pain left him unable to chew food; he had only been able to force down a bowl of soup during the previous two days. Now he felt weak as hell, and was starting to give serious consideration to visiting a doctor because he was beginning to think there was something broken in there. It didn't seem possible, but things were about to get worse.

"Next up, Marc Jensen," an announcer said.

Jensen lifted his head, took a deep breath, and pulled himself into the saddle. He rode to the chute feeling about as bad as he'd ever felt in his life. He backed his horse into the box, looked down at his steer, and gave a nod. He caught the animal and got it stopped, but then he reached for the nose and missed. Jensen held on for a few seconds as the steer pushed him forward through the dirt. Finally, Jensen let go and the animal ran away. Rat fucked. After the ride, Jensen slowly made his way back to Luke's trailer and went back to sleep.

The Snake River Stampede couldn't have gone any differently for Luke. After an opening-round time of 3.8 seconds won him seven hundred dollars, Luke settled his horse in the box with a good shot at qualifying for the weekend's short round. He rode out, caught his steer after a short chase, and threw the animal into the dirt. He stood, wiped his nose on his sleeve as he, too, was battling illness, and waited to hear his time. It was a 3.9—not quick enough for any round money, but it qualified him for the short round and left him in the top five of an average that paid about five thousand dollars.

An hour later, Luke loaded his horses into the rig. He pulled into a feed store and added six bales of hay to the stack on top of his trailer. It was going to be another long week on the road: Before making the trip back to Nampa for Saturday's final, Luke would travel to three Utah rodeos. As Luke pulled out of the Idaho Center parking lot, the cab seemed unmistakably quiet. Something was missing: Travis.

A few days earlier, Travis had ridden into Salinas with a desperate idea already fixed in his head. Like a gambler down to his last bet, Travis had decided a bad run in Salinas would serve as that last shove into retirement. And Salinas treated him like most every other city had during the previous few months. Travis managed to win about two hundred dollars for placing in his first-round run, but he never got out of the saddle on his second ride. No time. No money. No more.

As he walked from the arena, he yanked his cell phone from his pocket. He called the rodeo office and withdrew from every future rodeo he had entered, including Nampa, Salt Lake City, and Cheyenne. Then he walked alone down a long dirt road that led him past a group of kids swinging ropes near a horned bale of hay, a sad and hopeful portrait of rodeo's past and future. Yet, even as he left the arena behind, Travis knew he was not walking away from his last rodeo. There would be others, most likely the ones held on weekends throughout California. But, at that moment, he couldn't stand to think about rodeo and the steady disappointment it had dealt him all season. He cringed at the thought of another month-long summer road trip, especially now with a son and daughter at home growing up too fast. And worst of all was the losing, which only salts the wound and starts a thirty-six-year-old man to wondering what the hell he's even doing still rodeoing.

Travis kept walking until he reached the rows of trucks and horse trailers. He opened a few trailer doors until he found an unattended ice chest. He grabbed a Coors Light, took a seat on a tailgate, and took a long pull on the first beer of his retirement. Jensen walked up, already aware of what Travis had in mind.

"So, you ain't going to Nampa with us?" Jensen said.

"I'm retired, Jensen."

"Retired?" Jensen said, scoffing. "You ain't retired Cadwell."

"I'm retired," Travis said. "I already withdrew from everything."

"Even Cheyenne?"

"Even Cheyenne," Travis said, taking another drink of his beer.

"Oh, you'll be back," Jensen said. "You'll get the itch again."

Travis got a serious look on his face, and he looked at Jensen.

"I scratched that itch a long time ago, buddy."

And Travis wasn't the only one who hopped out of Luke's rig in Salinas. Jeremy also called it quits, telling Luke he was going back to junior college and no longer could work as Luke's driver. With Travis and Jeremy gone, and with Jensen sleeping in the trailer, Luke pulled out of the Idaho Center alone and settled in for the seven-hour drive to Salt Lake City. As he headed east on Interstate 84, he fumbled with the radio dial, looking for some country. Finally, a Garth Brooks rodeo song came on. Luke turned up the volume and sat back, singing every word of "Much Too Young (To Feel This Damn Old)," a song that better fit the plight of the man fighting fever in the trailer.

> *"And the white line's getting longer, and the saddle's getting cold . . ."*

MOUNTAIN HOME. GOODING. SNAKE RIVER PLAIN.

As Jensen slept, Luke wound his way through a cloudy southern Idaho morning. He passed through corn and hay fields broken up by winding river canyons. Then he reached a familiar stretch of I-84, and he looked out his side window just past the oncoming lanes of traffic. He stared at the landscape. There was nothing there but small shrubs and dried yellow grass. And a bad memory.

It was March 2002 and the Branquinho family was on its way home from the Dodge National Circuit Finals in Pocatello. A late-winter storm had blown through the region the night before. The temperature hung around fifteen degrees that morning as a blinding sun turned the wet pavement into ice. Casey was driving and both his parents were sitting in the truck with him. Luke had crawled into his trailer bed an hour earlier and was asleep when the truck lost traction at about 25 mph.

The truck skidded into a sideways slide, then spun around and hit the trailer. The jackknifed rig slid out of control off the side of the road and started to go over. Casey gripped the wheel as the front windshield scene vanished into the darkness of solid dirt.

Just as fast, it was daylight again as the truck finished its flip and landed on its wheels. Further off the road, the trailer came to rest on its roof. Casey checked on his parents, and they were fine. The doors were jammed, so Casey's dad kicked out a side window with his boot and got him and his wife outside. The three of them banged on the trailer's walls for what seemed like forever before they finally heard Luke's voice, saying he was okay. Luke had awakened the moment he felt the trailer's tires sliding across the ice. He knew something felt wrong. When he heard both sets of wheels cross the rumble strip and skid onto the gravel, he gripped his mattress and held it as tightly as he could. Luke bounced against the walls as the trailer rolled. It came to rest on its roof, and somehow Luke landed on top of the mattress when it settled on the ceiling. It was one of the scariest moments of his life. He didn't sleep well in the trailer for months. Even now, his ears perk whenever he's in the trailer and he hears the mad roar of tires crossing the rumble strip. The true danger of rodeo life lies not in the arena, but on the roads leading there.

HEYBURN. TREMONTON. SALT LAKE CITY.

As the rig entered the outskirts of Salt Lake City, Luke's cell phone rang. He reached onto the dashboard, grabbed his phone, and saw that it was Travis calling. Luke shook his head from side to side, and answered the phone in a sarcastically sweet voice.

"Hi Travis. . . . Well, I'm just driving to a rodeo buddy. Do you remember rodeos, Trav? . . . No, we're headed to Salt Lake. We were supposed to run our second steers there together, remember? . . . I know, you're a loser, remember? . . . Yeah, you quit. Remember? . . . Okay, so I don't have to keep reminding you, right? . . . Okay quitter. . . . Well, you know, it'd be a little better if you were here so I could make fun of you, but I'll be all right. . . . Well, now I've got to find somebody to haze for me in Cheyenne because you're a quitter. . . . I know it. Right back atcha buddy. . . . That's okay, Trav. I still hate you, okay buddy? . . . Okay, you little skinny fucker. . . . Okay, you little skinny prick."

Luke hung up the phone and flipped it back onto the dashboard, muttering to himself, "That guy's a fucking idiot." A disgusted look hung on his face. Now he was driving in downtown Salt Lake City looking for the fairgrounds, and he realized he'd taken a wrong turn.

"Goddamn it!" he said to himself. "I knew talking to him would screw me up."

Luke made a sweeping illegal turn in the middle of a four-lane road, ran a red light, and angered an intersection full of drivers in his wake. He shook his head, still muttering to himself.

All that week, any time Travis's name came up in conversation, Luke slumped his shoulders and got a sour, blank expression on his face. And, each time, he looked into the eyes of whoever mentioned Travis and said the same three words: He's an idiot. He couldn't find enough hurtful words to say about his friend because, deep down, he missed yelling and cussing ol' Trav. And that pissed Luke off something fierce.

AMERICAN FORK. PROVO. SPANISH FORK.

The sound of hooves on gravel outside the trailer woke Luke a little before 8 A.M. As the first cowboys headed to the arena for the Spanish Fork Fiesta Days Rodeo slack, Luke lay in bed, trying to squeeze a little extra sleep from the morning. He had spent the night with Lindsay, celebrating her twenty-first birthday in Salt Lake City. After she left at 3 A.M. to drive to Cheyenne, Luke had driven to Spanish Fork and managed about four hours' sleep. At 8:30, Frank Thompson—the 2000 PRCA steer wrestling champion—poked his head into Luke's trailer.

"Luke, you still sleeping?"

"No, I'm up," Luke said, in a groggy voice.

"Hey," Frank said, "I was just wondering if you're gonna paint it on your trailer every time you place at some rodeo? If you win Spanish Fork, you gonna print that on there, too?"

"There ain't that much on my trailer," said Luke, whose trailer had "NFR Qualifier" and "Pace Chute-out Champion" painted on one side.

Frank laughed, knowing he had no room to talk. Parked nearby was his gaudy rig, which displayed not only an enormous color photo of his face, but also a large picture of him, throwing down a steer.

"Your steer any good?" Luke said.

"No, not much of one," Frank said. "You know what you've got yet?"

"No."

"Well, I'm headed that way. I'll see what number you got and stop by on my way back."

"All right, thanks Frank."

Luke rolled over and fell back to sleep. Jensen sat on the couch, quietly wrapping an ace bandage around his leg to cover an abrasion that was roughly the size of a grapefruit. Still weak from the flu and all that stuff that happened in Salinas, he was simply working on feeling right again. A few minutes later, Frank poked his head back into the trailer.

"Luke," he said.

"Yeah Frank."

"Yours is eighty-four."

"He any good?"

"Looks all right."

"All right Frank, thanks. See you in there."

Luke got up, put his boots on, and walked with Jensen to the arena to join the other bulldoggers. As slack began at 9 A.M., a neck-scorching sun beamed above a large oval arena surrounded by wooden grandstands. Rusty handrails and light posts gave the arena an Old West feel.

Jensen's turn came first. He caught his steer and nearly had him stopped, but the animal surged, leading Jensen on a short ride. He finally wrestled the steer down in 8.8 seconds.

Luke went next. His steer stopped after running a few steps out of the chute, and Luke was ready for it. He jumped off his horse in time and got the steer under control. Then he reached out for the nose, but missed. He watched in disbelief as his steer trotted away.

A few minutes later, as Luke pulled out of the fairgrounds, he took his hat off and threw it at the front windshield. It landed on the dashboard. He looked over at Jensen.

"I should have won that fucker right there," Luke said.

"Yeah, I thought you had it."

"I just missed him," Luke said in disbelief. "I haven't missed one like that in a long time."

SPANISH FORK. PLEASANT GROVE. SALT LAKE CITY.

Pulling onto the interstate, Luke reached onto the floorboard and picked up a small plastic grocery bag. He stuck his hand inside and removed a Snickers bar the sun had turned to liquid. Thoughtfully, he examined it for a couple seconds. Then he held it up to the air conditioner vent to try to get it solid once again. He gave up after a few minutes, and began squeezing it into his mouth one gooey clump at a time.

Jensen sat and watched with a strange smile on his face, not saying a word. Then Luke's cell phone rang again. Jensen picked up the phone and looked at it for a second. He started laughing.

"It's Trav," he said, handing the phone over. Luke's shoulders slumped and he grimaced at Jensen.

"He's an idiot," Luke said, grabbing the phone.

"Hey Trav. . . . Just heading for Ogden, buddy. . . . No, didn't do any good. Missed one for first place. . . . Jensen? No, he was long. Nine seconds or something. . . . So, what are you doing, Trav? . . . Really? That sounds exciting. . . . What? . . . You are? . . . Why? . . . You're an idiot, you know that? . . . You just are. . . . Whatever. . . . All right, you dumb skinny fucker. . . . We'll talk to ya tomorrow."

Luke hung up the phone, looked at Jensen, and laughed in disbelief.

"He's an idiot," Luke said.

"What's he doing?"

"Says he's working."

"Bullshit," Jensen said. "Cadwell doesn't work."

"Know what he just told me? He said next week he was going

to start throwing steers again. He said he didn't have anything else to do."

Jensen laughed, shook his head, and looked out his side window.

"He just retired four days ago," Jensen said. "How many times you think he's retired now?"

"Thirty or forty," Luke said. "That guy ain't never gonna retire. He's gonna be eighty years old, all crippled up, still trying to throw down steers. And he'll still be cussing and bitching and moaning 'cause that's always been his problem. He can't let go of a bad run."

"He really can't," Jensen said, nodding.

"That's 'cause he's an idiot," Luke said.

"I've seen him get mad in practice and say, 'I quit,'" Jensen said. "Then he always comes back five minutes later and starts again."

"Hell," Luke said, "my rookie year, he was about to retire. Him and Tiffany were sitting in the stands in Reno, and he was going home. He would have quit, too, but Russell Solberg said he'd carry him, financially, emotionally, whatever. So he kept going. And that was the year he made the finals."

"Are you serious?" Jensen said, laughing once again. Luke looked over and nodded.

"He's an idiot."

LAYTON. CLEARFIELD. OGDEN.

The next morning, most of the same bulldoggers who competed in Spanish Fork had made the short trek to Ogden for another round of slack. Ogden sports an enormous arena rimmed with tall trees. The Wasatch Mountains rise dramatically to the east. After their events, cowboys water their horses in a creek that runs along the rodeo grounds. It was a beautiful setting, but not pretty enough to offset the ugly feeling looming inside of Jensen. He was beginning to wonder if things could get any worse.

When Jensen hopped off his horse onto his steer that morning, they both tumbled to the ground. They rolled around together for a while before Jensen got the animal back to its feet. He tried to throw the steer down, but the animal got some momentum and began leading Jensen on a wild ride around the arena. Finally, he got the steer stopped again, twisted its neck, and they both fell to the ground. Not that it mattered at that point, but he'd also broken a barrier. His final time: 39.1 seconds. It doesn't get much worse than that.

Luke, eager to make up for the previous day's mishap, drew another good steer and, this time, made the most of it. He slammed the animal down in 4.1 seconds, beating Stockton Graves by one-tenth of a second to win first place and $3,150. The next day he would win a round in Salt Lake City worth nearly $2,000 before driving to Nampa where he would set an arena record of 3.0 in the short round en route to another $6,100. His three-day total: $11,250. It doesn't get much better than that.

When slack at Ogden ended, Jensen rode back to the trailer and put up his horse. He sat quietly on the trailer couch for a while, staring off into space. If someone opened the door looking for something, Jensen snapped out of his funk to greet the person with a smile and a self-deprecating joke. He's always been a pleasant guy to be around, even when he's down, but right now he felt absolutely terrible. There was no other way to describe it.

That summer, he'd learned precisely how far into the ground rodeo can beat a man. And he'd tried his share of approaches to dealing with it all. He had punched walls. He had gotten drunk.

He had yelled and screamed. He had been through all the stages—denial, anger, depression, and acceptance—and still he kept plodding ahead. He didn't see it at the time, but people around him like Luke and Travis were impressed with how Jensen kept on trying long past the point where they would have quit.

But that came as little consolation to Jensen. Here he was, sitting in a trailer in the middle of Utah wondering what possible good could come from these endless lessons in defeat. Sometimes, as he rode into the box, ugly thoughts crept into his head: What was going to go wrong this time? Where does confidence go? And where does a man go to reclaim it?

That was what he was thinking when his cell phone rang. He picked it up and looked at it, seeing it was his older brother calling. He pushed the answer button and lifted the phone to his ear.

"Hello. . . . Nothing. Sitting around, really. . . . No, I didn't do no good. I drew a piece of shit. . . . No, I'm ready to come home. I've got two more to run in Cheyenne then I'm done. . . . You know, I just want to come home and sleep for a few days and then climb on a backhoe. It's been so fucking long since I've seen a check. . . . I know. I just want to look at a check again. I don't even care if I have to work for it. . . . Yeah, it's been pretty bad. What's been going on there with you guys? . . . Just working, huh? . . . Yeah. . . . All right then. I'll let you go. . . . Okay, we'll talk to you later."

Jensen hung up the phone and dropped it on the couch beside him, disappearing again into his thoughts. He replayed a few of the recent bad runs in his head, thinking about things he could have done differently. His mind was drowning in the waters of negative thought. He had said on many occasions that he'd be happy to not win a dime to get to see Luke win a world championship. And Jensen meant it. Trouble was, that exact scenario was looking like a real possibility.

Sometimes he got to wondering what the hell he was even doing out here. On several occasions, Jensen had called his dad, saying that he'd had enough and was coming home. But his dad, being a man who understood that an unchased dream could haunt a man his entire life, always talked his son into sticking with it, to keep moving forward. And then the man would move some more money into Jensen's account. For as low as Jensen's confidence was, his financial condition was worse. In the month of July alone, Jensen had spent more than two thousand dollars on entry fees and another one thousand dollars in road living expenses. He had three credit cards, all at their limits. And the only check he'd won all season was $970 for finishing third in Bakersfield in April. Essentially, his parents were sponsoring his rodeo career, which hadn't existed two years earlier.

It had been Luke who had helped talk Jensen back into rodeo. The two had met about five years earlier while attending West Hills Community College in Coalinga. Jensen had grown up on a ranch riding horses and working cattle, but Luke and Casey taught Jensen how to bulldog. He placed fifth at his first rodeo and qualified for the California Circuit Finals his first year. He quit bulldogging in 2000 to give his time to school, work, and a steady girlfriend. But the relationship ended, and Jensen found himself in dire straits.

During that stretch, Luke kept calling Jensen, inviting him to the ranch to throw steers. Jensen hadn't needed all that much prodding. Because even after he had quit rodeo, something still simmered deep inside the man. It's something that lives inside most any cowboy or cowgirl who puts any time and effort into rodeo: the dream of making the NFR. Just as some little boys grow up pretending they're playing baseball in the World Series, little cowboys throw ropes at plastic horns making believe they're competing in the finals. And now Jensen was twenty-seven years old, and the vision had not weakened. The sickest part of the dream was that it would not die. He fully understood the long odds, but he'd always been a gambler at heart. Hope can be a cruel enemy.

Two days later, Jensen woke up in Cheyenne, Wyoming, on a cool morning that held all the promise in the world. It was 7 A.M.—six hours before that day's performance—but Jensen couldn't sleep. As he got himself dressed, he couldn't stop smiling. Because he was about to take his shot at the Daddy of 'em All. He walked around the grounds of Frontier Park that morning feeling in his stomach the nervous ache of excitement and anticipation, sensations he hadn't felt since the moments before game time during his football-playing days. The summer's disastrous rides faded from memory, replaced by thoughts of what winning a round here would mean. That's what Cheyenne can do to a struggling cowboy.

At 12:30 P.M., Jensen stepped out of the trailer and pushed down his cowboy hat. He walked around back to find Luke posing for pictures for a Cinch Jeans photographer. Jensen sat on a wooden fence nearby and waited. As Luke took turns standing in front of trucks, trailers, and horses, modeling Cinch T-shirts, jackets, and dress shirts, a couple cowboys walked past him on their way to the arena.

"You doing a photo shoot, Fatty?" one of them said, smiling.

"Yeah, a little one," Luke said, seeming a little embarrassed.

"Okay, big smile now," the photographer said as she clicked away. "Okay, this time look at the barn."

Luke did his best, turning this way and that on cue, but modeling really wasn't his thing. He couldn't wait to get to the arena. As the photo shoot ended, Casey walked to Luke and Jensen wearing a big smile.

"You guys ready or what?" Casey said.

"Oh yeah," Luke said.

"Well then hell, let's go," Casey said.

With that, the cowboys set out on the thin asphalt roads that led to the arena. As they got closer, the pavement gave way to a dirt road. They walked along in silence until they reached a white wooden fence that held in an impressive collection of rather large steers. Luke and Jensen climbed onto the fence and sat on the top board. Casey wasn't entered that day, so he helped Luke and Jensen find their steers.

Jensen's was a big black steer, and he sat and watched the animal as it moved with the others around the pen. Luke's was a brown-and-white steer, a little smaller than Jensen's, but it still commanded a presence. Stepping down from the fence, Luke looked at Jensen and smiled.

"You can tell you're nervous when a little pee comes out the end of your dick," Luke said.

"Yeah," Jensen said, "I know it, buddy."

There's a lot that sets Cheyenne apart from other rodeos. Some of it is the mystique of a big-time event that has been drawing people from around the world since 1897. Some of it is the money—the winning steer wrestler often makes off with about twenty thousand dollars. And some of it is the unpredictable nature of the event itself.

The steers used at Cheyenne are huge and fresh. They've never been wrestled before, so there is no scouting report available. It's all guesswork. Some steers run their first time out of the chute. Others walk out slowly and examine their new surroundings at a leisurely pace. Some even stop and stand around awhile. Timing the run is nearly impossible. To make things tougher, the largest arena in professional rodeo also mandates that each steer is given a thirty-foot head start before the bulldogger can leave the box.

All this was on full display that afternoon as the first of three rounds of steer wrestling got under way. Luke and Jensen watched as steers led man after man on wild rides through the thick muddy arena. One cowboy trying to pull a steer down wound up on his back, looking up into the face of his steer, then flipped onto his stomach as the animal dug its hooves across the man's back to get away. Jason Lahr brought thousands of fans to their feet with a run of 6.7 seconds. Outside of that, no one in the first round had much luck.

"Folks, these steers weigh 450 pounds," the announcer said. "They are not your ordinary cattle. . . . These steers are large and in charge today."

An hour later, Jensen stood atop his horse in the arena, his arms folded and his eyes hidden behind sunglasses. When the announcer called Jensen's name, he pulled his sleeves tight and pushed his hat down on his head. Riding into the box, Jensen gave his steer a long look. Once he got settled, he nodded for the gateman. The chute opened and the steer walked slowly from the box. Jensen kept the reins pulled back. After taking a couple steps, the steer broke into a light trot and crossed the thirty-foot mark. Jensen kicked his horse into action and gave chase as the steer started to run. Jensen slid out of his saddle and caught the animal's horns. But while trying to gain control of the steer, he lost his grip and came up empty. He retrieved his horse, rode out of the arena, and stopped when he reached Luke.

"I was trying not to let him get away, but fuck," Jensen said, shaking his head. "He was kind of rearing up on me."

"Yeah, and he jerked you down," Luke said.

"Motherfucker," Jensen said again and again. "Motherfucker."

Jensen often goes to Luke looking for answers about a failed run, but there wasn't much to say this time. It just didn't happen. Jensen stood there with his hands on his hips, shaking his head back and forth. Finally, Jensen looked at Luke and threw his hands up in the air, exasperated.

"This fucking sucks," he said. "I just can't win. I just can't win."

At 3:30 P.M., the main arena gate swung open and Luke and a few other steer wrestlers rode inside, taking their spots along a fence. As Luke and Rodney Burks awaited their turns, they made small talk.

"So," Luke said, "you want me to do anything special?"

"Yeah," Burks said, "just blow on my steer a little when I get close."

"Okay," Luke said as both men started laughing.

Then the announcer called Luke's name. As he rode into the box, Luke took one last look at his steer's face. Then he backed his horse into the corner.

"Ladies and gentlemen," the announcer yelled, "the number one steer wrestler in the world. Los Alamos, California. Luke Branquinho."

Luke nodded and the chute opened. The steer walked out of the box, taking tiny steps; clearly, it was in no hurry. Shortly after crossing the advantage point, the steer sensed the horses racing after it and started running. Luke leaned out of the saddle and caught the horns, but the force knocked both him and the steer into the mud. Luke held on, pulled the steer back to its feet, and slammed the animal into the ground. The time was 9.9 seconds, which doesn't get it done in Cheyenne. Luke walked from the arena shaking his head and shrugging off the ride.

Neither Luke nor Jensen had any luck in their second runs at Cheyenne, either. At that point, Jensen just wanted to go home and lay up for a while. For Luke, who never has cashed a check at Cheyenne, it was merely a speed bump. He had earned about twenty thousand dollars in July, helping him extend his lead to more than twenty thousand dollars over the second-placed man, defending champ Teddy Johnson.

Luke remained hot during the early weeks of August, winning a couple thousand here and there. Then he took third in the average at Caldwell, Idaho. The $4,000 he won there pushed his season total to $89,264 through forty-two rodeos, breaking the existing regular-season record of $88,139 set by Cash Myers in 2002. By the end of August, with more than two months to go, Luke had upped his goal to $120,000 heading into the finals.

Lurking in the distance was Rope Myers's all-time record of $176,584 set in 2001. That season, Rope won $117,774 at the NFR, setting the NFR average record in the process (37.4 seconds on ten head) in perhaps the greatest season any steer wrestler has ever had.

Luke was well ahead of pace to break the all-time record until he made a run in late August at Kennewick, Washington. While trying to slow a steer there, Luke took an off-balance step with his left foot and heard two pops in his knee. They were loud enough that Lahr heard them thirty yards away. The pain wasn't unbearable, but something in the knee burned terribly. Luke iced it that night and, a couple days later, had a doctor look at it before a rodeo in San Juan Capistrano, California. The doctor examined the knee, and told Luke the medial collateral ligament was torn and there could be cartilage damage as well. An MRI later would confirm the diagnosis. Luke asked the doctor if competing on the knee would worsen the injury, and the doctor said probably not. So Luke bought a brace, had the knee taped, and went out that afternoon and won fourth for another twenty-three hundred. He left San Juan thinking the ordeal was a minor setback.

But that's where his good fortune ended. After San Juan, Luke fell into one of the coldest streaks of his career. He didn't win a decent check during the next month, managing less than fifteen hundred dollars in winnings from his next fifteen rodeos. Something seemed to go wrong everywhere he went. When his knee felt good, he drew a bad steer. When he drew a good steer, he had trouble chasing worries about his knee out of his mind, and that ruined his all-out approach to the sport. All the while, the pack closed the gap behind him.

Luke began taking time off. He spent much of the two months before the NFR resting the injury as much as he could, but his knee probably wasn't going to heal entirely without surgery. Heading into the home stretch, he resigned himself to a grim fact: If he was going to win a world title this year, he would have to do it with a bad knee.

CHAPTER 11

Travis Becomes
a Sex Therapist

POWAY, CALIFORNIA

FRIDAY, SEPTEMBER 24

T ravis opened his truck door, leaned into the backseat, and began rummaging through clothes, empty coffee cups, and fast-food bags stained with ketchup. As he searched for his knee brace, a sinking feeling formed in his stomach. In his mind, he pictured the brace resting atop a fence post at Mike Barnes's arena in Nuevo, where Travis had practiced the night before. Now it was 8 A.M., two hours before slack began at the Poway Coors Original Rodeo, and he was facing the prospect of making his first run without a brace since he injured his knee. At his first rodeo in two months.

Convinced it was a lost cause, Travis gave up and walked across the lawn where dozens of cowboys stood beside trucks and trailers, readying their horses. He opened the door of Luke's trailer and disappeared inside. Luke was in Omaha, Nebraska, competing in the Pace Picante ProRodeo Challenge, the summer rodeo series equivalent of the Pace Chute-out. Jensen and Casey had driven Luke's rig from Los Alamos, arriving at 2 A.M.

Travis stood in the trailer, still trying to figure out how to get his brace. But no one was at the Barnes's ranch, and there wasn't time to drive there. A sleepy-eyed Jensen leaned out of his bottom bunk to see who had come in. He smiled at Travis, and Travis grimaced in return.

"Mornin' buddy," Jensen said.

"Fuck," Travis said, "I left my knee brace in Nuevo."

"Now why'd you go and do a thing like that?"

"Probably got to drinking beer," Travis said.

"Well, that ain't very smart," Jensen said as he rolled out of bed and stretched his arms. As he made his way for the door to take his morning piss, he looked at Travis and shook his head.

"Fuck," Travis said.

"You know buddy," Jensen said, "things like that happen sometimes and you just have to go on with life."

"Oh really?" Travis said, giving Jensen a cocky smirk as he headed outside. The trademark cockiness had slowly faded from Travis's repertoire a few months earlier as one bad run after another built up until, finally, he just had to get the hell away from rodeo. He called it retirement, but really it was just a break: some time away from the sport he loves to hate. And hates to love. Jensen, who broke his long drought by winning a $650 check at Deadwood, South Dakota, had taken a much-needed rest as well. He had spent a couple weeks at his parents' house in Coalinga, where he had developed his new approach to rodeo: Fuck it, make the run, forget about it, have a beer. Now both he and Travis were in much better moods than the last time they saw each other in Salinas.

Jensen walked back into the trailer. Someone had told him slack began at ten, not nine, and that meant another hour's sleep. Travis walked into the bathroom where more bad news awaited him: The generator had run out of gas, so there was no hot water. Soon, the only sounds in the trailer were running water and a muffled voice screaming out things like, "Oh Lord!"

and "Brrrrrrrr!" and "Somebody help me!" It sounded as if a violent crime were taking place in the bathroom. Ten minutes later, Travis emerged in his underwear, still shivering.

"So, how you been Jensen?"

"Been good, Trav."

"You got any good pussy stories? You almost fuck anybody to death or anything like that?"

"Nope, nothing like that."

"Why not? You went to Pendleton, didn't you? Don't tell me you didn't get yourself some pussy in Pendleton. Even an old guy like me could get laid in Pendleton."

"No buddy," Jensen said. "I've been being good. I only went out one night in Pendleton."

"Why ain't you been goin' out?"

"'Cause my buddy left me," Jensen said.

"Who? Jeremy?" Travis said.

Jensen didn't say anything.

"Oh you meant me, didn't you?" Travis said. "That's sweet, buddy. Yeah, I'm sorry about that. But you know, you won't let me cradle you in my arms and feed you a bottle like T.C. does."

"That's not really my thing, buddy," Jensen said.

"No, me neither," Travis said.

A few minutes later, Travis and Jensen walked outside and joined the others. Schenk, Tyler, and Vince Walker sat on chairs and hay bales and drank morning coffee. Travis and Jensen got some coffee and joined them.

Schenk looked up at Travis, smiled, and stuck out his hand.

"Good to see you out here again," Schenk said, shaking Travis's hand.

"Feels good to be back," Travis said.

Casey stood about fifteen feet away, saddling his horse. With half an hour left to kill before slack, the men did what cowboys always have done during the slow times: They sat around and told stories.

"Hey Casey," Travis said, calling out. "So tell me this story about the stolen tow truck."

Casey smiled and laughed a little.

"Well, we were coming home from Pendleton. We'd been gone on the road for a month and we were all anxious to get home. So we're about to Redding and it's just about dark when we lose our alternator on our truck. We pulled off to the side of the road up there at Lake Shasta and let the battery charge. We make it another five miles and lose the alternator again. We're done for. As we pull onto the off-ramp, the truck just friggin' dies. We call AAA, trying to figure out what we're going to do. Finally we get a tow truck out there.

"So he had parked in front of our truck, and you couldn't see his tow truck from where we were all standing. We go walking up there with him, and the tow truck's gone. He starts freaking out, looks square in the eye at me, and says, 'Didn't I park my tow truck right here?' I was laughing, saying, 'Yeah, you did.' So he starts throwing a shit fit, running around like a chicken with his head cut off, asking people if they saw anyone steal his truck. And he called the cops and his boss. So then two trucks show up. The cops brought a guy back in handcuffs, but it turns out he didn't steal the truck. I don't know if they ever found the guy who stole it. I got up at seven the next morning and called mechanics and Ford dealers until about 9 A.M. Finally, I called Napa and told them we needed an alternator and some tools, and they delivered them to us. We fixed it ourselves and drove the rest of the way home."

When Casey finished his story, everyone laughed. The mention of the cops shifted the morning's theme to brushes with the law. That's how cowboy storytelling sessions go: Everyone sticks to a subject until something reminds someone of something else. The theme shifts, and the time passes. After Casey finished his story, Tyler spoke up.

"Ol' Shark here got me arrested in San Antone once."

Schenk started laughing and said, "Yes, I did."

"We were drinking at this bar and a fight broke out," Tyler said. "The cops got there and everyone scattered. The bar had this circular deal in the middle, and I ran around one side, trying to outrun the cops. I got outside and I was home free. I'm running away, looking behind me to see who all was getting caught. And I ran smack into a cop. It stopped me in my tracks. There was this guardrail right there. He whipped his cuffs out, tied one to my wrist and the other to the rail. I was done."

"I'm in the piano bar, partying, 'Whoo-hoo,'" Schenk said, waving his arms like he was dancing. "And I look out, and there's Tyler standing alone, cuffed to a rail."

"I spent that night in jail with the other drunks," Tyler said. "Next morning, they let us all out, but now I'm on foot. I walked across the street to a Holiday Inn. Everyone was having a continental breakfast, and I got in line like I had spent the night there. As I was eating, I asked someone, 'Hey, when's the shuttle to the rodeo?' Someone said it'd be here in five minutes. I said, 'Well, all right.'"

Everyone laughed. Travis dropped a fresh wad of Copenhagen into his mouth and took a seat on a folding chair.

"One time me and Vince were driving Rope's trailer around in Cheyenne. We didn't know it, but the thing is totaled. And we're driving around town, having a good ol' time and we get pulled over. The cops are pissed. They make us get out, and they slap the cuffs on us and put us in the car. We're sitting there like, 'Oh fuck, what did we do last night?'

"Finally, I asked what we were being arrested for. The cop looks back and says, this truck was involved in a hit-and-run accident. We look out the window at the trailer, and it's just destroyed. There's shit hanging everywhere, the sides are crumpled in. And we'd been driving all over town like that. So they drive us back to the scene, and when we get there there's more shit scattered all over the road. Pieces of the air conditioner.

"The officer looks at me and Vince and tells us we don't match the description of the driver. And just then, Sean Smith sticks his head in the window of the cop car and says, 'What's up guys?' The cop looks at him and says, 'But he does.'"

Everyone laughed again. The men told a few more stories; each of them had been arrested on numerous occasions. It probably could have gone on a while longer, but it was time to get to the arena.

Travis finished his coffee, walked to his trailer, and climbed aboard his new weapon: a quarter horse named H-Bar-B. He'd had the horse a few years, mostly using him in practice. He was plenty fast enough, but every time he got into the box, the horse acted up and wouldn't settle into the corner. This weekend was the horse's last chance; Travis hauled H-Bar-B down south for three rodeos to determine, once and for all, if he had a bulldogging horse.

By 10 A.M., the late-summer sun had risen above a shrub-covered mountain that borders one side of Poway's rodeo grounds. The grandstands mostly were empty except for several classrooms of students huddled together, ready to cheer most anything that happened. Slack began with the steer wrestlers.

Casey was the first man to go and he'd asked Travis to haze. As Casey raced from the box after his steer, the gap between him and his steer quickly widened. The horse Travis had borrowed for the haze stopped running, and Casey found himself on his own. He leaned out of his saddle and reached out his right hand for a horn, but the steer was too far away. At the last moment, he pulled up and rode away with a no time.

Tyler, standing by the chute, looked at a cowboy next to him and muttered: "Nice haze Cadwell."

As Travis rode back to the chute, he told Casey he was sorry. Casey shrugged it off, saying it was no problem. These things happen.

Travis walked past Tyler, looked at him, and shook his head.

"You see that horse stop like that?" Travis said.

"Yeah," Tyler said.

"That horse must have been used for calf roping," Travis said.

"Yeah," Tyler said.

Jensen rode into the box and backed into the corner. Once he was set, he nodded and gave chase, catching the steer quickly. But he had some trouble muscling the animal to the ground, and they finally hit the dirt in 7.1 seconds. A broken barrier only made things worse. Jensen got up, brushed the dirt off his hands, and walked out to catch his horse, muttering to himself. The children cheered him anyway.

After Tyler put together a 4.1-second run that would earn him first place and $1,640, it was Travis's turn. Standing near the box, he bent down and stretched his legs one last time, wincing a bit. Travis threw the reins over H-Bar-B's neck, climbed aboard, and rode into the box. He tried to back the horse into the corner. But each time, the horse began dancing around in circles as Travis fought for control. This went on a good minute or so.

"You need help?" someone shouted.

"I might need help getting another horse," Travis said, as H-Bar-B reared back on his hind legs. Everyone around laughed. Everyone but Travis, who patted the horse's neck and talked to him softly. Finally, Travis settled his horse into the corner. As he nodded, a new problem took shape: The steer that wasn't supposed to run much darted like a deer from the chute.

This group of steers belonged to Luke, who had leased them to Poway for the rodeo. So, after the morning draw, every steer wrestler called Fatty in Omaha to get the lowdown on their steers. When Travis called to find out about his, Luke had said it probably would run out a little and stop. Definitely not a runner. Of course, animals are unpredictable. Instead, Travis raced out halfway across the arena before he caught up to the steer, throwing the animal down in 6.6 seconds. No money, but his knee and his horse performed well, so it wasn't a complete loss.

Travis rode back to his trailer, watered H-Bar-B, and loaded him into the trailer. Many of the cowboys in Poway also had runs that day in Barstow and San Bernardino, a hectic day of rodeo. Travis hurried from the rodeo grounds, trying to beat the rush of Friday afternoon traffic heading from Los Angeles to Las Vegas. It didn't happen. Four hours later, Travis finally pulled into Barstow.

There is no shortage of god-awful places where rodeos are held each year. Vernal, Utah. Kingman, Arizona. Rock Springs, Wyoming. But Barstow just might be the worst of them all. The small desert town, known mostly as a place people pass through on their way to Las Vegas, is as hot as they come. The blazing sun overhead is unyielding. A dry wind that never seems to stop sucks the moisture out of every cowboy. With the temperature pushing toward one hundred, a 6 P.M. slack time feels like a death sentence.

A few minutes before slack began, Jensen rode his horse from the shade of Luke's trailer through a gravel parking lot to the outskirts of one of the tiniest arenas in rodeo. He tied his horse to a tree and hid in the shade. He took off his hat and wiped a good amount of sweat onto his sleeve. As he put his hat back on, Travis rode up on H-Bar-B and joined Jensen beneath the tree.

"Hey Jensen," Travis said, climbing down from his horse, "you gonna buy me a beer at the beer stand tonight in San Bernardino?"

"Trav, I honestly don't think I can get any money."

"Oh Jensen, c'mon now, you can do it. You're the kind of man who makes magic happen."

"I'm serious, Trav. I don't got any money. None. You know the other day I was driving the rig home and I fueled up in Washington. It was like two hundred dollars. I went in to pay. I take out my Mastercard—declined. I take out my ATM card—declined. So I take out my Chevron card—declined. I look at the lady and say, 'I don't have any money. What do you want me to do?' She says, 'I don't know.' What's a fella to do when he ain't got no money? So I said, 'Hold on.' I went outside and called my dad, got his credit card number, and wrote it down on a piece of paper. I brought it back into the store and put it down on the counter. I said, 'I don't know what you want me to do, but here's a credit card number. That's the best I can do.' She ran the card and it went through. She let me slide on it."

"Now see there Jensen, that's exactly what I'm talking about. A lot of fellas in that spot would have panicked, but not you. You made magic happen."

"Well, I ain't been making much magic happen this year, buddy."

"I know you can do it," Travis said. "And I'm not even talking about two hundred dollars. I'm only talking about two beers. That's what, seven or eight dollars? You can do that Jensen. You're a magic man."

A hundred feet away, a tractor finished smoothing out the sandy arena dirt. The setting sun dipped behind the mountains and the air suddenly felt ten degrees cooler, turning a miserable day into a bearable evening. Travis and Jensen climbed aboard their horses and continued talking.

"You got your phone working?" Travis said.

"No Trav, it's been dead all day. Fatty's been trying to get ahold of you."

"He has?" Travis said. "Good, I'd like to thank him for the scouting report on that steer in Poway."

"He tell you he wouldn't take off and run?" Jensen said.

"Yeah," Travis said. "You see him break?"

"Yeah," Jensen said, laughing. "He ran like a son of a bitch."

Both men laughed and shook their heads. Jensen looked over at Travis.

"You know the night Fatty hurt his knee?"

"Yeah."

"It was like midnight," Jensen said. "I went to the store and bought him ice and bandages. I gave them to him and he didn't even look up. Just said, 'Thanks.'"

"Well Jensen, you know it's all about Fatty. Always has been. Really, tell me when it wasn't about him?"

"Not since the first day I met him," Jensen said.

"This is terrible Jensen. He's two thousand miles away and the guy is still affecting us."

"It is terrible, Trav."

With that, Travis, Jensen, and the rest of the steer wrestlers rode into the arena to get things started. Jensen chased his steer to the far end of the arena, finally giving up on the run as he reached the fence. As Travis backed into the box, H-Bar-B gave him no trouble. But he had drawn another runner, and Travis didn't throw the steer down until 6.2 seconds had passed. Normally, the run would have been worthless. But the guys who followed Travis—among them Tyler, Casey, and Levi—all failed to catch their steers for one reason or another. Travis managed to hang on for fifth place, worth $275.

After his run, Travis led his horse from the arena to his truck. He gave H-Bar-B a long drink of water and loaded the horse into the trailer. He had roughly an hour to make the hour's drive to San Bernardino for that night's performance. Travis wasn't up until the following morning, but he promised a couple guys he'd haze for them that night. As he pulled out of the parking lot, he grabbed his phone and left Tiffany a voice mail.

"Hey Tif. I didn't do any good in Barstow. H-Bar-B worked really good, gave me a good run so I was real happy with that. I'll call you later."

As Travis raced along I-15 at 80 mph, he picked up his phone again and called Luke to see how he had done in the second round of the Pace ProRodeo Challenge.

"Hey, what're you doing? . . . Just got done doing the dirty thing? That's good. . . . How'd you do tonight? You win any money? . . . You're still in the top eight though, right? . . . You placed sixth in the average? What do they pay, top four? . . . Okay. . . . Me? No, haven't done no good. Did all right in Barstow. In Poway my steer kind of took off on me. . . . Yeah. You know how you said it wouldn't run like the others? Well, it did. But that's just how that goes sometimes. . . . I cussed you though. I told everybody how dumb you were. Don't even know your own steers. . . . Okay, bud, I'll talk at you later. Tomorrow afternoon then. . . . Okay, good luck."

Luke would find only a little luck in Omaha. Despite the recent slump, he still came into the Pace Challenge with a fifteen-thousand-dollar lead over Jason Lahr in the world standings. He finished second to win three thousand dollars on the opening night—his first big check since he injured his knee—but he stumbled to a 5.6-second run in the second round. The run kept him in the top eight and moved him into semifinals. There, he threw his steer in 3.3 seconds in what would have been an arena record and forty-seven hundred dollars, but he broke a barrier and was eliminated from the tournament.

Instead, Lahr won that semifinal round money with a 3.4. Lahr advanced to the final where he lowered the arena record to 3.2 in a first-place run worth another $10,575, giving him a total of more than $23,000 in Omaha. With that, the five-figure lead Luke had enjoyed most of the season vanished in a flash. He would leave Nebraska with $96,521—just $700 ahead of Lahr. The following week, Lahr would move into first by about $3,000, with one month left in the regular season. Luke would take two of those weeks off in early October to rest his ailing knee as the race for the gold buckle had become a lot more interesting.

But Travis wasn't thinking about any of that as he pulled into San Bernardino that night. It was a little after 8 P.M., and he could hear the "Star-Spangled Banner" as he drove into the rodeo grounds. He parked, unloaded his horse, and hurried to the arena just in time to haze steers for a couple of his friends. When the night's steer wrestling ended, Travis had one last chore before he could turn his focus toward drinking beer: He tied his horse to a fence and headed to the secretary's office to pay his entry fees. He walked into a cramped office where arena secretary Tracy Mitchell sat behind a cluttered desk. Travis took a seat across the table from her and slammed his hat on the table.

"Hello Tracy."

"Hi Trav."

"Well, I guess I owe you some money," Travis said. "But, really, I need you to give me some money. Can I write this check out for more?"

"Sure thing," Tracy said. "Hey, you wanna see what one of the bull riders paid his entry fee with?"

"Sure."

She leaned down by her feet and picked up a blue plastic grocery bag. She lifted the bag and set it on the desk between her and Travis, nodding for Travis to look inside. He opened the bag to find a large stack of rolled coins: quarters, dimes, nickels, and even some pennies. Travis looked up in stunned amazement.

"You've got to be kidding me!" he said.

"Nope."

"How much is that?" he said.

"Well, he had forty-eight dollars in cash, so there's got to be another fifty dollars or so. That was everything he had in the world to get on the back of a bull."

"I can't believe that," Travis said, filling out a check. "Can I get sixty dollars back?"

"No problem," she said.

"Just don't pay me in coins," he said. "That's what you should do for the next guy who cashes a check."

"Okay," she said, "I'll do that."

"See you later, Tracy."

"Have a good night, Trav."

Travis left the office and walked behind the grandstands to the beer stand where a couple dozen of his cowboy friends had a head start on the night's drinking. He ordered a Coors Light and joined a conversation with Casey, Robbin Peterson, Levi Rosser, and Travis's brother, Dan. A few feet away, Jensen and Adam Maher, a calf roper from Australia, roared in laughter as they told the story of their recent visit to a whorehouse in Winnemucca, Nevada. All around were small groups of cowboys telling stories as a few women who had grown bored with the rodeo stood nearby and listened, interacting some.

Every few minutes, the cowboys wandered from the conversations and returned with new beers, never straying more than twenty feet from the taps. Far off in the background, a decent-size crowd roared every minute or so as a roper made a great run or a bull rider managed to stay aboard. As the night wore on, the cowboys at the beer stand galloped toward inebriation.

When the rodeo ended, the party moved about fifty feet away to a large outdoor area where a country band played songs by Garth Brooks, Lynyrd Skynyrd, and others for people dancing atop a floor covered in straw. The moon rose at 11 P.M., throwing a little more light on the party. Bartenders started offering two-for-one drinks and now Travis, Casey, Jensen, Robbin, Schenk, and the others all were stumbling around laughing at everything with a beer in each hand, often spilling large splashes into the straw below.

The party dwindled to about forty people, and most of them were completely trashed. The men outnumbered the women roughly five to one. Those cowboys who were looking for sex all took their shots at talking up three young twentysomethings—who had arrived with dates, but spent very little time with them. Two of the women kept kissing each other, and some figured them for teases; but their flirtatious friend was harder to figure. Two larger women talked particularly dirty to any cowboy who approached them; they made no secret they had sex on the brain; one of them kept placing a drink in the cleavage between her large breasts, lowering her head and sticking out her tongue to reach the straw, taking a sip without spilling a drop. But, by midnight, the men had lost interest and those two women were talking and drinking alone. When the band stopped playing and sheriff's deputies moved through the crowd to shut things down, several people took their last shots at hooking up for the night.

One of the twentysomethings, a short woman with a drunk smile and a hot pink bandanna over her hair, walked up to a young steer wrestler named Josh Peek and gave him a big hug. The two had been dancing and flirting off and on throughout the night. Now the woman, who said her name was Maci, was telling him good-bye. Peek asked her to join him for a walk by the trailers. They both knew what that meant. She stood on her tiptoes to get a couple inches from his face. Twenty feet away, the man she had come to the rodeo with sat on a bale of hay and watched this most disturbing development with great confusion.

"I've got to go home with him," Maci said. "He's the one who brought me here."

"Okay," Josh said, nodding.

"But I want to kiss you," Maci said, leaning closer as Josh suddenly pulled away.

"Hell no," he said. "I'm not going to kiss you if you're going home with him."

They stood there and looked in each other's eyes, and neither one made a move. Then Josh grabbed Maci's hand, said "C'mon," and led her from the bar area into the parking lot. She started laughing, and never looked back at her date.

A few cowboys watched as the new couple walked across a road and headed toward the horse trailers. Twenty minutes later, Josh and Maci were laughing and rubbing all over each other, kissing and tingling in the darkness behind Luke's trailer. Not five feet away, a horse tied to the trailer ate grain from a bucket, ignoring the show. The horse was only one small part of the audience. All around, hiding in the shadows of goosenecks and long beds, at least ten drunk cowboys watched, snickering and giggling at the action. Josh and Maci knew they were being seen, but they were long past the point of caring about that. That's partly why they kept laughing.

As Casey and Travis had nearly finished the long drunken walk from the outdoor bar to Luke's trailer, Jensen caught their attention from his spot behind Levi's truck.

"Hey Casey," Jensen whispered, laughing as he pointed the way. "Come here. This is fucking hilarious!"

Casey and Travis started laughing, too; they knew where they were headed. The three men walked around the trailer to the back. They stopped as they happened upon Josh, standing with his legs bent and with Maci sitting on top of him in a straddle, grinding.

They looked up and broke into laughter. Casey, Travis, and Jensen ran back the way they came, laughing as they disappeared into Luke's trailer.

Casey crawled into Luke's bed above the gooseneck. He started playing a game of Madden football on the Playstation 2, but he passed out before he even finished the first quarter. Travis grabbed four Coors Lights from a thirty-pack and went back outside to drink with Schenk and Robbin. Jensen opened the freezer and pulled out a bag of small frozen burritos. He placed two in the microwave and waited. Just then, the trailer door swung open and Josh and Maci stumbled in. Maci walked into the back room and climbed into the top bunk. Josh followed her there. As he slid the back door shut, Josh looked at Jensen with a big smile on his face and whispered, "Man, I've got to be at the airport at 7:30 A.M." Both men laughed as the door closed. It was already 2:30 A.M.

A few minutes later, Levi walked into the trailer.

"That was funny," Levi said. "Where'd Josh take that girl?"

Jensen pointed his thumb to the closed door and said, "They're back there."

"No shit," Levi said, smiling. "Damn. Hey, what are you eating?"

"Burritos."

"There any more?"

"No," Jensen said. "But there's some frozen corn dogs."

"That sounds all right," Levi said, taking a seat on the couch.

Jensen stood and returned to the freezer. He stuck four frozen corn dogs in the microwave and turned it on. As he waited, the panting from the back room stopped. Levi and Jensen heard talking through the closed door.

"Where the fuck are you going?" Maci said.

"I'm sorry," Josh said. "I gotta pee."

The back room's door slid open. Josh walked out, looked at Jensen and Levi on the couch, and smiled big. Levi stood up and walked toward the other side of the trailer. He looked in on Casey, who was propped up against a pillow, sitting motionless with a video game control in his hands.

"Casey," Levi said. "You're missing all the action."

Casey opened one eye just enough to see. He smiled through the stupor.

"Yeah," he said, "it sounds like I am."

Casey slowly rolled onto his side and fell back to sleep, and he would not move again until the following morning.

"Corn dogs are ready," Jensen said.

Levi joined Jensen on the couch. They took turns dipping their corn dogs into a pile of ketchup on a paper plate. As the two men wolfed down their late-night snack and chased it with beer, they giggled each time sex noises traveled through the door.

"There better not be anything on my bed," Jensen said. "If there is, I'm going to be pissed."

"Dude," Levi said, his mouth full of food, "that's fucking sick."

"Let's not talk about it right now," Jensen said. "I'm trying to eat."

Maci's moans grew louder. With mouths full of food, Levi and Jensen halfheartedly cheered Josh on through the door, shouting things like, "C'mon Peek," and "Atta boy, Peek."

Just then, the trailer door swung open and banged against the side of the trailer. Travis and Schenk poured into the trailer like a couple of drunken hyenas.

"What the fuck is going on in here?" Travis shouted.

He turned and noticed the back room door was closed. He threw the door open, showing everyone in the room a shot of Josh on top of Maci in the top bunk. Travis stumbled into the room.

"Hey," he said, "is Peek a good fuck? That's all we want to know."

"Get out of here!" Maci yelled from beneath Josh as she swung an arm at Travis. He backed out of the room with his arms up, saying, "Okay, okay." Once outside the room, Travis turned and leaned his head back in to speak again, this time quietly, as if telling a secret.

"You know what he likes?" Travis whispered. "He likes it when you spank him on the ass."

They kicked him out again. But eventually, Maci and Josh started ignoring Travis as they continued to kiss and moan, silently deciding it would be easier to put up with Travis than try to chase him away all night long. Plus, they were drunk and horny. Travis sensed he was being allowed into the circle. He made eye contact with Jensen, Levi, and Schenk and smiled and closed the door, disappearing into darkness with the lovebirds. Everyone in the other room roared with laughter.

Five minutes later, the door swung open. Travis danced out, saying, "I saw titties, I saw titties." Jensen stood up to take a look, but Travis held out his hand to stop anyone else from going into the room.

"Gentlemen, we're not done in here," Travis said, holding his arms in the air like a quarterback trying to hush a crowd. "I'm sorry, but I'm afraid this is a private moment. We need our privacy right now. I'm really sorry, guys."

Travis's grinning face disappeared as he slid the door shut again. Once the three of them were alone again, Travis resumed his role as coach, telling the lovers how disappointed everyone outside would be if they found out there had been no penetration. To that point, Josh and Maci had not progressed beyond rubbing on each other with their clothes on. Something needed to happen to kick things into another gear, and it arrived in the form of Jeff Danoff. A Hollywood stuntman and one of the only long-haired steer wrestlers anywhere, Danoff walked into the trailer with several friends, a glass pipe, and a fat bag of high-grade marijuana. Within a few minutes, Luke's trailer had morphed into a smoke box loaded with red-eyed cowboys. Even those cowboys not indulging had red eyes from the thick smoke that filled the air.

"Hey," Maci yelled from beneath Josh, "I want some of that."

Travis borrowed the pipe and a lighter, and walked into the back room. Maci's hands were busy, so Travis began feeding her pipe loads of marijuana. Meanwhile, Josh was lying on Maci's side, his hands moving beneath the sheet that covered them. So Travis fed him some marijuana, too. The door remained open, and the party kicked into high gear as it spread to both rooms. Travis began leading cowboys in and out of the back room on quick tours, explaining like a tour guide how things were progressing. Some guys heated up more frozen corn dogs. Every couple minutes, someone flung the trailer door open and heaved empty beer cans into the parking lot. The pipe kept making the rounds. There was laughter and no music. There were friends and no enemies. There was sex and no inhibitions. At that moment, it was pretty easy to see why a fella might love the rodeo life.

Jensen sat on the couch and took another hit off the pipe. His eyes were glazed, and he felt perfect. Travis, now feeling good and loose, walked over and collapsed onto his lap. Travis looked at Jensen and started rubbing the hair on his head. They laughed like hell. Travis lost his balance and almost rolled onto the floor, but Jensen caught him. They laughed like hell again.

"Jensen, how long has it been since you got pussy?"

"Long time."

"How long?"

"Probably Salinas," Jensen said.

"Probably?" Travis said. "Probably? What the fuck is probably? Did you come in Salinas?"

"Yes."

"Did you have sex with another person in Salinas?"

"Yes."

"Okay, then, that's settled," Travis said. "So that's, what, three or four months? That's not very good buddy."

"No," Jensen said, laughing, "it's not very good at all."

"Jensen," Travis said, thoughtfully, "you know who you're going to marry?"

"Who's that Trav?"

"You're going to marry you a broke-down stripper."

"Is that right?"

"Oh no," Travis said. "Jensen, I think I'm gonna fart."

"Trav, I like you a lot buddy, but I don't want you to shit on me."

"I'm not going to shit on you, Jensen, I'm just going to fart."

"Oh, sorry Trav," Jensen said, standing up and dumping Travis on the floor. "I've got to go take a piss."

Jensen disappeared outside. Levi and Schenk walked out to join him. Travis went back into the room with the lovebirds, stood back, and admired Josh for a moment. Josh looked at Travis and started laughing, too. Travis thought Josh was being a pretty good sport about things. For Josh, it had been a hell of a day. Sitting on the outskirts of the NFR bubble with time running out, he had come to California and won roughly $3,000 in Poway and another $650 in San Bernardino. And now, he was having sex before an audience. Four hours later, he would be on an airplane to make an afternoon rodeo performance in Memphis.

"Josh," Travis said, shaking his head in amazed appreciation, "I want you to know I'm rooting for you to make the finals. After seeing this, I'm rooting for you."

"Thanks," Josh said, smiling and still rubbing on Maci as she moaned. "But Travis, really, you're making me lose my hard-on."

"I'm sorry about that, buddy," Travis said. "Are you in the top fifteen?"

"After today, I'm close," Josh said.

"Well," Travis said, "I hope you make it. Now, guys, I'm going to go outside and shut this door. When I come back, I want you guys to be naked. It's time to step to the plate. C'mon Josh, there's sixty thousand people out here cheering for you. But this ain't right. You can't do this with your clothes on."

"I've had five orgasms," Maci said, looking up at Travis.

"No you haven't," Travis said.

"Yes I have," Maci said. "I have."

"No you haven't," Travis said. "C'mon Peek, now show us something here. We're all tired of waiting."

Travis slapped Josh on the ass, opened the door, and emerged from the back room. A few guys leaned in to take a look, but Travis pushed them back. He took a long drink of his beer, and addressed the crowd wearing the serious tone and demeanor of a funeral director.

"Okay everyone, we need to be discreet about this," Travis said, slurring. "Let's be respectful now. This is a very private moment, and we need to be respectful about this."

"What's going on in there?" Jensen said.

"They're getting closer," Travis said. "But these things take time, Jensen. Now we've got a guy here who's trying to make the finals. We need to help him any way we can."

"Are they fucking yet?" Jensen yelled.

"Ssshhhh," Travis said, holding his index finger to his lips. "Now, we need to be discreet about this. Okay, what we need right now is a condom. But let's keep this quiet. We do not want to embarrass her. And we can't let her know what we're up to. We have to be respectful and discreet."

A couple cowboys went outside to find a condom. Someone returned a few minutes later and handed a rubber to Travis, who disappeared into the room again. Ten minutes later, the door opened just enough for him to poke his head out.

"Guys," he whispered. "Oh guys. Now this, this is a really private moment. Oh my God, is this ever a private moment. You'll have to give us a minute here."

The door shut, and everyone in the room laughed. Another ten minutes passed, and the door opened again. Travis backed out, still talking to Maci and Josh.

"Okay guys," Travis said, sliding the door closed. "I'm going to go now. But you know what to do. Hey, it's just you and me here. Just you and me."

Travis turned and took a long look around the room, pretending to notice the smoke cloud for the first time. He sniffed the air. He walked to the counter and picked up an empty beer can, and shook it from side to side. He formed a disgusted expression on his face and looked at Jensen, who was sitting comfortably numb on the couch.

"Jensen!" Travis said, looking around and shaking his head. "Just take a look at this place! Pot smoking. Fucking in the bunk bed. Late-night drinking parties. C'mon Jensen, what's wrong with you? Luke's trying to win a world championship right now. And you're just being a fucking fuckup."

Jensen threw his hands into the air and scowled.

"Can't I just have fun for one day?" Jensen yelled, looking equally disgusted. "Huh? What the fuck is wrong with having a little fun, Trav?"

"Jensen," Travis said, "this isn't about you. And it's not about me. It's about Fatty."

Travis sat down on the couch next to Jensen, looking dejected. No one said a word for a few seconds. Then Travis looked over at Jensen and spoke softly.

"Jensen, we're just trying to make a living here," Travis said. "That's all we're doing. Just some guys out trying to earn a living."

"I know it, buddy," Jensen said, softly. "I tell people this is hard work, and they don't believe me."

"I can't do this forever, Jensen," Travis said. "Look at me. Taking care of horses and getting people fucked. I mean, what the fuck?"

They both laughed, but the laughter died out suddenly as the sound of Maci's moaning intensified. She clearly was about to have an orgasm.

"Oh, to hell with this," Jensen said, standing up from the couch. "I'm going to bed."

Jensen threw the back room door open, and climbed into the bottom bunk. Josh and Maci either didn't notice or didn't care. Soon, Travis, Schenk, and Levi made their way into the back room. Holding beers and giggling, each of them watched the show for a few minutes. Now Maci was naked; so was Josh, except for the pigging string hanging around his neck.

Every few seconds, one of the watchers reached out and lifted the sheet as everyone snickered. Josh, who was on top, kept reaching out and pulling the sheet back over himself, trying not to lose his rhythm. Maci never noticed; she just kept moaning louder and louder with her eyes closed. He was inside her now, and they were too close to orgasms to care about anything else.

Jensen leaned out from the bottom bunk, looked up at Travis with a big grin, and started laughing, silently mouthing a "Yeeeeeeaaaaaaahhhh!" Travis reached down and rubbed Jensen's head, and they snickered some more. Travis emptied another beer, and set the can on the ground. He watched for another couple seconds, then started pretending he had lost patience.

"Josh, Josh," Travis said, tapping Josh on his leg. "Hold on, hold on. I'm sorry to interrupt, but it's time to do her doggy style."

Jensen roared from the bottom bunk. Levi and Schenk leaned on each other and lost it. Now Maci and Josh were laughing, too, but they tried to remain focused on the task at hand. Another few seconds passed, and Travis tapped Josh on the leg again.

"Guys, guys, really, hold on a second," Travis said softly as laughter again filled the cramped room. "Please, time out. She needs it doggy style. C'mon, it's just you and me here. I've been with you guys all night long. I'm part of this. It's just you and me. Lock the rest of the world away. Just you and me."

Maci stopped moaning, opened her eyes, and looked at Travis.

"You're making him go soft," she said.

"What?" Travis said.

"You're making him go soft."

"Oh, I'm sorry," Travis said.

"We need to take a break," Maci said.

"A break?" Travis said. "Yes, a break. That's a wonderful idea. And when we come back, I want to see some doggy style."

Everyone laughed as they filed out of the room and headed outside. The group disbanded. It was well after 4 A.M. Accepting that the bunk he'd planned on sleeping in was now out of service, Travis began wandering around the parking lot looking for his brother's trailer where there was an empty bed. Twenty minutes later, he was still stumbling around alone, laughing at himself and the wild night. And the funniest part was, four hours later, he would throw down a steer in 4.9 seconds to win $650, enough to pay for the trip.

With everyone else gone from Luke's trailer, Maci and Josh emerged from the back room, laughing at the weirdness of it all. She had thrown on some clothes, but he was mostly naked. He still had the pigging string around his neck, and he walked with both hands holding a hot pink bandanna that mostly shielded his genitals. In a hurry to get outside to pee, but still drunk and stoned, he banged into the door and nearly fell down. Maci looked back and they both laughed again. She walked back to him, and, arm in arm, they moved away from the trailer.

"Hey," he shouted into the night air, "are we goin' western or what, babe?"

She howled in delight and slapped his naked ass. They walked away, laughing.

An hour later, Robbin heard some kind of ruckus just outside his trailer. He got out of bed and walked over to a window. He looked outside and laughed. There were Maci and Josh, completely naked and fucking hard in the dim light of the moon.

CHAPTER 12

Man on the Bubble

Frank Thompson paced back and forth through the dirt, a 195-pound clump of nervous energy. He moved around the halls and warm-up area behind the Cow Palace arena, his eyes fixed on the ground, his mind weeding through a hundred scenarios. He tried his best to hide his emotions, but the intense expression on his face left one fact clear: Inside, he was a complete mess. A couple months on the NFR bubble will do that to a man.

As Frank passed by a group of steer wrestlers waiting for the short round of the Grand National Rodeo, he made eye contact with Luke, who was standing with his back to a wall. Frank flashed Luke a nervous smile.

"C'mon Kid," Frank said, "I need you here."

Luke looked up, smiled, and nodded. He knew too well what it felt like to finish sixteenth in the world standings.

"Good luck, Frank."

"Yeah," Frank said, continuing on his way, "I could use it."

He also could have used a bad performance from Luke; he and Levi Rosser were the only two cowboys within two seconds of Frank's lead in the average. And he needed to win the average and place at least fourth in the short round to keep his slim NFR hopes alive.

He had come to San Francisco about four thousand dollars out of fifteenth place. He had two rodeos left to make up the difference: the Grand National, and a smaller purse event at Brawley. Even if he managed to earn enough money to climb into the top fifteen, several other cowboys had secured spots at the final weekend's Pace Picante ProRodeo Classic in Dallas. If any one of them had a great run there, Frank's season would be done.

Ending a season in sixteenth place is lonelier than an all-night drive through Nevada on Highway 50. It's rodeo hell. In the long term, in some ways, it can prove more debilitating than a death in the family. Some guys who end up one spot short are able to come back the following year hungrier than before. But for many others, it's a career killer. Countless cowboys fade into rodeo obscurity and live out their days replaying runs from the season that could have been, their heads forever haunted by the lingering pangs that come with almost tasting a dream.

Frank knows a lot about that sort of thing. In 1991, he finished four hundred dollars short of the finals—knocked out of fifteenth place by legendary steer wrestler Roy Duvall at the last rodeo of the year. Frank spent the next few years fighting himself to get over the nagging disappointment that traveled with him everywhere. He was tired, burned out, and, worst of all, trapped trying to bulldog his way out of debt with a cloudy head. The whole deal ruined him for several years, but eventually he got past it. He finally made his first NFR in 1997 and, in 2000, he won more than eighty-five thousand dollars at the finals en route to a world title.

The passion Frank used to win that first gold buckle softened once the goal became simply winning another one. But it had come back that afternoon in San Francisco as he and eleven other cowboys walked through the moat toward the chute. Frank felt like his old self, his younger self; he wanted to win more than ever. And not just because an NFR appearance meant a shot at the big money as well as roughly fifteen thousand dollars in bonuses and future contracts from his sponsors, Wrangler, Justin Boots, and Senco. At thirty-seven, Frank is a man who talks of an impending retirement, and he knew this could well be his last run at the finals.

He is a friendly man with kind eyes; he wears a long brown mustache that extends to the bottom of his jaw, and a cowboy hat usually conceals the bald spot on his head. At heart, he is a family man. Once, after winning a round at the NFR, he invited his ninety-three-year-old grandmother onstage at the Gold Coast Casino and presented her with the go-round buckle.

Frank's chances looked good early. None of the first four bulldoggers managed to finish runs in less than five seconds. With each rider, Frank looked up at the scoreboard to gauge his lead in the average, exhaling to calm himself. It's a heavy thing needing your friends to fail, and Frank hated being in that position. Rodeo, unlike other sports, is not a scene where most contestants wish bad fortunes on their peers. Whenever steers are drawn, you'll see cowboys madly making cell phone calls to get other bulldoggers' thoughts on a particular animal. For the most part, everyone helps everyone, then they all go out and try to beat one another. Frank honored the code even in his most desperate hour.

As Spud Duvall—Roy Duvall's nephew—rode into the box, Frank climbed into the chute and wrapped the steer's tail around his hand, ready to give the animal a shove to help Spud. Frank clapped his hands together as Spud, who already had secured his trip to the NFR, broke from the box. He threw the steer down in 5.3 seconds, making that the early mark Frank had to beat. After another slow run, Levi rode into the box, trailing Frank in the average by 1.6 seconds.

"We've watched this young man grow up here," the announcer said. "This is Cotton Rosser's grandson. They practically raised this kid at the Cow Palace."

Levi nodded for his steer and chased it into the arena. He slid off his horse, got the steer stopped quickly, and slammed him into the dirt as the crowd cheered. The time: 4.2 seconds. Levi looked back at the scoreboard and smiled big. Frank looked at the same scoreboard and shook his head. Cotton Rosser, who sat atop a horse in the arena, smiled proudly as he clapped his hands.

"Look at that!" the announcer yelled. "Look at that! The Blistex buckaroo has done it."

The run gave Levi the lead in the short round, and put a little more pressure on Frank in the average. After another no time, Luke rode into the arena and backed into the box. He rode out and caught his steer, but the animal fell over the wrong way. Luke wrestled the steer on the ground, settling for a 7.0-second ride worth third in the average.

That set the stage for Frank. He climbed onto his horse and rode toward the chute.

"Here's the world champion from Cheyenne," the announcer said. "He really needs to win about six thousand dollars here. This rodeo could be the turning point."

Once Frank got set in the box, he rubbed his hands together and took a couple deliberate breaths. This was the moment. Frank always admired guys who could hit the game-winning shot at the buzzer or throw the touchdown pass in overtime. Now it was his turn to see what he could do with everything on the line.

He nodded for his steer, which got a slow break from the

chute before picking up speed. Frank raced out and caught the animal, skidding to a stop as the crowd began to cheer. He turned and threw the steer to the ground. He looked back at the scoreboard: 4.6 seconds. As he walked away, a relieved smile overtook his face.

"Whoa!" the announcer said. "He moves to the lead overall. Cotton, there will be many more days for Levi."

As Frank rejoined the other steer wrestlers, Cotton rode over graciously and extended his hand. He had been rooting for his grandson to win the rodeo, but seeing Frank stay alive in the NFR hunt was a decent consolation. Frank reached up and shook Cotton's hand as the stock contractor leaned down to be heard above the din of the crowd.

"I hope you make the finals, Frank," Cotton said into Frank's ear.

"Thanks."

Frank, Luke, and Levi all walked out of the arena together headed for the rodeo secretary's office to collect their checks. Luke stopped off in the trainer's room. He sat in a folding chair, pulled his pants down, and started taking off his knee brace. Ailing cowboys sat all around him in various states of disrepair. Luke looked up and noticed saddle bronc rider Cody Martin examining a healthy amount of bright red blood seeping from his toes into his sock.

"You hurt yourself Cody?" Luke said.

"I think my toes may be broke," Martin said, looking at his foot. "I'm not sure. I don't even want to look at it."

"How'd that happen?" Luke said.

"Horse reared up in front of the gate and it peeled my toes back."

Martin finally removed his sock, and found the injury was about what he had figured. The toenails from his big toe and the one next to it had been pried back, and fresh blood filled the new spaces each time he wiped the old blood away. He limped around the room until he found a rubber glove. He filled it with ice and sat down, placing the glove on his foot. Then he leaned his head back against a wall and closed his eyes.

Luke pulled his pants back on, tucked his shirt in, and picked his knee brace off the floor. He looked at Martin and shook his head.

"Well," Luke said, "good luck with that."

"Yep," Martin said.

Luke walked out of that office and disappeared into another room about twenty feet away. The cowboys there looked a lot happier—anyone in the room was about to collect a check. As Luke and Levi talked and waited, Frank walked in carrying his newest buckle.

"Nice job, Frank," Levi said.

"Yeah, nice job," Luke said.

Frank shook their hands and thanked them. A rodeo secretary walked over and started handing out checks. She gave Luke nearly three thousand dollars. That, coupled with the fifty-two hundred he won the week before in Kansas City, helped Luke reclaim his lead over Lahr in the world standings. Then the secretary handed Frank checks totaling about forty-four hundred dollars for winning the average and taking second in the short round. The money moved Frank into fifteenth place, ahead of Joey Bell, Jr. by $354.

But he still had plenty to worry about. Frank had not qualified for the big money of the Pace Classic, but three cowboys trying to catch him had: Bob Lummus, Randy Suhn, and Steven Campbell. Of the three, Lummus had the best shot of passing Frank at about eighteen hundred dollars behind.

That scenario became cloudier with Friday's first round at

the Pace Classic. As Frank ate dinner that night with his wife, Dawn, Spud called with news that Suhn had turned in a 3.4-second run worth first place in the round and $3,916, moving him within about four thousand dollars of Frank. Lummus did not earn a check in the round. Frank returned the phone to his shirt pocket and looked at his wife.

"Well," Frank said, "we're still alive."

The next morning, Frank caught an early flight to California. That night, as he was getting close to running his steer at Brawley, he noticed he had some voice mail messages. Frank listened and deleted the voice mails until he came to a message left by his son, Zane.

"Dad, I just called to tell you do good tonight. . . . You have to, Dad."

Even at six years old, the kid already lives for rodeo. Frank saved the message and laughed to himself. As if he didn't have enough pressure already.

A few minutes later, Spud called with the second-day results from Dallas. Luke had won the round and the average worth a total of about eight thousand dollars. Campbell broke a barrier and was eliminated from contention. Lummus and Suhn had not won any more money, but were among the eight cowboys who advanced to Sunday's semifinal round.

Shortly after hearing his season still was alive, Frank rose to the occasion in Brawley and put down a steer in 4.2 seconds for a second-place finish worth seventeen hundred dollars. But that was all he could do; he had run out of rodeos. As he started making his way home, Frank resigned himself to the fact that his fate was out of his hands. That added a helpless component to an anxiety that already had wracked his nerves.

After a mostly sleepless night, Frank caught a Sunday morning flight to Denver. A truck driver friend of Frank's picked him up. As the two rode toward Frank's home east of Cheyenne, the phone rang. Frank looked at the phone to see it was Spud calling, and felt his heart jump. He pushed the answer button and held the phone to his ear, somewhat afraid of what Spud might tell him. The news was not entirely bad. Suhn had gone long in the semifinals, ending his season with an 8.2-second run. But, facing elimination, Lummus had downed his steer in 3.9 seconds, splitting third and fourth place to win $1,762. That pulled Lummus to within seventeen hundred dollars of Frank. It also moved Lummus into the Pace Classic final along with Luke, Lahr, and Rope Myers. A first- or second-place run by Lummus there would kick Frank down to sixteenth.

Frank hung up the phone and sank back into the big rig's passenger seat, rubbing his hand over his face. The tension grew tighter with each call from Spud, and Frank already felt like a ruined man. He knew he had about an hour before the steer wrestling final began. He spent the rest of the ride home talking to his friend, trying not to think about the scene in Dallas. It was a futile attempt.

Half an hour later, the rig pulled in front of Frank's house. He thanked his friend for the ride, walked into his home, and set his bag on the service porch. He looked at Dawn and they flashed each other nervous smiles before they hugged. Frank visited with his eighteen-month-old daughter, Madi, and then Zane.

Before long, his thoughts turned back to rodeo. He began to pace the floor between the kitchen and the living room. He had never felt so nervous sitting on a rodeo deal, mostly because this time he had no say in the outcome. The moment was exciting, but tinged with a bittersweetness. Even before the outcome was decided, Frank knew either he or Lummus wasn't going to make it to the finals. Lummus was a good friend, and Frank hated the ugly feelings that came with needing Lummus to finish out of the money at Dallas.

As Frank kept waiting for Spud's phone call, Dawn's parents stopped by on their way into town. They sat on the couch together and visited with the kids as everyone waited to hear if Frank would make the finals. Dawn's mother and father, Jon and Yvonne Ware, watched as Frank paced madly. It was strange to see the normally laid-back cowboy acting so nervously.

"Frank, you're going to wear a hole in the floor," Yvonne said.

"I think he's walked five miles since we've been here," Jon said.

In a bid to keep herself from pacing, Dawn sat in an oversize chair and awaited the news. Finally, Frank's phone rang. It wasn't Spud, but Brad Goodrich, another friend who himself had just squeaked into the NFR by securing the fifteenth spot in the tie-down roping standings. The first thing Frank heard was the roar of the crowd. Then he heard Goodrich's voice, saying, "All right, here we go." As Frank got ready to listen live to the steer wrestling final, he moved into the kitchen. The moment didn't need any more tension, but Goodrich decided to give some play-by-play.

"Okay, Rope's backing into the box. . . . There he goes. . . ."

Frank worked intently to hear the rest, but the crowd noise drowned out Goodrich's voice. Next thing Frank heard was Goodrich shouting, "Oh my God! Oh my God! 3.2 seconds! 3.2 seconds!"

That was good news for Frank. He looked over at his wife and noticed how anxious she had grown. She's usually pretty well composed, but she clearly had become a nervous wreck as well; she appeared on the verge of tears.

"Rope was 3.2," Frank told her.

She nodded as Frank returned to the phone. Next up was Lummus. Frank strained to hear Goodrich.

"Bob's ready in the box. . . . Oh man, he got a really good start. . . . He hung a leg."

Again the crowd drowned out Goodrich's voice. Frank stood motionless, trying to hear Lummus's time. Finally, it came through: 4.1 seconds.

That left Lahr and Luke. Frank had talked to Ivan Teigen a few minutes earlier, and Teigen had said both Lahr and Luke— the season's hottest two steer wrestlers—had drawn good steers. One of them needed to beat 4.1 seconds. Frank knew he had a shot.

"Okay, Jason's in the box. . . . Oh, he's late. . . . He missed the barrier. . . . Whoa! He just slammed him. . . . 4.1 seconds. . . . He just tied Bob."

Frank groaned. As it stood, Lahr and Lummus were splitting second and third, which would give Lummus $3,525 and knock Frank out of the finals. The stage was set: It was all going to come down to the last steer of the last regular-season rodeo. And Luke was to be the deciding factor.

"C'mon kid," Frank said to himself as Goodrich delivered the call.

"Okay, he's backing into the box. . . . He's still getting set. . . . There he goes. . . . He's got a good start. . . . Whoa! . . ."

Frank strained to hear Goodrich, but the crowd noise drowned him out. It went on for several excruciating seconds. Frank could hear Goodrich trying to yell something, and then he and Frank started talking at the same time. The crowd still was too loud.

"What was he?" Frank said. "What was he?"

Finally, the crowd noise died down enough for Frank to make out some of the sweetest words he'd ever heard.

"You're in," Goodrich said. "You made it. You're in."

Luke had finished the run in 3.9 seconds. That earned him another $7,050, stopping Lummus two-tenths of a second short of making the NFR. Frank tried to thank Goodrich, but the crowd noise made a conversation impossible. Frank hung up the phone and, as he turned to everyone in the living room, a huge grin overtook his face.

"I'm in," he said.

Dawn laughed a little as her eyes filled with tears. Frank walked over to the chair and looked at his wife, who was fighting for composure. Her upper lip still quivered a bit. She imagined she would feel better if she could just throw up. For all the demands of being a rodeo cowboy, it's the wives who sacrifice the most. They raise the children while their husbands are gone. They keep the house going, the bills paid. They often work full-time jobs to keep the steady money coming in. The NFR is the one reward that can significantly sweeten the sacrifice. To come so close and not make it can be a spirit crusher.

Instead, Dawn wiped away the good kind of tears. Frank climbed beside her in the big chair. He lifted his arm and she moved in closer. As they hugged, Frank looked over at her as their tension receded, replaced by a sudden and beautiful realization.

They were going back to Vegas.

CHAPTER 13

Pay Dirt (Part 1)

LAS VEGAS, NEVADA

FRIDAY, DECEMBER 3

NATIONAL FINALS RODEO, FIRST DAY

An early December night on the sidewalks of the Las Vegas Strip used to mean an eerie stroll through an illuminated but deserted ghost town. The weeks between Thanksgiving and Christmas mostly were a time of rest for those within the casino industry. Blackjack dealers, bartenders, and cabbies took extended vacations. Maintenance workers gave hotels fresh coats of paint and new carpet. It always was the quietest time of the year.

All that changed in 1985, the year the National Finals Rodeo moved from Oklahoma City to Las Vegas. And Vegas, having no idea of the massive cowboy pilgrimage headed its way, was not prepared. Everywhere that year, people waited in lines to spend their money. Gamblers stood around crowded tables of half-opened casinos looking for action, prompting pit bosses to sit and deal blackjack. Large groups of people parked themselves outside hotels and waited for taxis, rather than the other way around. Many restaurants had closed expecting the usual lull, and those that remained open struggled to keep up with the rush. More than 140,000 people attended the NFR that first year, and tens of thousands more rodeo fans came just to join the party. The Las Vegas Convention and Visitors Authority figured the NFR pumped $14 million in nongaming revenue into the region.

Though few realized it before 1985, rodeo and Las Vegas made an ideal match. Cowboys are a breed that doesn't mind dropping serious money as long as everyone around is having a hell of a time; Vegas was created for that sort of mind-set. The city was ready for the onslaught the following year, and every year since. Now, as December approaches, the message boards out front of most every hotel and casino change to welcome rodeo fans. Cowboy-themed parties take place around the clock all over town. People wearing cowboy hats fill every casino on the Strip, and the whooping and hollering that follow victories at the craps table often startle quieter gamblers. The party grows larger every year. More than 3 million people have paid to attend the finals since they arrived in Vegas. The NFR arguably has become the hottest ticket in town; scalpers and ticket brokers make a killing, charging five hundred dollars and above for choice seats on weekend nights. Even after each night's rodeo begins, people can be found wandering outside the Thomas & Mack Center looking to buy tickets.

For contestants, the odds of getting shut out of the finals are far greater. Thousands of cowboys and cowgirls collectively shell out millions of dollars trying to win enough money to qualify for the NFR, but there's only room for 120 contestants. The mind-numbing riches possible at rodeo's Super Bowl more than justify the expense and wear that come with a hard year living on the road. To make the NFR truly is to strike pay dirt.

First place in a finals round pays $14,777. Winning the aggregate title is worth $38,000. In all, $5.1 million is up for grabs in seven events that unfold over ten days. That explained the excited buzz that moved through the wintry air behind the

Thomas & Mack Center a few minutes before the 2004 NFR got under way.

Dozens of contestants rode around in a crowded circle, talking to one another as they warmed their horses in an enormous white tent set up outdoors, about a hundred yards from the arena. The tension grew with the muffled sounds that escaped the arena party and traveled outside into the ears of every contestant: The first few chords of "Viva Las Vegas," the excited howling voices of rodeo announcers Bob Tallman and Boyd Polhamus, and the first roar of the crowd as the lights went out for the spectacular laser and fireworks show that opens each performance.

Just outside the tent, the plastic door of a portable toilet swung open and Luke stepped out. His face showed no signs of anxiety, but his bladder hinted otherwise: For the past hour, Luke had disappeared into the toilet every fifteen minutes or so to take a nervous piss.

He moved to a far corner of the tent, sat on a bale of hay, and slipped a large blue brace over his knee. Once the brace was in place, he stood and pulled his pants back on.

The brace was one of several recent accessories: Luke also wore a wedding ring on his finger; he had married Lindsay a week earlier on a wintry day in Los Olivos, California, before about three hundred family and friends.

Luke snapped together the buttons of his newest NFR jacket as he walked over to meet Jesse Peterson, who stood and waited, holding the reins of his horse, Gunner. Luke had chosen Peterson's horse as his best shot at the finals. Gunner is a speedy beast that lit up Montana racetracks for three years before being converted to a steer wrestling horse. Peterson describes Gunner as a once-in-a-lifetime horse.

Luke stuck his foot in a stirrup and climbed aboard. As he

did, he heard a loud ripping noise. He looked down and shook his head in disbelief at the gaping hole in his black jeans that stretched from his knee to his ankle. There was no time to find a change of pants.

As contestants began leaving the tent to line up for the grand entry, Luke hopped off his horse and found Ronnie Fields, who was wrapping his injured wrist with adhesive tape. Luke borrowed the tape and frantically began trying to cover the hole. As he did, PRCA announcer John Shipley moved in to help.

"I used to be a trainer," Shipley said. "Can I help you with that?"

"Sure, just hold the hole together if you could."

"No problem."

Luke tore off long strips of tape and covered the hole as best he could, knowing it looked ridiculous. Looking outside, he noticed contestants already had started riding into the arena. He was scheduled to carry the California flag, an honor bestowed upon him for earning more money than any other contestant in the state. Out of time, he slapped one more piece of tape on his pants, patted the ugly white mess down, and climbed aboard his horse. Grabbing the flag, he looked at Shipley.

"How's that look?" Luke said.

"Well," Shipley said, "it'll give Bob and Boyd something to talk about."

"Yeah, no shit," Luke said, laughing.

With that, he grabbed his flag and galloped down a long dirt ramp toward the tunnel that led to the arena. Inside, Tallman and Polhamus held microphones and stood together in a spotlighted perch just outside the arena, the ringleaders of a country circus. With voices that boomed through the air, the announcers took turns shouting out the flag bearers' names and states as the contestants galloped in.

"Here comes Todd Suhn from Colorado!"

"It's Jason Lahr from Kansas!"

When his time came, Luke burst into the arena with the other Californians.

"It's Baby Branquinho from California!" Polhamus shouted as Luke galloped in with the flag held high in the air. The contestants filled the arena in the shape of a large horseshoe as the crowd cheered their arrival. When it was done, the arena gates opened again, and the contestants tipped their hats and raced from the arena to make way for the bareback riders to kick off the action. Inside the arena, the rodeo is a well-orchestrated event: Gates swing open and riders move in and out on cue. But behind the scenes, much like backstage at a musical, it's a bit of a fire drill. As riders moved about in all directions, Luke galloped up the ramp leading from the arena, tossed his flag to someone, hopped off his mount, and quickly tied the horse to a fence. He put on his coat as he and the other steer wrestlers moved in a brisk, silent walk along a green strip of carpet that led to an entrance behind the timed-events chute.

By the time Luke got back inside, he wore a look of intense concentration. He had come to Vegas this time ready to take home more than money; the gold buckle was his to win or lose, and he knew it. When the regular season's dust had settled, he had won a record $125,625. It marked the first time he'd entered the NFR as the top-ranked steer wrestler. Even with the knee injury, Luke was the man to beat.

However, the favorite coming in often drives away from Vegas without the buckle; the ten days of the NFR can pass like an eternity, particularly for those atop the standings. Everyone is gunning for the leader and his lead, adding pressure where none is needed. There's the matter of what big money lost in split seconds can do to the mind; a couple bad breaks or missed opportunities can leave a cowboy questioning fundamentals like technique and strategy even as he's sitting aboard a horse, ready to make another run. The ten days also mean countless conversations with TV and newspaper reporters, as well as some rodeo fans, who collectively hound the front-runners with many of the same unanswerable questions: Can you do it? Are you gonna win it all this time? Will the knee hold up?

For Luke, those distractions were mild at best compared to the real threat to his title quest: the other fourteen steer wrestlers at the finals. For starters, the field held three former world champions: Frank Thompson, Rope Myers, and defending champ Teddy Johnson. Any man wearing a gold buckle enjoys a distinct advantage in experience as he already knows what it takes to win a championship. Of the three former champs, Johnson was the closest to the lead, sitting in third place nearly thirty-six thousand dollars behind Luke. Far closer was the second-place man, Jason Lahr, who spent the end of the season battling Luke for the lead. Lahr, thirty-two, was a six-four, 230-pound powerhouse making his fourth NFR appearance since 1999. Coming in, Luke led Lahr by slightly more than fourteen thousand dollars, a figure that can evaporate in one night at the finals. Stockton Graves, twenty-five, entered the NFR in fourth place, enjoying the best season of his eight-year career. The $88,437 he won during the regular season nearly doubled his career earnings. Todd Suhn, thirty-one, came into the NFR in sixth place. The 2004 Cheyenne steer wrestling champ was making his ninth consecutive NFR appearance, the longest active streak of anyone in the field. He also had the highest career earnings, quickly approaching the $1 million threshold.

Ronnie Fields, thirty-one, entered his first NFR in seventh place, having firmly established himself as one of rodeo's fastest emerging stars. After not competing in high school or college, he took up steer wrestling in 1997 at age twenty-four, after watching his older brother and his friends practicing. The $72,500 he earned during the regular season is more impressive considering he had made less than twenty-five thousand dollars since joining the PRCA in 2002. He likely would have emerged sooner if not for two significant factors: It took him awhile to get into financial position to be able to afford rodeoing full-time, and he also underwent total reconstruction surgery on his right knee in 1999. Spud Duvall entered his second NFR in eighth place. Like Fields, Johnson, and Graves, Spud hails from Oklahoma, long considered one of the premier hotbeds of steer wrestling. He learned the sport from his father, Bill, and his uncle, steer wrestling legend Roy Duvall.

The rest of the field consisted of talented cowboys with slimming title hopes as each came in more than sixty thousand dollars behind Luke. There was K. C. Jones, thirty-three, Sean Mulligan, twenty-nine, and Shawn Greenfield, thirty, all of whom had competed in the NFR before. Sitting in twelfth position was Ivan Teigen, who was forty-six years old, by far the oldest man in the field. Teigen has nearly $750,000 in career earnings, including seven finals appearances. Rounding out the field were Lee Graves, thirty-three, the only Canadian qualifier, and Trevor Knowles, twenty-four, the youngest steer wrestler at the finals.

Everyone in the field had at least an outside shot at the title; though it's extremely difficult to come from fifteenth to first at the NFR, it's a road that has been traveled. Luke simply hoped this wouldn't be the year someone pulled off those theatrics.

Limping slightly through the dirt as he neared the arena, Luke passed one rodeo legend after another. He and eight-time team roping world champ Speed Williams walked past each other and nodded.

"Get to it, man," Speed said.

"All right," Luke said.

As he passed pens of steers and calves, Luke walked by sixteen-time NFR bulldogging qualifier Rod Lyman. Sitting atop a horse, Lyman looked down and grinned.

"Good luck, Luke," Lyman said.

"Thanks Rod."

Luke reached the warm-up area behind the chute, and stopped when he got to Peterson and Gunner. As the last bareback riders went, Luke glanced across the chute and saw seventime calf roping champ Fred Whitfield getting ready to rope. The two nodded at each other. Then Luke felt an old familiar feeling: He handed Gunner's reins back to Peterson, squeezed past the other contestants, and ran to a portable toilet to take one last nervous piss. He returned a few minutes later as Frank, the night's first steer wrestler, rode into the arena.

"In an event with three world champs, we start with one," Polhamus said. "In Y2K, he won the buckle that says champion."

Frank rode out and caught his steer well, but his hand missed the nose as he prepared to throw the animal down. He recovered and finished the run, but not before 8.3 seconds had elapsed. After Knowles failed to catch his steer and Lee Graves broke a barrier, Greenfield brought the crowd's first roar with a 4.1-second run that vaulted him into the lead. But the first pen of NFR cattle was loaded with fast, brawny steers that dominated the competition. Teigen and Mulligan both failed to break five seconds on their runs before Jones moved into second with a 4.4. Spud followed with a 4.8, but got knocked from third when Fields answered with a 4.6, a fast run considering he used his foot to push the steer down after it hung on its feet. None of the next four-riders—Myers, Stockton Graves, Johnson, and Lahr—finished below 5.4 seconds. That set the stage for the night's final bulldogger.

"California, I want to see your hands in the air," Polhamus said as Luke got set in the box. "It's Luke Branquinho."

"In four years," Tallman said, "he's won half a million dollars."

Luke nodded and the chute opened. The steer got a slow break, and Luke was on him in an instant. He caught the animal and threw him to the ground as the clock stopped on 3.5 seconds. Polhamus yelled into the microphone as the crowd went wild. But the cheers turned to a collective groan as it became known Luke had broken the barrier, giving Greenfield the first-round victory. In the slow-motion replay, it appeared Gunner got out cleanly before the barrier rope skimmed off Luke's left boot and stirrup, the slimmest of margins. However small, the misstep was significant: Not only did it cost Luke $14,777, but the ten-second penalty wiped away his chances of finishing high in the aggregate standings, meaning someone besides him would claim the thirty-eight-thousand-dollar aggregate prize. As he walked out of the arena that night, he shook his head in disgust. He knew he had just opened the door for everyone else.

NFR, SECOND DAY

Luke stepped out of the rodeo secretary's office suddenly feeling a lot better about the night's prospects: He had drawn a beauty of a steer. He buttoned his coat as he walked through the frozen air toward the contestant's warm-up area. He couldn't wait to tell Travis the news, so Luke called on the way.

"Hey Trav. . . . How's it goin'?. . . Oh, pretty good. Just fixin' to get ready. . . . Yeah, guess what? I'm happy. . . . No, I'm real happy this time. . . . It's a good little steer. . . . Yeah, well, there's a lot of good steers going tonight, but I'm happy. . . . Yeah. . . . Yeah, I'm going to leave the same way I did last night. You gotta go after it. . . . I know. . . . All right, I'll call you after I go. . . . Talk to you later."

Luke called Travis before and after each run at the NFR. The calls usually were brief, an update on Luke's steer and which bulldoggers had drawn well. Despite being 450 miles away in Oakdale, Travis knew a lot more about what was going down in the NFR's steer wrestling competition than most of those in attendance. The two did talk some about Luke's game plan, but now that the average money was gone, the only sensible strategy was to go balls-out for the go-round cash. In fact, Travis believed Luke's first-round broken barrier probably would help more than it hurt because it eliminated any reason to play things safe.

As Luke reached the warm-up tent, he came upon another man whose opinion he trusted—Spud, a man known for his steer wrestling as well as his steer tracking. He keeps a book that rates every steer he sees at every rodeo throughout the year. As far as current NFR stock went, Spud was one of the experts.

"Hey Spud," Luke said, reaching out to shake Spud's hand. "How's it goin'?"

"It's goin' good," Spud said. "Yours is 219, right?"

"Yep. How's he look?"

"Oh, he's good," Spud said. "I've got him as real average. Here, I made a list."

Spud reached into an inside coat pocket and pulled out a crumpled sheet of notebook paper. It held his four-category speed rating for each steer—slow, average, average plus, and runs hard—with additional notes on how strong the animal was on his feet. Of course, steers don't behave the same way each time, but it helps to know their tendencies.

"I would compare this steer to the one you had last night," Spud said. "You could be 3.5 on him."

Luke smiled. That was sweet music to his ears.

"Who is mine comparable to that I should be watching?" Luke said.

"Maybe Stockton Graves's steer," Spud said. "And Frank's. And Jason Lahr's."

As they talked, Teigen walked by after making a visit to the steer pen.

"How's he look, Ivan?" Luke said. "Good?"

"Yeah, I like him," Teigen said. "Spud says he's pretty good."

"Well," Luke said, "that's the thing about Spud. When he tells you he knows, he knows."

Every bulldogger who stopped by Spud that night was in a particularly good mood. That's because the second pen of NFR steers was loaded with animals that ran slow and fell fast, which meant an electrifying night of steer wrestling was about to begin.

Lee Graves was the first man to go. Riding into the arena, he reached out and caught the steer's left horn first, landed, and threw the animal down in 3.9 seconds.

"Exactly what he did last night, but he's penalty free," Tallman said while Graves tipped his hat to the crowd and walked off.

Greenfield, fresh off his opening-night win, got a late start out of the box and had to settle for a 4.5. Next, Teigen's high hopes faded when he reached out for his steer's left horn and missed, landing hard in the dirt.

Next up was Mulligan. As he rode out, he caught the steer's horns simultaneously as he landed, grabbed the nose, and yanked the steer off its feet onto its side. The scoreboard read 3.8 seconds, giving him the lead by one-tenth of a second.

"He doesn't need a Mulligan, he'll take that one," Polhamus shouted as the crowd cheered. "That was a long drive with a Big Bertha."

Jones and Spud followed with disappointing runs, and then Fields rode into the arena. He caught his steer fast, turned the animal left until its head was just over Fields's hip, and then he shifted hard to the right, driving the animal into the ground in 3.7 seconds. The brutish display pleased some fans and made him the night's new leader.

Not to be outdone, Suhn tracked down a slow-moving steer and took him to the ground in similar fashion. He rose from the dirt after a 3.7 gave him a share of the lead.

"Whoa!" Polhamus yelled. "Lookie there! Like a bunch of middle linebackers!"

Next man up was Myers, who has made a career of coming up big in the clutch. He rode into the arena and gave chase as his steer slowed its pace at the last moment. Myers recovered, secured the animal's head, and gave a powerful twist that slammed the steer onto its side. The crowd went wild as Myers looked up at the scoreboard: 3.6 seconds. He walked off to a roar, becoming the third man of the night to grab the lead by one-tenth of a second.

Myers's chances to win the round looked good, and they got better as the next three riders—Stockton Graves, Johnson, and Lahr—failed to get below the four-second mark. With three bulldoggers left, Luke rode into the arena.

"Now here's California's only bulldogger here," Polhamus said as Luke settled Gunner into the corner of the box. "He's the only Californian you'll need."

Luke nodded and kicked, and Gunner charged from the box. The horse quickly caught up to the slow-moving steer. Luke slid from the saddle and, as he reached for the horns, the steer raised its head slightly. Luke grabbed the steer's horns and planted his feet into the dirt, skidding to a fast stop. He grabbed the nose, wrenched the steer's neck, and flipped the animal onto its side with a thud no one heard because the crowd, sensing another big moment, already had started coming to life. When 3.1 flashed on the scoreboard, the Thomas & Mack Center erupted in a deafening roar as Luke jumped to his feet, held his hat in the air, and surveyed the crowd.

"Look at this!" Tallman shouted in amazement. "Look at this! One-tenth of a second from an arena record! C'mon Vegas, tell him you like it!"

As Luke walked from the arena, a TV camera caught a shot of Myers—who had just got knocked out of the lead and roughly three thousand dollars—grinning big and clapping his hands in admiration of Luke's ride. That's what it's like at the NFR. The next two riders, Frank and Knowles, failed to get below four seconds, giving Luke the second-night victory. He climbed onto a horse and held his hat in the air as he paraded around the arena.

"So the opera comes to a close in the big man's event," Tallman said as Luke finished the victory lap to more loud applause. "It is the newlywed. That's right, the guy that just got married. Well, Luke, there's reason for you to dance. We'll see you tonight at the Gold Coast."

Three hours later, the Gold Coast Hotel and Casino was a western madhouse. It was Saturday night, and thousands of people crammed into the joint as the din of jackpot bells, countless conversations, and two cover bands cluttered the air. In the main casino area, a sea of black-and-white cowboy hats seemed to float about on waves of smoke. A full staff of bartenders could not keep up with an insatiable demand for drinks, so workers set up large silver troughs on the carpet of the sports book area, filling them with ice and Coors Lights. On television screens throughout the casino, the most recent NFR performance played in a twenty-four-hour loop, and there were always people watching it.

At 11 P.M., in a large showroom deep in the casino, Tallman and Polhamus picked up their microphones and took the stage to present the night's winners with NFR go-round buckles. Rodeo fans packed the place; every few minutes, the sound of broken glass elicited howls of drunken laughter. After Cimmeron Gerke received his buckle for winning the bareback round, Tallman looked over at Luke and Lindsay, who were standing in the wings, and waved them onstage.

"Okay," Tallman said, "the large newlywed is up."

Luke walked onto the stage between Tallman and Polhamus, but Lindsay retreated a few steps and tried to hide against a wall. Tallman looked back at her and grimaced.

"Bring your bride," Tallman said, seeing Lindsay shaking her head with purpose. She appeared honestly set against it.

"He just got you fourteen thousand dollars," Tallman said, softly taking her elbow and leading her onto the stage. "Where he goes, you go."

Lindsay reluctantly moved into the spotlight, taking a place beside Luke.

"What we want to do is talk about that broken barrier last night," Polhamus said, pointing the microphone at Luke.

"Yeah, I already told her I was sorry about that," Luke said.

Tallman looked at Lindsay and put his arm around her.

"He cost you," Tallman said. "You could be at twenty-eight thousand right now."

Lindsay nodded.

"Did you whip him?" Boyd said.

"Not yet," Lindsay said playfully as the crowd laughed.

"So Luke," Tallman said. "How is marriage treating you so far?"

"Well, I go to bed early and I don't drink, so it's been good," he said.

"How long have you been married now?"

"Um, this will be a week today," Luke said as the crowd hooted and hollered.

"You need us to help you out with anything?" Polhamus said. "You need a little talk with Bob and Boyd?"

"Actually," Luke said, politely, "I think we're doing pretty good there, thanks."

NFR, THIRD DAY

On a cloudy gray Sunday afternoon, Luke stood outside the Gold Coast with his father, John, and cousin, Johnny Joe Barlogio. A valet driver rounded a corner in a black BMW SUV and parked at Luke's feet. Luke climbed behind the wheel, his dad got in the passenger seat, and Johnny Joe sat in back. A minute later, Luke zoomed out of the parking lot and began weaving madly through late-morning traffic in the BMW, a loaner from a relative.

"Hang on," Luke said, looking around the cab, "this car goes really fast."

"It's like a black rocket," said Johnny Joe, who had ridden with Luke and Lindsay from Los Alamos to Las Vegas. "Hell, we got here in five hours."

"I think we made it in seven hours," John said, furrowing his brow as he did some quick math. "Five hours? Oh, good lord."

"We were only going eighty-five," Luke said.

John shook his head in disbelief and reached above his right shoulder. "I think I'm going to put on my seat belt."

Just after pulling onto I-15, Luke cut across three lanes of pavement to get to the fast lane. He looked down at the speedometer and laughed.

"See that," he said. "We're already going ninety. Doesn't feel like we're going that fast, does it?"

John didn't say anything. Johnny Joe looked out a side window to see the blur of a concrete barrier whizzing a few feet from his door.

"It does when I look to the side," he said.

Ten minutes later, Luke pulled off the interstate and wove through city streets until he arrived at the afternoon's destination: Sam's Town Hotel & Gambling Hall. Luke came to Sam's Town to sign autographs, the activity that takes more of his waking NFR hours than any other. As they pulled into Sam's Town, Johnny Joe read a marquee inviting fans to come meet eight-time bull riding champ Don Gay.

"Man, I bet a lot of these kids are too young to even remember Don Gay," Johnny Joe said. "The first year I was riding bulls, I was at a rodeo in Santa Maria. Don rode there and this bull, it was an NFR bull, it whipped him down hard. Busted his face all up. There was blood and shit everywhere. I rode the same bull, and I think I placed second on him."

Luke got a funny look on his face as he listened to the story. He looked into the rearview mirror at Johnny Joe.

"You guys rode the same bull?"

John started laughing.

"Man, I bet that looked pretty funny," John said.

"I guess he must have been sitting up front," Luke said, looking over at his dad. "That's probably why his face got all busted up."

"Yeah," John said, nodding, trying to keep a straight face, "that makes sense."

Johnny Joe tried to finish the story, but the laughter kept drowning him out. Finally, he gave up as Luke parked the car. John and Luke still were laughing as they stepped outside. John and Johnny Joe walked off to find a blackjack game as Luke made his way to a large white tent where Sheplers was hosting a western-clothing sale. As part of a new sponsorship deal with Cinch Jeans, Luke spent ninety minutes sitting at a table and signing autographs.

As a man walked into the tent, he stopped to shake hands with Luke and get an autograph for his son.

"Man, that was a hell of a run last night," the man said.

"Ah, thanks," Luke said, handing the man a signed photo.

Next, a woman who looked to be in her thirties stopped at Luke's table.

"Hello," she said.

"Hello," Luke said.

"Can I tell you what to write?"

"Sure."

"Well my husband's a bulldogger too, but he didn't have a good season," she said. "Write, 'Dear Mike, better luck next year. Luke Branquinho.' "

Luke wrote the message, signed his name, and smiled as he handed the woman the photo.

Nearly everyone who entered the tent recognized Luke, and most stopped at his table to congratulate him on his NFR go-round victory. When Luke spotted Frank signing autographs at another table, he walked up to him with a sly smile on his face.

"Hey Frank, do you want my autograph?"

Frank retaliated as Luke walked off.

"Hey Kid," Frank said, "do you want me to sign the back of my gold buckle?"

But Luke already had traveled too far away to hear Frank, who shook his head and laughed. Frank is one of the only people around still calling Luke by the nickname Kid. Luke was nineteen years old when he burst onto the pro rodeo scene, and veteran cowboys—some more than twice his age—thought he acted like a goofball; he got away with it because everyone knew how good he was going to become, but they all started calling him Kid. In time, he put on weight and more people started calling him Fatty.

Unable to assault Luke verbally, Frank grabbed a pen and one of his photos. With great delight, he scrawled a message to Luke.

To Kid,
2000 World Champion steer wrestler
Frank Thompson

Frank asked his wife to walk over to Luke's table and deliver the photo. Five minutes later, a stranger walked up to Frank holding a signed photograph of Luke. The man handed it to Frank, who smiled as he read the message.

To Frank,
3.1 second go-round, 2004 NFR
Luke Branquinho

But Frank would have the last laugh at that night's performance.

Teigen kicked things off with a 4.0, followed by Mulligan and Jones, who each clocked 4.2-second runs. Then Spud enjoyed his best run of the finals, throwing a big steer down in 3.6 seconds to take the lead. As he walked off to a rousing ovation, he grabbed his hat and thrust it into the air in a show of celebratory relief.

"Oklahoma!" Tallman's voice boomed through the arena. "Are we here on a Sunday?"

The next man, Fields, tracked a big, fast steer to the middle of the arena and muscled it down in a flawless 4.1-second run. That brought up Myers, who took advantage of a slow steer, throwing the animal down in 3.6 seconds to grab a share of the lead. As Myers stood, he kissed his finger and waved it to the applauding crowd. It was his second straight night with a run of 3.6 seconds.

After Stockton Graves settled for a 4.2, Johnson rode into the arena, a defending champ looking to make some noise.

"He hasn't won a penny in the first two rounds," Polhamus said as Johnson got set. "C'mon brother."

Johnson reached for his steer's horns, but missed and overshot the animal. Johnson landed empty-handed in the dirt, a couple feet in front of his steer. He turned, took a step back, and caught the steer's right horn with his left hand before the animal had a chance to run away. As the applause grew, Johnson held on, worked himself around the steer, and finally wrestled the animal onto the dirt. The 9.4-second run wasn't worth any money, but it delighted fans of the never-say-die spirit.

The next man up was Luke. He had drawn a big steer that liked to run, which is the last thing a cowboy wants to see blowing out of an NFR chute.

"Here comes the man," Polhamus said. "He's got a twenty-thousand-dollar lead and an Army of One on his back. This is Luke Branquinho."

Luke nodded and the steer broke hard and fast. Luke got caught a little out of position as he grabbed the horns, and he skidded a few feet through the dirt, trying to slow the steer. Making matters worse, the steer held on a leg when Luke tried to throw him to the ground, and he had to settle for a 5.2.

Luke walked out of the arena as Frank rode in. He backed into the box, needing a 3.5-second run to erase the disappointment the first two nights had left him feeling.

"Here's Frank Thompson from the Daddy of 'em All," Tallman said. "Just get a check."

Frank nodded and surged into the arena after his steer, which hopped and jerked its head up as it sensed Frank was about to make the grab. The unexpected move jabbed a horn into the left side of Frank's face. He stayed with it, pulled in the horns, and turned the animal left. The crowd came alive as it recognized Frank had caught his steer closer to the chute than anyone else that night. Frank finished the run off strong, grabbing the nose and slamming the animal down. As the crowd roared, he looked up for the red numbers of the scoreboard. They read: 3.4 seconds. Frank grabbed his hat and whipped it through the air, an expression of elation and relief shining on his face. That's what an instant $14,777 can do to a man.

"He's usually so stoic," Polhamus said as the crowd continued its ovation. "It's good to see some emotion brother. We love it."

NFR, FOURTH DAY

The contestants' warm-up tent and the interactive village—where spectators can eat, drink, and take part in rodeo games and promotions before NFR performances—are located on opposite sides of the Thomas & Mack Center. Getting from one place to the other is about a five-minute walk for most people. However, it's an entirely different matter for NFR contestants, constantly being stopped by folks with widely varying agendas.

As Luke left the interactive village, he wove his way through the crowd, making it about ten steps before a man stopped him. The man reached out to shake Luke's hand and open a conversation. The man clearly was a fan and Luke talked with him for several minutes, even though it was getting late.

"Well, it's real good to meet you," the man said. "We always see you on TV. When your shirt's pulled up, your forearm looks about as big as my thigh. I'm like, 'Yeah, this is a man who can handle a five-hundred-pound steer.'"

"Oh, thanks," Luke said, nodding.

"Well, I won't take any more of your time, I just wanted to meet you," the man said, looking Luke carefully in the eye. "I just want you to know, it's guys like you who make this whole thing worthwhile for us fans. Don't ever lose your humbleness."

"Oh, I won't," Luke said, shaking the man's hand. "Thanks. I hope you enjoy the rodeo."

As Luke moved through the crowd, someone stopped him every fifteen or twenty feet. A woman asked him to sign a program for her son, so he did. Another woman reminded him she used to babysit him, then asked if he knew where to get tickets; he didn't. A couple fans stopped him to say they were rooting for him; he thanked them. Finally, two young women who had been seeking out NFR jackets approached, and shyly asked if he had any extra tickets; he didn't.

Luke finally reached the contestants' area with about two minutes to spare before the opening ceremony. Half an hour later, as Will Lowe finished his victory lap for winning the bareback, the arena gates opened and the fourth night of steer wrestling got under way.

The big steers from the first night were back, and that meant a lot of bulldoggers had their hands full—or empty, as it would turn out. The first man out was Jones, whose trouble started when his steer stopped abruptly after leaving the chute. He managed to grab the steer's right horn, and he held onto it with both hands as the animal dragged him about fifteen feet to the side of the arena before Jones finally let go. That set the tone as none of the first eight bulldoggers managed times below four seconds. Of the eight, Suhn had the best showing with a solid 4.0-second-run, his third of four seconds or better.

Then Luke rode into the arena. As he settled into the corner, he looked at the horns of the steer Greenfield threw down in 4.1 seconds to win the opening night.

"Here's Lukie, one-tenth of a second off an arena record two nights ago," Polhamus said. "He's twenty-nine thousand dollars in the lead."

Luke nodded, kicked, and charged into the arena, quickly riding alongside a slow-moving steer. He slid from the saddle and grabbed the left horn. As his right arm cradled the steer's other horn, Luke planted in the dirt, reached for the nose, and twisted, whisking the steer off its feet and onto its side. The clock froze on 3.7 seconds. The crowd roared as Luke hopped to his feet and raised his hat into the air. He walked off smiling and clapping.

"California, where are you?" Polhamus said. "He didn't make some money right then, he just got paid."

The Fatty Curse seemed to take care of the rest of the pack. Three of the next six bulldoggers missed their steers completely. Knowles was the only one who came close to catching Luke that night, but Knowles settled for a 4.1 when his steer momentarily held onto its feet before falling. With that, Luke headed back to the Gold Coast, delighted at having extended his lead over Lahr to forty-four thousand.

By 11 P.M., a harsh desert wind pushed most everyone in Las Vegas inside as the temperature dipped below freezing. Luke and Lindsay ran through the night to the back door of the Gold Coast showroom, opened it, and hurried inside. They huddled together in a hallway, but a cold blast of air hit them every time someone opened the back door. They looked around for better shelter and ducked into a tiny side closet stuffed with stacks of music equipment. A moment later, a shivering Tallman walked into the hallway and spotted the closet.

"I'm coming in here with you guys where it's warm," Tallman said, squeezing inside. Tallman is a legend, the undisputed voice of professional rodeo. He has announced the NFR eighteen times, including the past nine. When Tallman talks, rodeo people listen. As everyone waited for the night's ceremony to begin, Tallman looked at Luke and smiled.

"You're gonna do it," Tallman said quietly. "I'm not saying you're there yet, but you can relax now. The way I got it figured, you could win it with five fifth-place runs."

Luke nodded.

"Thanks Bob. You know, I'm just going to keep running 'em one at a time."

"And that's the way to approach it," Tallman said. "But I don't want you to just win the title. Now this is just me, this is just Bob talking here, I want you to smash the record. I want you to go out and do something that's never been done. Something like win three hundred thousand dollars. Something that's going to stick for ten years. That's what I'd like to see you do."

"Thanks Bob," Luke said.

The two shook hands, and Tallman headed onto the stage before another packed showroom audience. A couple minutes later, Tallman looked to the side of the stage at Luke and Lindsay.

"Well, it's time to bring out our steer wrestler," he said.

As Luke walked onto the stage, he grabbed the microphone from Polhamus and addressed the crowd.

"You know these guys are a bunch of perverts, don't you?"

The crowd laughed as Polhamus retrieved his microphone. He took the offensive with a series of fat jokes aimed at Luke. He asked the deejay to cue some dancing music and goaded Luke to shake his big butt for the crowd.

"Wouldn't you guys like to see that?" he asked, drawing a big crowd response.

"C'mon Luke," Polhamus said. "Shake your booty."

Luke looked around, somewhat embarrassed, but he knew this wasn't going to go away. Finally, he turned his back to the crowd, bent down a little, and gave his big butt a couple shakes. The audience whooped and hollered.

As that went on, Tallman spotted Lindsay watching from the side of the stage, partially hidden by a curtain. He looked at Luke.

"Why doesn't your wife come out onstage anymore?"

"I embarrass her."

"Why do you embarrass her?"

"Well," Luke said, "just look at me."

Tallman looked at Lindsay again and raised his eyebrows to say he was waiting. Lindsay walked onto the stage next to Luke. As she did, Tallman noticed she was wearing an NFR go-round buckle.

"Well, I see where the first buckle went," Tallman said, putting his arm around Lindsay. "Where did you get that?"

"From you," Lindsay said, pointing to Tallman. She clearly was becoming more comfortable with the public part of being a rodeo wife.

"Well, this one's yours," Polhamus said, handing Luke another buckle and shaking his hand. "I'm looking forward to calling you champion. A lot of people are."

NFR FIFTH DAY

Back in Oakdale, Travis waited to hear the results of the fifth go-round, which wasn't being shown live on TV. As he did, he prepared to give T.C. a bath. Once he had his thirteen-month-old son undressed, Travis knelt on the tile floor and used his hand to check the water in the tub. As he added cool water, he looked over at T.C. several times, thinking it was sort of strange the boy was being so quiet. The entire time, T.C. stared straight ahead, like he was in a trance. Travis reached over and lifted his son beneath the armpits to set him in the tub. About that time, Travis heard something hit the floor beneath his son.

Travis caught a whiff and a glimpse of T.C.'s surprise and instantly lost all control; a surge of vomit erupted from his mouth, some of it landing on T.C. Travis crawled to the toilet and began heaving the rest of that night's dinner, holding T.C. with one arm to keep him from the mess; the boy laughed the entire time, thinking it was a game. Travis usually isn't squeamish and mashed-up excrement in a diaper never bothered him, but something about a full belly and the sight and smell of a very adult-looking turd on the tile floor set him off.

A few minutes later, Travis still fought dry heaves as he cleaned the boy off. Before making a second attempt at a bath, Travis returned to the bathroom. He got down on his hands and knees and started cleaning the mess, realizing that, at that moment, he was about as far from the finals as a cowboy could get. He looked up in exasperation.

"Fatty," Travis said aloud, "I hope you're having a better night than I am."

Much better, as it would turn out. Of course, so was nearly every other steer wrestler in Vegas that night.

Fields started the fifth go-round by throwing a big steer down in 3.7 seconds, another impressive performance for a man who continued to look nothing like an NFR rookie. Suhn, battling Fields for the aggregate lead, followed by throwing his steer down in 3.8 seconds.

"Oh, this could be a record night," Tallman said over the loudspeaker.

Indeed. Myers went next and looked good early until his steer put up a good battle on its feet, forcing Myers to settle for a 4.5. Then Stockton Graves shot into the arena, chasing the same steer Luke nearly broke the arena record on in the second round. Graves threw the steer down in 3.9 seconds, but there was a feeling in the air that 3.9—normally a hell of a time—wasn't going to make much money on this night.

The next man up was Johnson, who had yet to make much of a presence at these finals. That changed in a hurry as Johnson shot out of the box, caught his steer, and threw it down in 3.7 seconds, tying Fields for the lead. Johnson stood, clapped his hands a couple times, and shouted something to himself as he walked off.

"The 2003 champion of the world," Polhamus shouted as the crowd responded. "He's no teddy bear, he's a grizzly. There's the wake-up call!"

Another man off to a surprisingly slow NFR start was Lahr, who rode into the box after Johnson. He had not drawn any great steers during the first four rounds, and his luck didn't improve any on the fifth. He caught up to his steer a little late and managed to put it down in 4.4 seconds, but that wasn't worth much on this night.

As Lahr walked off, Luke rode into the arena. As he did, a collective murmur rumbled through the crowd. Fans elbowed one another, telling those they came with that this was the man to watch. Clearly, he had captured the rodeo world's attention.

"California, here he comes, Luke Branquinho," Polhamus said as Luke backed into the box. "He has a forty-thousand-dollar lead on the number two man. Here is a man that can get 'er done."

The arena's big screen showed a close-up of Luke's face, a portrait of concentration. He sat on Gunner in the corner and waited as a man worked to get the steer's head pointed forward in the chute. The arena's tension level rose a bit, but Luke had good reason to take his time: As luck would have it, he had drawn the steer Fields put down in 3.7 seconds in the second round.

Once set, Luke nodded and kicked, and bolted into the arena. He leaned from the saddle shortly after he passed the chute. Lowering himself over the steer, he slapped his right arm on the animal's right side and grabbed the steer's left horn with his other hand. He clutched both horns as his feet hit the ground and rotated slightly to the left. Then, in one motion, he grabbed the steer's nose, flexed his legs, and leaned backward. The two crashed hard into the dirt. The flag came down.

A moment later, Luke's sneering face popped into view above the head of his downed steer. It was the same unmistakable sneer that had appeared on rodeo highlight reels all season, and in every casino in Vegas during the past week. As he looked up for the time, the sneer morphed into a smile. The scoreboard read: 3.3 seconds. The Thomas & Mack Center exploded in noise and scattered standing ovations. Luke stood, held his hat in the air, and smiled as he walked away. When he got near the chute, he clapped his hands and shook his ass a little in celebration.

"He shook that same booty last night," Polhamus said.

"It's going to be Luke Branquinho's Gold Coast Hotel," Tallman said as Luke left the arena.

Nine of fifteen bulldoggers turned in runs of less than four seconds that night, but no one beat Luke's 3.3. After the performance, the round winners sat at tables and signed autographs for fans as they filed out of the Thomas & Mack Center. Autograph sessions before a rodeo differ greatly from signings that follow a rodeo as many fans have drunk away their inhibitions. One woman asked Luke if he would sign her chest, so he stood and wrote his name just above her right breast. A few minutes later, a woman walked up with a drink in her hand and sat down at Luke's table, making herself comfortable. Luke recognized her instantly: The night before, he had signed her underwear.

"Hi," Luke said, "how's it goin'?"

"Great," she said. "Hey, I just wanted to say sorry about having you sign my underwear. I was drunk last night."

"Ah, that's no problem," Luke said. "It happens."

"But I was wondering," she said, reaching into her pants and pulling out her underwear, "if you could sign these, too."

Luke looked at Lindsay who was standing nearby, and they both laughed.

"Sure," Luke said, leaning in to sign the woman's underwear. "You have a good night."

"Oh, I will," the woman said as she wandered off.

Later, at the Gold Coast, Luke took the stage and received another NFR buckle. At Polhamus's prodding, Luke gave a celebratory butt shake, which for some reason Polhamus was trying to build into a trademark. Luke was winning too much money to give it much thought, so he went along with it. It was around midnight when Luke and Lindsay held hands and tried to make their way through the crowded casino to go to their room at Treasure Island. Giving up, they retreated and took a shortcut through a slightly less populated area full of people sitting around tables, drinking and talking.

At that moment, Luke could have walked anonymously through most any city in the United States. But in Vegas, he couldn't make it ten feet without being recognized. As Luke and Lindsay passed through, people at every table immediately noticed Luke and showered him with fawning treatment usually reserved for rock stars. Three couples at one table rose and gave him a standing ovation. He smiled and thanked them as he passed. A group of older men at another table gave him thumbs-up signs, congratulating him with marveled expressions on their faces. He nodded politely and waved to say thanks. As they continued on, a man stood and patted Luke on the shoulder. As Luke and Lindsay reached the end of the room, several more people in the place clapped their hands in respect, knowing the nightly NFR clinic he had been putting on was unprecedented and probably wouldn't happen again anytime soon. He had won forty-four thousand dollars and three NFR buckles in five nights, and was a split-second miscalculation from winning a fourth. His lead over Lahr had ballooned to fifty-five thousand, and the next-closest man, Myers, was seventy thousand behind Luke. Halfway through the NFR, the steer wrestling competition seemed to hold about as much suspense as an execution.

CHAPTER 14

Pay Dirt (Part 2)

NATIONAL FINALS RODEO, SIXTH DAY

Luke's enormous lead did nothing to calm the nerves of two of the more anxious fans in the Thomas & Mack Center: his mother, Brandy, and his father, John. As the couple sat together in the last row of the lower box section, waiting for steer wrestling to begin, emotions raged inside them. Simply knowing how close their son was to the title, and knowing how quickly it could fall apart, had made wrecks of them both.

For Brandy, trying to hide it would have been a lost cause. She is the sentimental sort, the kind of lady who cries over television commercials. All that week, she kept a handkerchief in one pocket, and a fresh supply of Kleenex in the other. Sometimes when talking about Luke, she would turn away in midsentence, reach into her pocket, and begin drying a new flood of tears. For his part, John tried to act calm, but it was a poor sell. Since arriving in Vegas, he had been a little grumpy and fidgety for no apparent reason; driving to the rodeo, he lost his patience in backed-up traffic, cursing other drivers. For him, the worst part was that he had no say in the outcome: He could only sit, stir, and watch. Anytime Brandy looked over and noticed John's index finger tapping the armrest of his seat, she quickly reached for a handkerchief to dab away the tears that came with knowing her husband also was a mess on the inside.

From across the arena, Luke's parents intently watched the area around the chute, monitoring their son's every move. Their emotions stirred wildly as they saw his black shirt move higher into the air as he climbed onto the saddle. After Lahr finished a solid run of 3.9 seconds that would earn him thirty-eight hundred dollars, the arena gates swung open to let him out, and to let Luke in.

"Horse power going into the box," Polhamus said as Luke got set. "Here's the number one cowboy."

Luke and Gunner charged into the arena. He slid from the saddle to the dirt, throwing his steer to the ground in 3.9 seconds. The crowd cheered him as he stood, but he did not join the celebration. He knew before anyone else that he had left the box too soon, his second broken barrier of the finals.

John craned his neck to see beyond the second-deck overhang, and he saw the scoreboard stopped on 3.9. A rush of excitement ran through him until he heard Tallman's groaning voice, lamenting a missed opportunity. Coming out of the box, Gunner's head had dropped as the horse dug its front feet into the dirt; at the same instant, the barrier rope snapped free and glanced off the horse's nose. The misstep cost Luke another check worth thousands of dollars.

John looked over at his wife, who was drying her cheeks with a handkerchief. He clinched his lip, grimaced, and shook his head. She looked down at his hand and noticed his index finger tapping the armrest, a little harder than before.

Though, for them, the night's drama had ended, there was still plenty of excitement left in the NFR's sixth round. After

Frank took his steer down in four seconds, Knowles put together a fast start and a slow steer en route to a 3.5-second run that vaulted him into the lead for the night's purse.

The next man up was Lee Graves, who had won a couple of decent NFR checks but otherwise had been fairly quiet. He rode out of the box and caught up to his steer in a flash, leaned out, and grabbed the horns. Upon landing, he turned, wheeled, and powered the steer into the ground.

"Whoa!" Tallman yelled to a rousing ovation. "That's a wake-up call!"

A delighted expression overtook Graves's face as he scrambled to his feet. He glanced at the scoreboard to see a friendly sight: 3.2 seconds. His eyes shot back to make sure he'd cleared the barrier, and the celebration began. Graves grabbed the hat off his head and whipped it through the air, raising his arms toward the roof. The huge smile on his face told the story.

Graves left the arena and took a spot behind the box. Nervously, he watched the action through the fence as, one by one, the next five bulldoggers failed to challenge him. Then Suhn, the night's final contestant, rode into the arena. Suhn had drawn a good steer and he had a great run going until the takedown. When he twisted the steer's neck, the animal's back legs buckled and it fell to its knees. Several tenths of a second elapsed before Suhn managed to roll the steer onto its side, finishing at 3.7 seconds. The run earned Suhn a decent check, and it also extended his growing lead in the aggregate standings.

But Lee Graves was the night's big winner. He hopped onto a horse and rode a victory lap around the arena, smiling the entire way as his fans waved Canadian flags. The nearly fifteen thousand dollars he won that night more than doubled his total through the NFR's first five nights.

NFR, SEVENTH DAY

Luke placed the cap on his Sharpie and rose from a table at the U.S. Army's corner of the interactive village; his nightly signing obligation was done. He picked up his jacket, turned, and saw the crowd patiently waiting for him. Another dozen or so family and friends had arrived for the final weekend of the NFR. As Luke walked over to join his family, Kassidy, his six-year-old goddaughter, met him first. She proudly showed him a handmade cardboard sign that read: BRANQUINHO'S THE BEST!

As Luke said hello, the girl's mother reminded her to give Luke's belly a customary hug. Kassidy smiled, leaned forward, and wrapped her arms as far around Luke as they would go, burying the side of her face in his belly. Everyone around smiled; Luke smiled, too, then wrinkled his nose at a nagging thought that bugged him.

"I look fat on TV," he said.

"You look fat in real life," said Tony, his older brother.

Luke nodded, resigned to his stature. A man always can count on his family to tell it like it is. Tony moved in and shook Luke's hand.

"Hey, good luck tonight," Tony said.

"Hey, thanks Tony," Luke said.

"Yeah, good luck," said Casey, who was standing with his girlfriend, Beau. The two had met during the season, and their relationship had progressed even quicker than Luke and Lindsay's. Beau wore a new engagement ring, another sign that the Branquinho bachelors were dropping fast.

Luke hugged his mother and father, and headed off through the crowd to get ready. He walked away with a limp that had worsened with the NFR's nightly pounding. To that point, the knee injury hadn't hampered his bulldogging, but it hurt like hell each time the adrenaline of competition receded.

An hour later in the arena, as Luke got ready to climb aboard Gunner, Lahr finished off his first stellar ride of the finals, a 3.4-second beauty that brought the crowd to life.

"He needed that shot in the arm," Polhamus said as Lahr walked out of the arena with a relieved smile on his face. To that point, Lahr had managed just $8,000 in NFR earnings after finishing the regular season with more than $111,000. Still the closest man to Luke, Lahr's ride put some added pressure on Luke as he backed into the box.

"Luke Branquinho may have a $51,000 lead, but he's not safe," Polhamus said. "Don't take this wrong, but everyone here wants to see you shake your butt."

Luke did not disappoint, turning in a solid 4.1-second ride. With round seven pitting the bulldoggers against the NFR's big, nasty pen of steers, Luke figured his performance was going to win him some money. As he walked from the arena, he could hear Polhamus's voice, egging Luke on. So he stopped in the middle of the arena, looked to the side, and gave his butt a little wiggle. The crowd loved it.

"His mother is gonna grab me by the ears the next time she sees me," Polhamus said.

But this wasn't Luke's night. Instead, it belonged to Teigen, a friendly gray-haired man who was throwing steers down before Luke was born. Teigen—at forty-six, the oldest bulldogger at the finals by nine years—entered the night having managed just six thousand dollars through six rounds. That changed in a hurry as Teigen caught his steer, planted, and wrenched the animal's neck so hard it landed partially on its back. The crowd roared its approval when a 3.3 flashed onto the scoreboard—one-tenth of a second faster than Lahr.

"Forty-six years old!" Polhamus shouted above the crowd. "Forty-six years old!"

Teigen walked off, smiling as the speakers blared the chorus of a KC and the Sunshine Band song: "That's the way, uh-huh uh-huh, I like it."

Teigen's magical run knocked Lahr into second, but he still earned roughly $11,700 on the night—his biggest check of the finals. Luke settled for fifth and thirty-eight hundred dollars. Lahr's run not only trimmed Luke's overall lead to forty-two thousand dollars, but it also moved Lahr to within three-tenths of a second of Suhn's lead in the aggregate standings.

World championship scenarios change nightly at the NFR. And here, with three rounds to go, new possibilities emerged: If Lahr could stay hot and win the aggregate title and its thirty-eight thousand dollars, then he would need to make up about four thousand in go-round money on Luke during the final three nights to steal the title. Suhn wasn't out of the championship picture, either: If he could hang on and win the aggregate and a couple of go-rounds, he had an outside shot of catching Luke as well.

Suddenly, the race that was all but over was getting interesting again.

NFR, EIGHTH DAY

For all the high-stakes theatrics that play out inside the arena walls, rodeo's world titles often are decided in a small room situated across a short cement walkway from the Thomas & Mack Center. It is a nondescript place of drab paint, short carpet, and rows of folding tables and chairs. This is where the steers are drawn an hour before each NFR performance. As far as the adage "better to be lucky than good" is concerned, the draw is where most of the luck comes in. The significance of the event was not lost on the contestants, and many of them arrived shortly before the night's stock was doled out.

Luke, Frank, Lahr, Suhn, and a handful of other steer wrestlers gathered near a portable wall inside the small room. They listened as several officials seated around a table started the proceedings. A man opened a box containing white poker chips, each bearing the number of a steer. Another man reached in, drew chips, and handed them to rodeo secretary Irene Singer. She called out the names and numbers as they were drawn. Luke, scheduled to go first at that night's performance, heard his steer drawn first.

"Luke Branquinho," she said. "Number 268."

Hearing the number, Luke quickly flipped through a stack of papers to see what other contestants had done with the steer. A giddy feeling grew inside him as he saw the results. Both Mulligan and Suhn had thrown number 268 in 3.8 seconds. Also pleasing Luke was the fact that he had been performing about a half second faster per steer than many of the NFR's bulldoggers.

As Luke walked over to the holding pens to take a look at his steer, he pulled out his cell phone and called Travis.

"Hey. . . . He's good. Todd Suhn had him. They've been 3.8 on him. . . . Uh, I think Suhn had him in the fifth round. . . . He's pretty skinny, all black with big horns. . . . You remember that steer? What'd you think? . . . Yeah, I know. And he's real average on the ground. . . . I'm about to go inside and look at him. . . . Okay, I'll talk to you after the perf. . . . All right, Trav, talk to you later."

As the bareback riders took their turns that night, Luke and Peterson stood together and talked. Every once in a while, Luke glanced into the chute to look at his steer. That night, Luke was scheduled to be the first man out, and that suited him just fine. He could almost taste the title. All of a sudden, he felt that old familiar feeling. He ran off and disappeared into a portable toilet. He returned as Cody Demers was finishing his victory lap for winning the bareback go-round. As Demers rode out of the arena, Luke climbed aboard Gunner and rode into the arena with Peterson.

"We're starting it off with Luke Branquinho," Tallman said. "He has a forty-two-thousand-dollar lead. Jason Lahr and Todd Suhn are breathing down Luke's neck a little."

That was about to change. The chute doors swung open and, holding true to form, steer number 268 broke slowly into a run. Luke and Gunner were on him in a flash. The crowd grew louder as Luke leaned out and caught hold of his steer, planted his feet, and drove the steer sideways into the dirt. The scoreboard stopped on 3.3 seconds. Luke stood, whipped his hat through the air, and yelled something that got lost in the roar. He walked off, knowing he'd done his part.

Moments later, Frank answered with a beauty of his own, downing his steer in 3.5 seconds.

"It's going to be one of those nights," Tallman told the crowd.

And it was. After Lee Graves turned in a 3.7, Greenfield brought the biggest ovation of the night when he threw his steer down in 3.1 seconds—tying Luke for the fastest run of the finals.

"How loud can you get?" Polhamus screamed into the microphone to be heard above the crowd. "How loud can you get? 3.1!"

"Sounds like seventeen thousand people from Oregon," Tallman said.

As the round continued, Mulligan and Fields added 3.8s that, on any other night, would have earned them some money. Suhn threw his steer down in 4.1, which kept him in first place in the aggregate. Myers scored a 3.5 before Stockton Graves and Johnson put down 3.7s. In all, nine of the first fourteen bull-doggers finished faster than four seconds.

That set the stage for Lahr, who sat in the box, staring at the back of his steer's head. As Lahr got set, Polhamus laid out the situation.

"Ladies and gentlemen, this steer is a pig," Polhamus said, drawing laughter from the crowd. "This steer runs like he's Seabiscuit. This steer is no fun."

For Lahr, however, his draw was anything but a laughing matter. When he nodded, the steer shot out of the chute and broke hard. Lahr raced out and finally caught up about two-thirds of the way down the arena. He leaned and grabbed the steer's horns, pivoted in the dirt, and threw the animal down in 4.2 seconds. It was a hell of a run, but it didn't get the job done.

"He won't get a check in the round," Tallman told the crowd, "but Branquinho will."

Though another go-round win eluded him, Luke finished second to add $11,700 to his total. His lead returned to nearly fifty-four thousand dollars. With two nights to go, Lahr was the only man who had a shot to catch Luke. And it was a long shot.

NFR, NINTH DAY

The NFR is a marathon of sprints. It is rodeo's version of the movie *Groundhog Day.* But instead of Bill Murray's character re-living the same day again and again in Punxsutawney, Pennsyl-vania, NFR contestants fight themselves to stay fresh in the face of living ten consecutive days that feel somewhat identical. On top of the vaguely surreal feeling that comes with living two weeks out of a casino hotel, there are daily autograph signings, television and newspaper interviews, sponsor obligations, point-less conversations, buffet lunches, and, of course, the nightly rodeo in front of seventeen thousand fans. Factor in the year's miles and injuries. Then add the nightly pressure of having fourteen guys gunning for you as you try to secure a world title. It's a recipe for exhaustion.

As it wound down, Luke stood next to a horse, a weary look in his eyes. He moved around more slowly than usual, visibly favoring his injured knee. By the end of it, the NFR starts to feel like a full-time job, and rodeo cowboys are not fans of that sort of thing. He popped the top of a Red Bull and drank it down without taking a breath. He chased it with a big wad of Copen-hagen. After he put the can in his pocket, he pulled out his phone and called Travis.

"Hey skinny fucker. . . . They're all gonna hate me for this, but I've got the one. . . . Yeah, he's real good. . . . Lee Graves was 3.2 on him. Someone else was 3.8, I think. . . . Yeah, that's him. Average speed and real average on the ground. . . . Think so? . . . I think so. . . . Good deal. . . . All right. You watching it? I think it's on live tonight. . . . Okay, well I'm gonna get ready. I'll talk to you in a while. . . . Okay, thanks. . . . See ya, Trav."

Though the days were blending together, there was some-thing different about this night: For the first time in his life, the world title actually was within reach. All Luke had to do was fin-ish higher than Lahr in one of the last two go-rounds, or have Lahr finish out of the money once, and the championship would belong to Luke. Travis told Luke he wanted him to go out and do something flashy like clinch the buckle with an arena record, especially with ESPN2 showing the performance live. But Luke gave Travis's scenario no thought. He'd ridden so many adrenaline peaks and valleys during the previous nine days, he felt flat and all he wanted was to sew the damn title up and be done with it. To want something so badly for so long can wreck a man when it's actually within his grasp.

Just after 6 P.M., the arena gate swung open and Knowles rode in to kick off the bulldogging. He threw his steer down in 4.1 seconds. After Lee Graves missed his steer and Greenfield broke a barrier, Teigen battled a big steer to a 6.2.

As Luke stood around the box, awaiting his turn, other steer wrestlers kept coming up to him, shaking his hand and wishing him luck. But there was something different in the way they acted that clicked with Luke. The closer it got to his ride, the more nervous he became. And it was something a trip to the outhouse could not fix.

Mulligan broke a barrier. Jones got a slow break and settled for a 4.7. The next man up was Spud, who tore into the arena and threw down his steer in 3.9 seconds to bring the crowd into it for the first time.

"C'mon folks," Polhamus said, "give him something for taking the lead."

Next, Fields blew out of the box, skidded to a stop, and stuck his steer on its side. The scoreboard read: 3.5 seconds. The crowd roared in delight for Fields, who would put together another dandy in the final round to win the aggregate title by one-tenth of a second over Suhn.

"Whoa!" Tallman said. "Look at this! He goes to the lead for the Gold Coast."

Suhn and Myers surged into the ninth-round money with back-to-back 3.9s. After Stockton Graves and Johnson both went longer than five seconds, Lahr rode into the arena needing everything to go his way.

"Either Jason Lahr or Luke Branquinho will be the world champion steer wrestler," Polhamus told the crowd as Lahr got set. "He's six-two, 230 pounds. A Coors fan's favorite cowboy."

Lahr nodded and his steer broke from the chute. He rode out and caught the animal as they skidded to a stop. After throwing the steer down, Lahr glanced at the scoreboard to see 4.2 seconds on the screen. That was the time Luke had to beat.

"That's sixth-place money," Tallman said as Lahr walked back toward the chute. He left the arena as Luke rode in.

"All right California, are you ready?" Polhamus said as Luke backed his horse into the box. "Folks, he can put the cinch on the mule right now. Let's watch him do it."

Once Gunner was set, Luke looked forward and took a few deliberate breaths. He exhaled with purpose, like a man trying to get hot coals to ignite. In the stands, John began tapping his finger on the armrest. Brandy clutched a handkerchief. Lindsay got so nervous she felt sick to her stomach.

Back in Oakdale, seeing a close-up of Luke's face for the first time, Travis leaned toward the television to get a better look. He saw fear. In this season, and throughout the past, there had been big victories, and many had come in the clutch. But during Luke's young career, there had been big moments where nervousness took over, where the pressure got to him. It was the last demon he had not yet conquered.

"Oh no, Fatty," Travis said aloud, "not this time. Don't do this now."

Luke sat atop Gunner and glanced at the back of his steer's head. The fact remained: He was nervous, and he knew it. He tried to envision the run that was about to take place.

"In four short years, he's won over six hundred thousand dollars," Tallman said, filling the time. "California, where are you?"

Applause came from all around as Luke nodded and charged from the box. He caught the steer's horns and skidded to a stop, but he was a little shaky on the handle. He fought with the steer a few extra beats before he regained control, reached for the nose, and twisted the animal until it flopped onto its side. The scoreboard's red numbers rolled over, like the last row in a slot machine, until stopping on 3.9 seconds. The time flashed like a jackpot. The crowd came to life.

Moments later, the first California steer wrestling champion in fifteen years rose from the dirt and held his hat high above his head, looking up at the video screen. He began walking back toward the chute as the crowd cheered him on, some of them rising in appreciation. He stopped in midstep, bent a little, and gave his ass a couple of shakes and smiled. Now the crowd roared its approval.

"I've just done some quick math," Polhamus said as Luke reached the end of the arena.

"Ladies and gentlemen, the world champion steer wrestler just shook his butt at you. They can't catch him."

As Luke began receiving the first of hundreds of congratulatory handshakes and shoulder pats, Frank capped a wild night with a 3.4 that won the round. That knocked Luke back a spot, and he settled for another fifty-three hundred. The next day he would draw a big fast steer and finish out of the round money, but it would make no difference: He was the world champion.

Luke walked out of the arena into a barrage of questions from TV and newspaper reporters. As he was downstairs finishing the interviews, some of his family members left their seats and congregated in the main upstairs bar area of the Thomas & Mack Center. About fifty people crowded loosely around the long bar, some talking in groups, some flirting, some watching monitors showing the rodeo.

John and Johnny Joe stood together, away from the crowd, and sipped on Pepsis. Casey ordered a stiff drink, walked over, and joined them. John, the proud father, kept calling relatives and close friends just like he'd done the night Luke was born twenty-four years before. Johnny Joe kept shaking his head, amazed at what Luke had done. Casey ran through the numbers aloud, nodding to himself, saying, "Yeah, there's no way they can catch him."

As the men stood together, waiting on little brother, they talked softly and nodded. Slowly, uncontrollably, their expressions shifted as they began to comprehend what Luke had accomplished. He had won a world title and set the all-time steer wrestling earnings record of $193,614, topping Myers's old mark by $17,000. John reached up and wiped the first tears away. Johnny Joe followed suit, sniffing and nodding. Casey looked at his dad and smiled until his eyes filled to the point he no longer could see. The three cowboys began laughing at one another for crying.

A couple minutes later, the elevator door opened and Luke stepped out, finishing up a phone call with Travis. Luke hung up as he walked toward his family, clods of dried mud falling from his boots onto the tile floor with each step. As John watched his youngest son approach, a lifetime of amazing memories flooded back to him: Luke always had accomplished things younger than others. Like the time Luke, a second grader, arrived home at sunset atop a three-wheeler, asking for helpers to bring back a wild boar he had shot; how no one really believed him until they saw the 250-pound pig lying dead in the grass, a buck knife plunged deep into the side of its head. Or the time Luke, at age nine, shot his first bear. John thought of the countless hours spent hazing for his youngest son in the family arena, and how he and Luke had won junior-senior team roping buckles together from the time the kid was old enough to throw a loop.

Luke reached Casey first. The two shook hands as Casey wiped his eyes and said congratulations. Next, Johnny Joe walked up to Luke and gave him a big hug, sobbing.

"That made me cry," Johnny Joe said.

"A run like that made me cry, too," said Luke, upset he hadn't done better than 3.9 on his steer.

Finally, Luke reached his dad, who was wearing on his belt the first NFR buckle Luke ever won. They met face-to-face and looked into each other's eyes for a moment. Then they kissed: a quick one on the lips. John's eyes filled with tears again as he hugged his son tightly. Neither man let go for a while.

"Congratulations son," John said into Luke's ear.

"Thanks Dad."

Luke looked around until he saw Lindsay walking toward him, wiping her eyes. She was still crying when she placed the side of her face against his chest and hugged him. He wrapped his arms around her, and slowly they rocked back and forth. She looked up at him and smiled. He leaned down and whispered something in her ear, only loud enough for her to hear. She smiled again and kissed him, then returned her face to his chest.

Everyone around Luke continued to cry. As Luke stood there hugging his wife, he waited for the overwhelming emotions he always figured would come with winning a world championship. He had dreamed of the moment his entire life. But now that it was here, he had to admit it felt a little strange. There was no sweeping rush of joy, no pure surge of adrenaline. At that moment, the only overwhelming sensations he felt were exhaustion and relief.

As time passed, it would all make more sense to him: The lasting joy lives in the memories of the hunt, not the kill. And, for Luke Branquinho, the long hunt finally was over.

CHAPTER 15

A Season That Never Ends

NORCO, CALIFORNIA

SUNDAY, JANUARY 16, 2005

On a warm sunny afternoon, a crowd of cowboys gathered around the chute at Ingalls Arena to see who would win the title at the California Circuit Finals, the last rodeo of the 2004 season. Though twelve cowboys qualified for the short round, the title evolved into a showdown between two men: Luke and Travis. Luke had thrown down two steers in ten seconds. Travis finished his first two runs in 9.9 seconds to lead the world champ by one-tenth of a second heading into the final. The two men led the rest of the pack by more than a second.

After Luke made his run, he rose from the dirt with a smile. As he watched Jackpot gallop to the far end of the arena, Luke had a good feeling about the new year. Jackpot now belonged to him; a couple weeks earlier, Luke had bought the horse from Bryan Fields for sixty thousand dollars, using all but about eight thousand of his NFR earnings. Helping Luke to a 4.0 in the final, the horse already had paid a dividend. The run put the pressure on Travis.

As he walked into the arena to retrieve Jackpot, he shook his head and looked at Luke.

"Fatty, you prick," Travis said.

"Oh, he's just making sure you're worthy of it," said Casey, standing near the chute.

"I don't care," Travis said, "he's still a prick."

Luke smiled again as he reached Travis. The two men stood near the chute and got Jackpot's stirrups ready for Travis's ride. When all was set, Travis climbed into the saddle and rode into the box. Once he backed into the corner, Travis felt something wasn't quite right.

"He feels like he's squatting," Travis said, looking behind him.

"No," said Luke, standing at his side, "he's good."

"Really?" Travis said. "Feels like he's squatting."

"No, he's right," Luke said.

Travis took Luke's word for it and nodded for the gateman. The steer blew out of the chute and Travis and Jackpot raced into the middle of the arena to catch up. Travis made up for it on the ground, throwing the animal down hard and fast as the crowd cheered. He looked over for the scoreboard and nodded when he saw a friendly number: 4.0. He beat Luke by one-tenth of a second to win the circuit title.

As Travis walked back toward the chute, Luke was the first one to approach him.

"Man," Travis said, "I thought I led him too far right there."

"I did, too," Luke said. "But no, you made a nice run."

"Thanks."

Travis walked from the arena as a handful of cowboys congratulated him: Tyler and Schenk, and a few others. Casey walked up, laughing with a big smile on his face.

"Oh yeah," Casey said, shaking Travis's hand, "you're worthy, ain't you?"

Travis smiled. The last one to congratulate Travis was

Brad McGilchrist, a cowboy who had practiced a lot at Travis's house the past year. McGilchrist, who finished thirty-second in the 2004 world standings, grinned as he stuck out his hand.

"Man, Travvie," McGilchrist said, "you bulldogged really good this weekend."

"Wasn't bad, was it?" Travis said.

McGilchrist got a sincere expression on his face, and nodded like a man who knew something.

"You're back, ain't ya?" McGilchrist said.

Travis shook his head and laughed as he started to walk away. Then he stopped, and turned back to McGilchrist with a serious look.

"Yeah Donk," Travis said, "I'm back."

An hour later, Travis and Luke collected their prizes: buckles, saddles, and applause. Then they made their way down the hill at Ingall's Arena to the parking lot; they had steers to run in Denver the following night.

As everyone loaded horses and clothes into Luke's rig, the scene looked quite different from a year before when Luke and Casey made the trip to Denver alone. This time, Luke climbed behind the wheel. His wife sat in the passenger seat. Travis fastened T.C. into a car seat and sat beside him in the backseat. Schenk sat on the other side. McGilchrist climbed into the trailer and went to sleep.

Before long, the dirt and gravel gave way to city streets that emptied into the endless hum of Interstate 15. Outside, the setting sun struggled to push light through the smoggy air that hung above the mountains east of Los Angeles. And Luke's rig rolled past traffic at 75 mph in the fast lane, rumbling toward another new beginning of a season that never ends.

FINAL 2004 PRCA STEER WRESTLING WORLD STANDINGS

RANK	NAME (HOMETOWN)	REGULAR SEASON	NFR	OVERALL
1	Luke Branquinho (Los Alamos, CA)	$125,625.08	$67,989.33	$193,614.41
2	Jason Lahr (Emporia, KS)	$111,347.19	$43,935.85	$155,283.04
3	Ronnie Fields (Oklahoma City, OK)	$72,543.31	$73,372.07	$145,915.38
4	Todd Suhn (Brighton, CO)	$73,755.89	$68,942.72	$142,698.61
5	Rope Myers (Van, TX)	$78,589.69	$60,838.82	$139,428.51
6	Stockton Graves (Newkirk, OK)	$88,437.10	$41,750.97	$130,188.07
7	Shawn Greenfield (Lakeview, OR)	$59,581.53	$53,747.92	$113,329.45
8	Teddy Johnson (Checotah, OK)	$89,819.32	$18,233.77	$108,053.09
9	Spud Duvall (Checotah, OK)	$70,260.84	$32,912.15	$103,172.99
10	Trevor Knowles (Mt. Vernon, OR)	$56,453.78	$38,731.87	$95,185.65
11	Lee Graves (Calgary, AB)	$58,535.68	$30,429.35	$88,965.03
12	K. C. Jones (Las Animas, CO)	$65,596.00	$22,961.05	$88,557.05
13	Frank Thompson (Cheyenne, WY)	$50,054.63	$37,659.29	$87,713.92
14	Ivan Teigen (Capitol, MT)	$58,721.59	$20,259.75	$78,981.34
15	Sean Mulligan (Aurora, SD)	$60,118.87	$7,945.00	$68,063.87

(continued)

OTHER NOTABLES

NAME (HOMETOWN)	MONEY WON
23. Josh Peek (Pueblo, CO)	$40,384.87
31. Bryan Fields (Conroe, TX)	$33,492.92
32. Brad McGilchrist (Sheridan, CA)	$32,630.85
57. Ron Schenk (Moorpark, CA)	$19,304.41
58. Levi Rosser (Wheatland, CA)	$18,721.77
63. Clyde Himes (Stanton, TX)	$18,061.06
103. Tyler Holzum (Oakdale, CA)	$11,455.56
109. Travis Cadwell (Oakdale, CA)	$10,904.34
127. Austin Manning (Las Vegas, NV)	$9,547.58
143. Robbin Peterson (Mira Loma, CA)	$8,241.51
182. Casey Branquinho (Los Alamos, CA)	$6,481.48
365. Brock Andrus (St. George, UT)	$2,636.00
473. Marc Jensen (Coalinga, CA)	$1,618.00

AFTERWORD

Attesting to the grueling nature of rodeo, just two of the six main cowboys featured in this book were competing in rodeo when the 2005 season ended: Frank Thompson and Brock Andrus.

Frank again found himself on the NFR bubble, but he could not summon the magic and luck this time around. He finished the season in nineteenth place with a little more than forty-nine thousand dollars. Brock healed up, won more than nine thousand at the Reno Rodeo, and finished with about thirty thousand dollars.

Luke started the year slowly, but he had climbed into the top twenty by late July when he suffered a torn pectoral muscle that required season-ending surgery. During his first extended break from rodeo in years, he fit in a Colorado hunting trip with Jensen, who was working full-time for his father's backhoe operation. After a six-month layoff, Luke began training for the 2006 season.

Jason Lahr entered the 2005 NFR in first place with $123,000 in earnings, nearly breaking Luke's regular-season record. However, Lee Graves stole the show at the NFR, winning a record $126,412 in Las Vegas en route to a world title and $206,415. With that, Graves replaced Luke as the sport's single-season earnings record holder.

Casey Branquinho, who did not rodeo full-time in 2005, married Beau in the spring in a ceremony that brought the gang together again.

And Travis earned about fourteen thousand dollars through April, his best start in years. But he quit steer wrestling to focus on raising his family, renovating houses, and farming his twenty-five-acre cherry orchard. Within six months, he began to enjoy the sensation of waking up without feeling pain everywhere. He says his rodeo days are behind him. Then again, he's said that before.

ACKNOWLEDGMENTS

First off, my biggest thanks and apologies are reserved for my family: Amber and our two sons, Sky and Murphy. To do the reporting necessary for this book, I often had to be gone for weeks at a time, and that put a large strain on us all.

I want to thank everyone at St. Martin's and Thomas Dunne Books who helped put this book together, particularly editor Sean Desmond, whose content suggestions significantly strengthened the finished product.

I owe a huge debt of gratitude to my agent, Jay Acton, for his assistance in getting this book published and for rescuing me from the throes of daily journalism for at least a few years. Because of you, I am more hopeful of the future.

A mighty thanks to my favorite photographer, Bart Ah You, who created the pictures featured in this book. I wouldn't have wanted to work on this project with anyone else.

I am grateful for the support I received the past two years from my colleagues at *The Modesto Bee*, particularly Mark Vasché, for allowing the use of photos that originally appeared in *The Bee*, Susan Windemuth for creative scheduling and for occasionally moving deadlines in my favor, Patty Guerra, Brian Clark, and Dave Jones for editing suggestions, Jose Escoto and Steve Kosko for technical support, and Ron Agostini, who first encouraged me to meet Travis Cadwell.

ACKNOWLEDGMENTS

This project simply could not have happened without the help of dozens of rodeo cowboys who embraced what I was doing, even though none of us knew exactly what that was. Be it a ride to some faraway rodeo, a place to sleep, or enduring another damn conversation about the finer points of steer wrestling, those within the rodeo community always made me feel welcome even though I was a lot more rock and roll than country.

Particular thanks to Casey Branquinho, Marc Jensen, Frank Thompson, Tyler Holzum, Ron Schenk, and Brock Andrus. Also, special thanks to Mike Bacigalupi, my link to the cowboy world for this book as well as numerous newspaper stories over the years.

Several people from the Professional Rodeo Cowboys Association assisted me greatly, particularly John Shipley, Anne Bleiker, and Tina Morin.

I want to point out the endless accommodations made by two cowboys who made *Blacktop Cowboys* a reality: Travis Cadwell and Luke Branquinho. The intimate tone could not have happened without the trust you showed by opening all aspects of your lives. I hope you enjoy reading this book as much as I enjoyed writing it, and I hope you feel it accurately captures the essence of the lives you lead as well as the cowboy experience at large. Writers do not usually get to have so much fun at "work." So, for all the all-night drives, the 85 mph Hold'em games, and the countless beers, I want to say thanks to the fat man and the skinny fucker for one hell of a ride.

Finally, I'd like to thank two men who helped me get to this point in my life: my father, Darell Phillips, and my grandfather, George Murphy, Jr. I miss the hours and years I spent eavesdropping on the two of you as you sat in living rooms and discussed newspapers. At times, I like to pretend you are out there guiding me in some way, though I don't really believe in that sort of thing. I wish I could put this book in your hands as proof that I learned so much from both of you, but you died while I was still too young to do anything but pretend I didn't care that much about writing. For that, I am truly sorry.